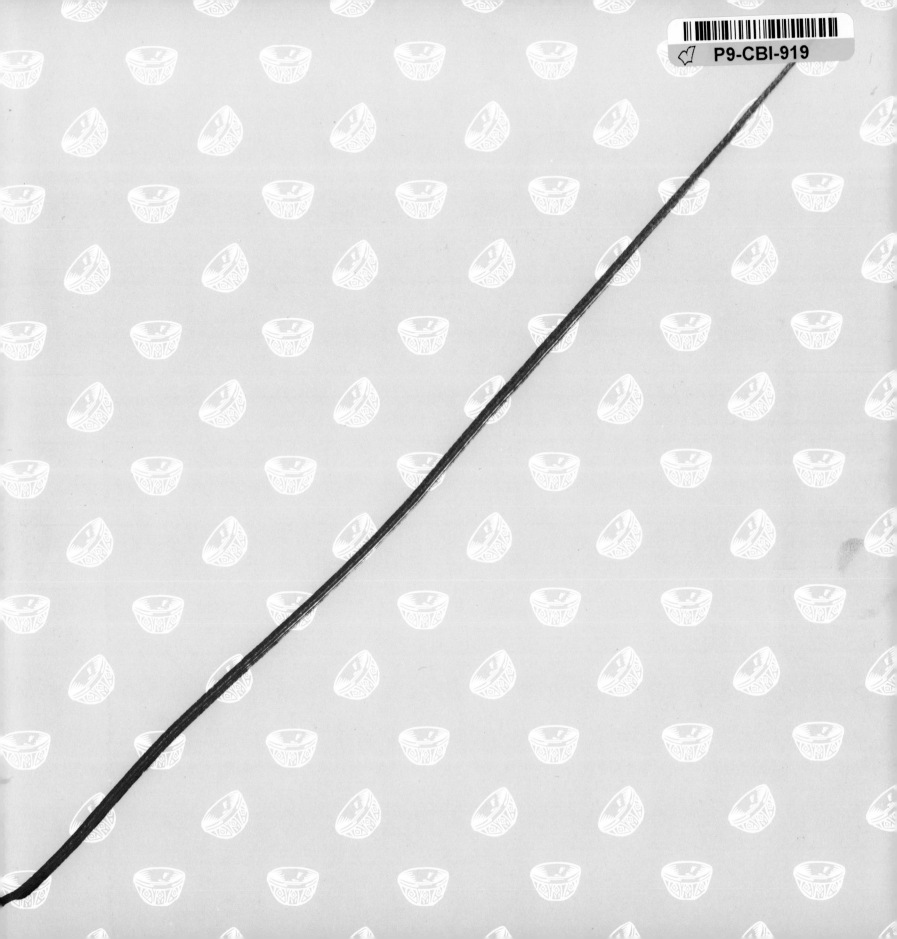

BREAD

● *Dresdner Stollen*

BREAD

150 Traditional Recipes from around the World

GAIL DUFF

MACMILLAN PUBLISHING COMPANY
NEW YORK

Maxwell Macmillan International
New York Oxford Singapore Sydney

For Mick and Lucy, who seemed to eat nothing but bread for six months

Typesetting, design and original photography copyright
© 1993 by Breslich & Foss

Conceived and produced by Breslich & Foss
Golden House
28-31 Great Pulteney Street, London W1R 3DD

Project editor: Catriona Woodburn
Art director: Nigel Osborne
Design: Sally Stockwell
Original photography: Nigel Bradley for Visuel 7
Styling for original photography: Sue Skeen
US editorial: Helen Huckle
Illustrator: Carol Wilhide

Macmillan Publishing Company
866 Third Avenue, New York, NY 10022

Printed in Italy

Typesetting by BMD Graphics, Hertfordshire, England

Film origination by Dot Gradations, Essex, England

Macmillan Publishing Company is part of the Maxwell Communication
Group of Companies.

Library of Congress Cataloging-in-Publication Data
Duff, Gail.
Bread / Gail Duff.
p.   cm.
Includes index.
ISBN 0-02-533585-5
1. Bread.   2. Cookery, International.   I. Title
TX 769.D77   1993
641.8′15—dc20   93-9232
                                                          CIP

Macmillan books are available at special discounts for bulk purchases for sales promotions, premiums, fund-raising, or educational use.
For details contact:

Special Sales Director
Macmillan Publishing Company
866 Third Avenue, New York, NY 10022

10 9 8 7 6 5 4 3 2 1

CONTENTS

FOREWORD

Anyone can make bread. There is no magic to it at all.
You don't need expensive equipment, and for some recipes you don't even
need an oven. If you have never baked bread before, it is best to
learn the basic recipe first (see page 12).
From this humble beginning, you can widen your horizons,
and take yourself on a culinary adventure of tastes, smells and
textures from around the world.

In the most up-to-date of baking plants today, the whole process
of bread-making is completely mechanical.
Ingredients are mixed at high speed into a dough, and the bread is

actually baked "on the move," whilst passing slowly on
a conveyor belt through a huge oven.
When the loaves are done, they are turned out of the pans,
sliced and bagged – all by machines.

By contrast, I visited a rural bakery at a watermill.
There was one baker who made a hundred loaves, almost totally
by hand, before 9:30 every morning, and his process was so simple that
it could have been taking place in my own kitchen.
He weighed out fresh yeast, flour, salt and fat.
He didn't even activate the yeast. He switched on the mixer and
added water by eye, before giving the dough a kneading
of about five minutes. He then turned it out
on to a wonderful old wooden baker's table and
gave it a final kneading by hand. An array of wreaths,
four-strand braids, cottage loaves and bloomers, were formed
in a matter of minutes.

These extremes of craftsmanship and commercialization
exist all over the world. We need them both.
Sadly, there are too many people wanting bread for everyone
to enjoy the luxury of a local baker, but
if you are lucky enough to be able to buy handmade bread regularly,
you'll know the difference.
Best of all, of course, is the satisfaction of taking a home-baked
loaf out of the oven in your own kitchen.

MAKING BREAD

The ingredients that you really need for making a good loaf are remarkably simple: flour, yeast, salt and water. However, to produce different textures and flavors, other ingredients can be added in varying amounts. Sugar, eggs, and fats such as butter, lard, oil or shortening, can give an altogether richer dough; and using alternative liquids such as milk, beer, white wine, or even brandy, will subtly influence the flavor.

To make a specific kind of loaf, you need the right kind of flour. Flour is milled from grains. The most commonly used is wheat, but bread can also be made from rye, barley, oats, buckwheat or cornmeal, though almost always in combination with wheat flour.

Every cereal grain is made up of the outer layer called the bran, the main starchy part called the endosperm, and the germ. The bran contains B vitamins and minerals, the endosperm is rich in carbohydrates and the germ, although the smallest part, is the richest in B vitamins, vitamin E and protein. It is obvious that to obtain the most complete goodness you have to eat all of it, and that is why many people over the past few years have chosen whole-wheat bread. However, when you eat a balanced diet, there is no reason why you should not include a whole range of breads – whole-wheat, white and in between. There are particular breads, the richer ones especially, for which only white flour will do. Others can be made successfully with a mixture. Once you have tried a few of the recipes in this book you will be able to adapt them to your own tastes.

That is all I will say about the health aspects of the various flours. The rest of the information is about choosing the right kind for the right recipe.

FLOUR MADE FROM WHEAT

There are really three types of wheat: durum wheat, soft wheat and hard wheat. Durum wheat is grown in many places, including the United States and Canada and is used in making dry pasta. Soft wheat has a lower protein content than the hard wheats, and when it is ground it makes a fine, powdery flour that is best suited to cakes and biscuits and to some breads which are risen with baking powder or baking soda. In the recipes throughout the book I have referred to this non-self-rising flour as "plain cake flour." You can make your own cake flour from all-purpose flour, by substituting 2 tablespoons cornstarch for 2 tablespoons flour in every cup. The wheat needed for bread making is known as hard wheat. Hard wheat has a high content of two proteins. When water is mixed with the flour, these combine to form gluten. Yeast mixed into this dough causes the release of carbon dioxide, and as this happens the gluten forms a stretchable network that expands and sets when the bread is baked. The flour has to be strong enough to take and hold the expansion of the dough. Called strong, bread-making or bread flour, when you feel it in your hands it has a grainier texture than soft flour and it contains no rising agents. Strong bread-making flour can be used for any of the recipes in this book that call for "all-purpose flour."

All-purpose Flour: Widely available in the United States, this is a mixture of strong and soft wheat flours and is used throughout this book as the basic white, non-self-rising, bread-making flour. White flour is produced mainly from the endosperm of the wheat. The bran and most of the germ are removed in the milling process. Depending on the country of origin, white flour is made up of between 70 percent and 78 percent of the wheat grain. White flour was once uniformly chemically bleached, but in many countries this is no longer the case. Naturally, it is a pale creamy color.

Whole-wheat Flour: Whole-wheat flour is made up of 98 percent to 100 percent extraction of the wheat grain, and contains the bran, endosperm and germ of the wheat. There are two different methods of producing whole-wheat flour. Most flour in the world today is ground on roller-mills. The grains are split open and by the end of the process the white flour, bran and germ are separated. Some flour is left white, while some is made into whole-wheat flour by mixing the bran and germ back in. Roller-milling has been accused of creating high temperatures that damage some of the nutrients in the wheat, but water-cooled rollers now counteract this.

Stone-ground whole-wheat flour is produced from wheat that is ground between mill stones. The whole of the grain is crushed, thus the bran, germ and endosperm are never separated. To produce stone-ground white flour, the whole-wheat flour is passed through a highly efficient sieve.

The vast majority of bread-making flour available is roller-milled unless otherwise stated on the package, but stone-ground flour is also widely available in health food stores and in many supermarkets.

Graham Flour: Graham flour is a whole-wheat flour that has been more finely milled. It is called after Dr. Sylvester Graham a nineteenth-century clergyman from Massachusetts who, at a time when everyone was after white bread, persistently extolled the virtues of brown.

Wheatmeal or Brown Flour: Wheatmeal or brown flour can have an extraction of 79 percent to 90 percent, and it is usually about 85 percent. It contains all the endosperm and germ and a little of the bran and makes lighter-textured loaves than whole-wheat flour. This type of flour was most popular during the 1970s and early 1980s but is now quite hard to come by. You can get similar results in baking if you mix together about one half all-purpose flour and one half whole-wheat flour.

Cracked Wheat: Cracked wheat consists of coarsely broken up wheat grains. They are scattered on top of whole-wheat loaves for decoration and can be soaked and added to whole-wheat flour to make a moist, nutty-flavored loaf.

Organic Flour: Organic flour is produced from wheat that has been grown without chemical fertilizers or pesticides. Both white and whole-wheat organic flours are available in limited quantities.

Self-rising Flour: Self-rising flour is a soft flour into which have been mixed rising agents, usually baking soda and an acid (such as cream of tartar) which neutralizes its flavor. Self-rising flour is more commonly available in the South and usually applies to cake flour used in making cakes and biscuits. Self-rising all-purpose flour, however, is also available.

Semolina: Semolina consists of the larger parts of the endosperm which are sifted out during the milling process. Semolina is the flour of choice in making fresh pasta, but is rarely used in bread making. I've included one recipe in the Middle Eastern section.

● *Grains of wheat*

FLOUR MADE FROM OTHER GRAINS

Mixed Grain Flour: Mixed grain flours are generally based on a wheat flour of about 85 percent extraction and contain malted grains of wheat and rye. One brand name for this type of flour is granary flour. Bread made with mixed grain flour rises well and the pieces of whole grain produce an interesting texture. Any of the plainer breads in this book that are made with all-purpose flour can be made with mixed grain flour.

Rye Flour: After wheat, rye is the most popular grain for bread making. However, it contains gum-like substances that inhibit the development of gluten and so, used alone, makes a very close-textured loaf. It is often mixed with wheat flour. Rye flour comes in various grades of coarseness. Light rye flour is produced mainly from the endosperm and is a pale fawn color. Rye meal, or dark rye flour, is made from the whole grain. It is a gray-brown color and similar in texture to whole-wheat flour.

Barley Flour: Barley flour is usually available from health food stores and specialty stores, but is rarely used by commercial bakers. It is a pale, gray-brown color and makes a rather gray loaf. Because it does not contain enough gluten-producing proteins, barley flour is usually mixed with wheat flour when making yeasted breads. However, it can be used successfully for unleavened breads or thin soda breads.

Oatmeal: Oatmeal comes in a variety of textures, ranging from fine, cream-colored flour to more coarsely-ground grains known as pin-head oatmeal. Oatmeal lacks gluten but it can be mixed successfully with wheat flour to make bread with a soft, moist texture. Rolled oats can be used in the same way.

Buckwheat Flour: Buckwheat flour is a dark gray flour, sometimes speckled with black pieces of bran, which is silky smooth to the touch. Bread made from it will not rise greatly due to the lack of gluten-forming proteins, but buckwheat flour does make delicious yeasted pancakes. For bread, it is best mixed with a wheat flour.

Cornmeal: Cornmeal is produced by grinding the whole kernels of sweet corn. It is a coarse, pale yellow flour which is entirely lacking in gluten-producing proteins. For yeasted breads it is often mixed with wheat flour. Cornmeal is popular for breads raised with baking soda or baking powder.

RISING AGENTS

Yeast: In order for dough to rise, gas has to be produced within it to swell and stretch the gluten network. Today, yeast is the most common rising agent.

Yeast is a growing organism which occurs naturally in the air and on the skins of certain fruits. It will begin to grow when it comes into contact with moist, starchy substances and, as it grows, it produces carbon dioxide. A warm, moist, flour-based dough is a perfect environment.

Over the years, bakers have used homemade yeasts and the by-products of brewing in order to rise their breads successfully. Nowadays, yeast is made commercially and bread making is no longer a hit and miss affair. Yeast is available fresh or dried.

Fresh Yeast: Fresh yeast comes in the form of a light brown, moist, compressed lump which can be crumbled easily. You can buy it by the ounce from bakeries, health food stores and specialty stores. Wrap it in wax paper and store it in a plastic bag in the refrigerator and it will keep for up to two weeks. If you cannot obtain fresh yeast, use half the amount substituting dried yeast.

Dried Yeast: Dried yeast comes in the form of small brown granules. Check for the expiration date on the package. Dried yeast needs to be left far longer than fresh yeast for it to activate. Once in the specified amount of liquid, leave it to stand for about 15 minutes (see page 12).

Quick-rise Yeast: Quick-rise yeast is made from a strong yeast strain that rises in about half the usual time and can be added dry to the flour. Follow the instructions given on the package as to amounts needed.

OTHER RISING AGENTS

Baking Soda: Baking soda is an alkaline rising agent which, like yeast, gives off carbon dioxide when moistened and heated.

Baking Powder: When baking soda is used on its own, it produces an alkaline "soapy" flavor. In many soda breads, sour milk or buttermilk is used – their acids neutralizing the soda's flavor. Cream of tartar will produce the same effect. Commercial baking powder is made from baking soda and cream of tartar mixed with a small amount of starch, such as cornstarch, to keep the mixture dry and flowing.

Most baking powders sold today are "double acting." The first action occurs when the powder comes in contact with liquid, the second during the heat of baking.

Sourdough Starters: Sourdough starters are an easy-to-make alternative to buying fresh yeast. You will have to wait a little time before they get going, but once you have begun you can have bowls of starter at various stages of development. There are several unique starter recipes throughout this book, but the two that follow here are the most popular and universal methods.

Sourdough is "alive" and needs to be replenished with more flour and water or it will eventually "die."

Potato Sourdough Starter

1 medium potato, scrubbed, not peeled
warm water
4 cups (1 pound) all-purpose or whole-wheat flour or rye meal
2 cups (8 ounces) sugar

Halve the potato. Place in a saucepan, cover with water and boil until it is tender. Drain it, reserving the water. Peel the potato, put it into a medium-sized bowl and mash it. Make up the potato water to 3¾ cups with more warm water. Stir it into the mashed potato and then stir in the flour and sugar. Cover the bowl with plastic wrap and put it into a warm place for about three days or until it is bubbling and smells slightly sour.

You can use your starter immediately or stir in another handful of flour and a little more warm water to keep it going (use approximately equal amounts of flour and water). If you don't use it all at once, you can keep the starter going for months, or even years, by stirring in more flour and water.

Rye and Yeast Sourdough Starter

3¾ cups warm water

1 ounce fresh yeast or 1 tablespoon dried

4 cups (1 pound) rye flour or meal

1 small onion, peeled and halved

Pour 2 cups of the water into a large bowl and sprinkle in the yeast. Leave this to stand — five minutes for fresh yeast and 15 for dried. Beat in half the flour and add the onion halves. Cover the bowl with plastic wrap and leave it in a warm place for 24 hours. Remove the onion and stir in the remaining flour and water. Cover the starter again and leave it in a warm place for two to three days or until it is bubbling, has a slightly sour smell and has tripled in volume.

Although this sourdough starter requires yeast initially, you can keep it going by replenishing it as you use it, with equal amounts of flour and warm water. This starter is not really authentic, since it uses commercial yeast, but it is often used. It should be combined with wheat flour for most breads.

OTHER INGREDIENTS

Liquids: The main liquid used for bread making is water. However, some or all of this can be replaced with milk or the equivalent volume of beaten egg. Generally, one large egg has a liquid capacity of 2 fluid ounces. Breads that contain milk or egg are softer than those made with water, but may not have such good keeping qualities. Milk does not inhibit the rising properties of dough, but large quantities of egg may. With egg breads you will find the dough slow to rise at the kneading and first rising stage, but it will nevertheless rise considerably in the oven. It is worth bearing this in mind when you are shaping rich breads or choosing a baking container. In some more unusual recipes, beer or white wine are used as the liquids, but these are rare.

Fats: Butter, vegetable shortening, lard and olive oil are all put into breads to enrich them. The hard fats are either melted and added or they are kneaded in at room temperature. Olive oil can be added with the liquids or kneaded in after the dough is mixed. All fats may inhibit the initial rising of the dough.

Salt: Unless salt is added to the flour, your bread will have a bland, sweetish flavor. More salt is generally added to plainer breads than to sweet breads, but all breads should contain some. Fine salt can be mixed with the flour or dissolved in a little of the warm liquid before mixing. If you use a coarse salt, always dissolve it in the liquid first.

Sugar: If you use fresh yeast, there is no need to add any sugar at all to plain breads. The yeast will work quite happily on the warm water and moist dough. Dried yeast, depending on the brand that you use, may or may not need a teaspoon of sugar to get it going. Read the instructions on the package, but it is also worth experimenting. If you do add sugar, use white for white bread so that you do not spoil the color. For whole-wheat or mixed grain breads, you can use white or brown, or honey or molasses.

For sweetened breads, the sugar is usually added to the flour at some point during the mixing of the dough. Where a recipe just says "sugar," ordinary granulated sugar is called for. Where special sugars are required it will be stated. Like eggs and butter, sugar may well inhibit the initial rising of the dough, but will not affect its ability to rise on baking.

Equipment

For a basic bread recipe you will need:

scales

a measuring jug

a small mixing bowl

a large mixing bowl

a tablespoon or a round-bladed knife

a large, clean, smooth surface on which to knead the bread

a clean, dry cloth

an oven

If you find kneading bread difficult you can use a food mixer or large food processor fitted with a dough hook.

Professional bakers use a dough scraper. This is made of either metal or a very durable but flexible plastic material. It is about 5 inches long, thin, and about 3 inches wide. It is used for scraping the dough out of the mixing bowl and pulling it together on the work surface. Some dough scrapers can be used to cut thinly-rolled dough. A dough scraper is not essential but, if you make a lot of bread, treat yourself to one.

There is no need for any kind of mechanical equipment. To my mind, bread making is an enjoyable craft which demands a little skill but which gives much pleasure. At the time of writing, bread-making machines are becoming very popular in the United States. For the person who enjoys freshly-baked homemade bread, but has limited time, these may well be the answer. However, the proportions of flour to other ingredients differ from those needed for oven-baked bread, which is the subject of this book. Should you wish to use one of these machines for making your bread, consult the manufacturer's instructions for recipes and methods.

For yourself, make sure your hands are clean and take off any rings that might get in the way. Wear short sleeves or sleeves that stay up when pushed or rolled up and take off any bracelets. To stop yourself from getting floury, wear an apron.

MAKING BASIC BREAD DOUGH

Let us look at a basic recipe and take it step by step. The importance of yeast activity, kneading, and leaving dough to rise in a warm place are fundamental to bread making and the following method can be applied to all the recipes in this book.

Ingredients

1 ounce fresh yeast or 1 tablespoon dried
1¼ cups warm water
sugar, optional
1 tablespoon salt
4 cups (1 pound) all-purpose or whole-wheat flour or a mixture, plus extra for kneading – most recipes never state this, but you will always need more

1. Weigh out the yeast.
2. Pour half the water into a small bowl. Crumble the fresh yeast into it or simply sprinkle over the dried yeast. If you need the sugar, sprinkle it into the water with the dried yeast. It is not necessary if you are using fresh yeast. Leave this mixture for the yeast to begin to work. The standard times for this are about 5 minutes for fresh yeast and 15 minutes for dried. However, I rarely leave fresh yeast for longer than 2 minutes and dried for longer than 10 minutes. If you feel safer leaving them longer, go ahead.
3. Dissolve the salt in the remaining water.
4. Place the flour in a mixing bowl. If it is a cold day and your room temperature is low, it will help to warm the flour slightly, by a radiator or open fire, or on top of a boiler or wood-burning stove.
5. Make a well in the center of the flour. Pour in the yeast mixture and mix in a little of the flour from the sides of the well. Pour in the remaining water with the salt dissolved in it and, using a long, round-bladed knife or a tablespoon, begin to mix everything together to make a dough. Bring it all together into a rough ball with your fingers. It will be a lumpy, uneven mixture of dry pieces and wet pieces.
6. Sprinkle some flour on your work surface. Turn the dough onto it, scraping it from the sides of the bowl. Push it together into a rough round.
7. Knead the bread. When you knead the dough you are producing a smooth mixture, assisting the development of gluten, and pushing out any pockets of air that might eventually make a hole in the loaf. Begin by pushing the dough away from you with the palms of your hands and pulling it back with your fingers and, in the very short space between the two processes, giving it a quick squeeze. Do this about six times. Fold the ends of the dough over the top, give the dough a quarter turn and start pushing, squeezing and pulling again. After five minutes you should notice that the flour and water have become evenly mixed and that the texture of the dough is changing.

You can actually see the gluten developing in strong, flexible strands. The more you knead, the more the bread will be able to rise. Most people knead for 5 to 7 minutes, but do not go over 10 minutes.

If you have judged your liquid content correctly and the dough is a plain one you will not have to use much extra flour as you knead. Use just enough to keep your hands and the work surface dry. See the notes below for richer doughs: Kneading in the Bowl.

8. When your dough is ready, return it to the bowl to rise or "prove." Some people like to put it into a greased plastic bag, and some like to rinse out the bowl and grease it. Neither of these are necessary. Unless otherwise specifically stated in the recipe, just return the dough to the original bowl.
9. Cut a cross shape in the top of the dough. Ancient folklore tells us that this is to keep the devil out. Actually, it helps the dough to rise.
10. Cover the bowl. I have always used a clean, dry cloth for this. If the bread rises above the bowl, the cloth simply gets pushed up. If you have used plastic wrap, the rising dough will stick to it. You can also place the bowl in a plastic bag which works quite well.
11. Place the bowl of dough somewhere where it will keep warm. If you have turned the oven on but not the rings, stand the bowl on top. It can also go by a radiator, on a covered wood-burning or solid-fuel stove, on the heating boiler, or on a sunny windowsill, as long as the position is draft-free. Leave the dough until it has doubled in size. The average time is about an hour, but plain doughs very often rise in half the time.
12. Knead the dough again. It is now ready for shaping (see pages 16 to 21).

Before you go on, here are some notes and variations:

Adding Salt: When you are making up the basic recipe, as above, fine salt can be mixed into the flour and the liquid added separately.

Amount of Liquid: 12 fluid ounces per 4 cups (1 pound) of flour is about right, but some flours, especially some brands of whole-wheat, soak up liquid fast and need a little bit more. If, after all the liquid has been added and you have begun to bring the dough together in the bowl, it still feels a bit dry, add another 4 tablespoons gradually. After a while, you will come to know your favorite flour and get used to the feel of your dough. I would rather err on the wet side than the dry. When the dough is on the work surface it is easy to knead in more flour, but adding water to mixed dough is exceptionally difficult and very messy.

Alternative Way of Mixing: Once you are absolutely certain how much liquid your flour is going to require, you can, if you like, mix your bread in the Scandinavian way, which saves on time and washing up, but is slightly more messy on your hands in the initial mixing. For this, the yeast and water are mixed in a large mixing bowl. After the yeast has risen, the extra water is added and the flour and salt are stirred into it. You then carry on as usual, mixing everything together to make a dough.

Adding Fats: If your butter, vegetable shortening and lard are sufficiently soft, you will be able to add them to the flour without melting them first. Melting is time consuming, messy, wasteful and not necessary. If you are only adding a small amount of fat, cut it into small pieces and put it into the well together with the liquid. As the bread is kneaded, it will mix in easily. Where a large amount of butter is added it is often kneaded in after the dough has become smooth. Punch the dough down on the work surface and dot one third of the butter on it. Fold it up and knead it until the butter is completely incorporated. Knead in the rest of the butter in the same way. Oil is added in a similar way: punch the dough on its surface and make a little dip in the center. Add as much oil as the dip will take, knead it in and carry on in the same way.

Adding Sugar and Dried Fruits: These can be added to the flour before the liquids. Other recipes call for them to be kneaded in. Do it in the same way as kneading in butter.

Kneading in the Bowl: When you have a very liquid dough you can knead it in the bowl. You will often have to use this method where you have an enriched dough containing a lot of butter, eggs and sugar. Hold the bowl in your left hand and rotate it towards the right hand. With your right hand bring a portion of the dough from the sides into the middle. Work in the pattern of rotate-knead-rotate-knead. It is quite hard work but eventually you will find that the structure of the dough begins to change and, even if it is still moist, it will lose its stickiness. Cover the dough and let it rise. It will probably take longer than a dough that is less rich. Once it has risen, you will be able to knead it successfully on the work surface, but even so, treat it gently and do not squeeze it too hard.

EATING AND STORING BREAD

Most breads are not suitable for eating as soon as they come from the oven. I can think of notable exceptions such as croissants, Danish pastries and some of the flat, Middle Eastern and Indian breads, but most of the more everyday breads should be given a cooling-off period first. Very fresh, warm bread tends to be doughy in texture and, if you cut a warm loaf, the next slice will be unusable as it will harden as it cools. So, for loaves, resist the temptation for at least an hour and for rolls, 20 minutes.

Bread is at its peak as soon as it has cooled and ideally it should be eaten within two days. You can store it in a special earthenware bread crock, or in a wooden bread keeper, whatever is best for you. It will keep equally well in a sealed plastic bag in a cool larder.

Most bread freezes well. Wait until it is completely cool and then seal it in a plastic bag. Frozen bread can be thawed in the bag at room temperature or unwrapped in a low oven. If you are desperate, use the microwave. There is no need to use the defrost setting. One of my plain whole-wheat loaves takes 4 minutes on the high setting. Follow your manufacturer's instructions or carry out some experiments, beginning at a short time and working up.

Bread will keep for up to three months in the freezer.

SHAPING AND MOLDING BREAD DOUGH

After the long rising and the second kneading (see page 12), it is time for you to stamp your own character on the bread, by shaping it. Certainly, some special breads, such as the French brioche or the Austrian *gugelhupf*, do have their own particular molds and pans, rarely used for other recipes, but the basic bread dough that is the staple of so many households can be as

● *Kneading the dough*

creatively used as potter's clay. Use a baking sheet, a baking pan, a mold or even a flowerpot, slash the top of the dough or sprinkle it with grains and seeds to make a loaf that suits your mood or occasion.

Baking Sheets, Pans and Molds

Using a Baking Sheet: Loaves baked on a flat baking sheet, not confined in a mold or pan will rise both upwards and sideways. Commercial bakers call them "crusty," meaning that there is a good, crisp crust all over the surface. The texture of the crumb (the inside of the loaf) is slightly more airy than that of loaves baked in a container.

A good-quality baking sheet should last you for years. Choose one that is made from fairly thick metal so that it will neither wobble out of shape as you are lifting a heavy loaf nor warp in a hot oven. The best surfaces are either textured and dull or coated with a non-stick silicon-type material. You will also find it practical to buy as big a one as will fit inside your oven.

You will find many recipes that tell you to grease and flour or simply grease your baking sheet, but this really isn't necessary. Over many years of baking, I have found that a fairly thick sprinkling of flour is all you need. Apart from being time-consuming and messy, greasing may well shorten the life of your baking sheet because of the extra scrubbing needed to get it clean afterwards. If you are using white flour which is very fine, you can add a little coarse semolina or yellow cornmeal to add to its non-stick properties. Any type of whole-wheat flour, wheat or rye for example, will work well on its own.

Plain yeasted loaves and buns, and also soda breads baked on floured baking sheets, will never normally stick. If your dough is rich and moist, you may simply need to ease off the bread using a wide palette knife.

After baking, wipe off browned flour with a soft, damp cloth.

If, however, you are over-zealous with an egg-based glaze, it may well form a cooked brown ring on the baking sheet. The bread will come off easily enough, after which the sheet should be soaked in warm soapy water for about half an hour. You should then be able to rub the egg off with a soft cloth assisted occasionally by a scouring pad. Do not scour the sheets with metal pads or you will spoil the surface.

Making a Dome Oven: Early "hearth breads" were baked underneath an iron pot or kettle which was piled high with hot ashes. You can achieve a similar effect by inverting a large earthenware or Pyrex bowl or a clean earthenware flowerpot over the loaf on your baking sheet. This will surround the baking loaf with steam, causing it to rise beautifully and producing a thin, crisp crust and moist crumb.

Practice first, simply by putting the bowl or pot on to the empty tray. Make sure you can lift it properly and that it will fit into your oven. Rearrange the oven shelves if necessary.

To remove the hot bowl from an equally hot tray, slip a sturdy palette knife between the two and gently lift up one side of the bowl.

Using Pans, Molds and Other Containers: Bread pans make even-shaped loaves that rise upwards only and have thinner crusts on the base and sides that are enclosed in the pan. The most popular shape is the rectangular, so-called two-pound bread pan, which actually takes a loaf made

with 1 pound of flour. One-pound pans are available, but this smaller loaf size is not very practical for everyday bread. You can also buy sets of six or eight miniature pans and the resulting loaves can be used as bread rolls or sliced to make garnishes and canapés.

Choose sturdy pans, preferably with no seams and with a non-shiny, textured surface. Silicon-coated pans also work well and both types should last a long time. Before using, the pans should be greased. Some recipes specify using butter to fit with the ingredients and character of that particular loaf. For making plain loaves, however, simply brush the insides of the pans with a thin coating of good-quality cooking oil, such as sunflower oil. The cooked loaves should be quite loose in the pans and will turn out easily. After use, the pans will not need to be washed and regular use will build up their non-stick qualities. If, however, some dough (perhaps from a rich, sticky mixture) does stick, soak and wash the pans as for the baking sheets and make sure that you oil them well the next time that you use them.

Bread can also be baked in round cake pans and French charlotte pans, prepared in a similar way. Also good are shallow round pans, such as the German spring-form pan, which give an even shape to the base of the loaf, but allow the top to rise both up and sideways. The French expanding cake hoop gives a similar effect. It consists of a wide, steel band coiled round into an adjustable circle and should be used in conjunction with a baking sheet.

If you like to make a bread with a soft, thin crust and a close crumb, you can use a hinged mold. Hinged molds are usually cylindrical in shape and completely enclose the dough, thus producing a perfectly even-shaped loaf that cuts crossways into round slices.

Two special types of bread pan which are used in this book are the slightly conical-shaped and fluted French brioche and the Austrian gugelhupf mold, again slightly conical, with a central column and spiral fluted patterns around the sides. Ordinary ring molds can be used as a substitute.

Many of these bread molds are now available in materials which are suitable for use in microwave ovens, usually some sort of durable and heat-proof plastic. Some of these can also be used in conventional ovens up to a certain temperature. If you frequently use both a microwave and a conventional oven, these dual purpose molds, particularly for the specialty breads, are a good buy. However, always check the manufacturer's instructions before use.

A popular way of cooking whole-wheat loaves during the health food boom of the 1980s was to bake them in flowerpots. Use earthenware pots that are unglazed on both outside and inside. If you are bringing them in from the garden, make sure they are clean, dry them well after washing and leave them in a warm place for 24 hours to dry out completely.

Flowerpots, like bread molds, need to be seasoned before you use them. Grease or oil them well and put them into a preheated 400°F oven for 45 minutes. Once they are cool they can be used in the same way as the bread pans. However, only use them for plain breads and do not wash them after use – just wipe them round with paper towels.

Specially-made earthenware bread pots are obtainable from some cookery stores and potters. They are unglazed, round, with a flat base and sides that slope slightly outwards towards the top, and come in several different sizes. Use them in the same way as flowerpots.

● *Adding eggs or milk to dough will produce a softer, richer bread*

SHAPES, SLASHES AND FINISHES

Elaborate bread shapes come from all over the world. The examples on the following pages are the most universal and some of the simplest to make in your own kitchen. Most bread shapes are baked on a baking sheet, but decorative tops will enhance bread baked in pans and molds as well. Slashing the top of the risen dough, glazing it and scattering it with grains and other ingredients will add considerably to the final appearance.

Bread is nearly always shaped after the second kneading (see page 12) by which time it will be non-sticky and pliable. Work on a dry, floured surface with clean, floured hands.

Whether you are dividing the dough into portions, rolling it flat or making long, sausage shapes, it should never be stretched. Dough that is stretched into its final shape may well shrink back during baking and its surface often looks pulled and broken. Bread should be eased naturally into shape and, where it needs dividing, it should always be cut using a sharp knife.

After the second kneading, dough can be handled easily, so make the shape you want on the work surface first and transfer it to the baking sheet when it is done. If you do not like a shape, you can quickly knead it into a ball and begin again, but do not over-knead it and do not add any extra flour at this point or it will become too dry.

Once a shape has been formed and is on the baking sheet, do not touch it again, unless you are going to slash the surface. Too much prodding of rising dough will cause it to deflate or become lop-sided.

Slashed Patterns

A slashed pattern not only gives a better visual effect, but also gives more crust. For effective scoring, you will need a razor blade or wide craft knife – the sharper the better.

Depending on the final shape required of the loaf, the surface can be cut either before or after rising. If it is *after* rising, take care not to press on the surface of the loaf.

Shallow slashes simply give a pattern to the finished loaf. Deep slashes – up to ½ inch – can affect the overall shape.

Ideas of patterns are given with the basic bread shapes that follow.

Round loaves

To make a basic round shape, after finishing kneading, tuck the uneven sides of the dough underneath, turning the loaf round as you do so, so that you end up with a smooth dome of dough. Turn it round several times, gently easing it into shape with your hands.

The patterning on round loaves is generally carried out after rising. The following are the most popular patterns.

The Crown

Score a circle about 1 inch in from the sides of the loaf so that the center part will rise slightly above the outside.

The Coburg

This is one of the standard English bread shapes. It is made by scoring a cross on the top of the loaf. Begin by scoring a straight line right across the top. Then score the second line in two separate parts, working from the outside of the loaf to the center. A deep score will cause the four quarters of the loaf to pull slightly apart when baked, and give the loaf a square shape.

A shallow-cut loaf will stay rounder. The cross need not go from side to side but can be confined more to the center of the loaf, in which case, cut it quite deep.

The Miche

The *miche* or *pain de campagne* is a French loaf which has its top scored in six sections. After rising, slash one long line across the top, but not quite to the edges. Make two slashes on each side of this line, from just inside the edge of the loaf to the center – so equally dividing the top of the loaf in six.

The Ring

If you do not have a ring mold, you can form a ring by hand. Shape the dough into a round. Push the handle of a wooden spoon down through the center. Insert two fingers, then three and eventually your whole fist. Having said that dough should never be stretched, this is the one occasion where stretching is permissible,

The Cottage Loaf

This is a peculiarly English loaf. Divide the dough in two pieces of one third and two thirds. Form each into a round and place the smaller on top of the larger. Push the handle of a wooden spoon down through both pieces to the bottom and then slightly enlarge the hole with your fingers. (According to Eliza Acton in *The English Bread Book*, 1857, the hole was sometimes made even bigger by the baker pushing his elbow through it!) Cottage loaves are slashed before rising. Score in straight lines from the top to the bottom, taking in both sections of the loaf and making the scores about ¼ inch deep and 1 inch apart all the way round. Leave the loaf to rise and, just before baking, press down gently, but firmly, in the center. This helps to maintain an even shape while the bread is baking.

backwards and forwards under your hands, working all the time from the center outwards to make a long, even shape. Flatten it out again to make a long rectangle. Fold in both ends to the center and press down hard again. This folding ensures all sides and corners are even. Roll up the dough tightly from one long side to make an even cylinder.

The Bloomer

How the bloomer obtained its name is a mystery and Elizabeth David in her book *English Bread and Yeast Cookery* looks at its fascinating etymology without reaching any firm conclusions. My favorite origin is that it was named after the bicycling attire of Mrs. Amelia Bloomer – having the appearance of one half of what became known as "a pair of bloomers." This is probably not the correct one, but it makes a good story. The bloomer is a large, cylindrical loaf, tapering at both ends, and has parallel diagonal slashes which are made after rising. To make a tapered cylinder, follow the instructions above, and at the final rolling bring the ends of the dough toward you with your palms and push the center away with your thumbs so that you have a thick crescent. Straighten the loaf, making the side that pointed toward you the underside. Then roll the loaf backwards and forwards under your hands until you get the right shape, keeping your hands

but you will have to be careful. With your fingers inside the hole and your palms on the edge of the ring, gently enlarge it until it is about 6 inches across. Do this slowly, letting the dough rest between pulls. The dough can be left plain or, after rising, marked with shallow diagonal slashes round the edge.

The Checkerboard

The checkerboard or college loaf is slashed with four parallel lines across the loaf and then another four at right angles to these, making a squared pattern. If this pattern is cut deep the result will be a knobbly, crusty top.

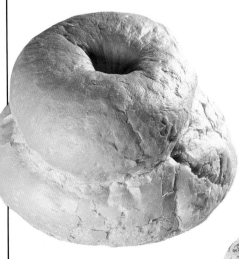

Elongated Bread Shapes

The instructions for making a cylinder of dough sound complicated at first, but with only a little practice you will be able to do it quickly.

Basic Cylinder Shape

First make a round of dough and let it rest for about 5 minutes. Then, on a floured board, flatten the dough with your hands to a thickness of about 1 inch. Roll it up and then roll it

mainly on the ends. Put the loaf on a floured baking sheet, leave it to rise and make a few short diagonal slashes all along its length, about 1½ inches apart, just before putting it into the oven to bake.

BREAD

The Vienna Loaf
Also called a lemon loaf because of its final shape, this loaf is made like a bloomer, the only difference being that there is one long, lengthways slash down the center.

The Cottage Brick
This is like a square cottage loaf and is mentioned by Elizabeth David as being more popular in London, in its day, than the round cottage. Divide the dough in two square pieces of about one third and two thirds. Put the smaller one on top of the larger. Make a hole through the center with the handle of a wooden spoon and gradually insert your hand flat, vertically down through the loaf, to make a lengthways slit along the length of the top. This type of cottage loaf is not slashed or scored.

The Long Crusty
Make the basic cylinder shape and lay it on a floured baking sheet. Take a sharp pair of scissors and make diagonal cuts all along the top of the loaf, about 1 inch deep and 1½ inches long, meeting at the points to make a zigzag pattern. Leave the loaf to rise before baking.

The Baguette
This is the long loaf originating in France, but well-known all over the world. Make a cylinder of dough and leave it to rest for about 10 minutes. On a floured surface, gradually roll the dough backwards and forwards, continually returning your hands to the center and gradually moving them outwards. Lay the loaf on a baking sheet and slash the top before leaving to rise. The four slashes in a baguette are diagonal, but only just so, making them very long and overlapping each other.

The Spiral
This is another version of the round loaf, but it is made by first making a long, thin cylinder and then coiling it round from the center outwards – to form a spiral.

The Braid
Divide the dough in three equal parts and roll them into long, thin cylinders. Lay them parallel to each other. To make an even shape, begin braiding from the center outwards. As you near the end, stretch the tips slightly and press them downwards and together. To complete the braid, turn the unfinished ends toward you. Finish as for the first half of the braid.

The Epi

This comes from France and its name means "ear of wheat" as that is what it resembles. Make a long cylinder and lay it on a floured baking sheet. With a razor blade, make flattened diagonal cuts three quarters of the way through the dough and about 2 inches apart all along the length. Pull the pieces to alternate sides.

The Pain Brie

This is a specialty of the Calvados region of France and is usually made with yeast. To make the shape, form a tapered cylinder as for the bloomer and leave it to rise. Just before baking, make parallel slashes down the whole length.

The Polka

Another French pattern, this is an elongated cylinder, longer than the bloomer but thicker and shorter than the baguette. Its surface is scored into a diagonal checkerboard pattern just before baking.

Flat Breads

The types of dough used for breads such as pita bread, naan bread and other flat Middle Eastern types are very similar to a basic white bread dough. They are very springy and bouncy and sometimes seem to have a mind of their own. Nevertheless, they must be rolled. Use a wooden cylindrical rolling pin and flour both it and the work surface well. Roll out the dough after the second kneading. If, halfway through, you find it keeps springing back into its original thickness, cover it with a clean, dry cloth and leave it to rest for a few minutes before continuing. This type of bread should in no way be stretched.

Instructions for a variety of flat breads will be found in specific recipes throughout this book.

Pizzas and Pies

Dough for pizzas and pies has to be rolled out very thinly and not stretched. Depending on the springiness of the dough, you may have to do this in several stages, letting the dough rest for a few minutes in between.

Breads Baked in Pans and Molds

For a well-shaped loaf, your dough should be shaped to fit your pan before you put it in. Although it sounds obvious, make sure that you have the right-size container for the amount of dough that you are making. Most recipes will state the size of container required, but a useful guide is that a mold should be twice the size of the volume of the kneaded dough.

Round containers: Shape the dough in a round, as above. The top can be slashed in a similar way to the tops of round loaves baked on a sheet.

Long containers: Roll the bread into a cylinder of the appropriate size, as above. The top can be slashed diagonally or once straight down the middle. To give a double top effect, the dough can also be divided into two high rectangles which are put in the mold side by side.

Ring molds: Form the dough into a tapered cylinder that, when formed into a ring, is the same circumference as the mold. Coil it round the mold, overlapping the ends, and push down gently to distribute the dough evenly.

Gugelhupf molds: There are two ways of filling these, the first is as for the ring mold. The second is to form the dough into a long cylinder and cut it in crossways slices which are then spread with a filling. These are then put in the mold in overlapping layers and gently pressed down. (See Gugelhupf recipe page 45.)

Brioche molds: Rich, soft brioche dough is baked in a similar shape to a cottage loaf, but its texture demands that it is cooked in a container. Take about three-quarters of the dough, form it into a round and put it in the mold. Form the other piece of dough into a pear shape, with the thin end tapered. With your fingers, make a hole down through the center of the dough in the mold to make a well slightly larger than the tapered end of the smaller piece. Insert the smaller piece of dough in the hole so that its rounded end forms a knob on top of the larger piece. (See Brioche recipe page 33.)

Rolls, Buns and Doughnuts

When you are making rolls and buns, cut the dough into even-sized pieces using a sharp knife and then lightly knead each piece separately.

Round Rolls

Roll the dough round and round between your palms to form a ball. Place it on a floured surface, and turn it round several times with your palms to give an even, round shape. Lay the rolls on a baking sheet without flattening them. Round rolls can be left plain or the tops can be slashed with a single line, a circle or a small cross shape after the first rising.

Clover Leaf

Cut the dough in smaller pieces. Form each into rounds and lay them on the baking sheet, just touching each other, in groups of three.

Cluster

Lay the rolls in a circular pattern on the baking sheet, just touching each other. As they bake, they will join together, but can easily be pulled apart when required.

Long Rolls

Roll the dough between your palms to form a ball, as above. Lay the dough on a floured work surface and roll it backwards and forwards under your hands until it is of the required length and thickness. A long diagonal or lengthways slash can be added on long rolls after the first rising.

Ring Doughnuts and Bagels

Make the dough into rounds. Push your forefinger down through the center of each. Enlarge the holes until they cover about one third of the diameter of the dough.

Knots

Form the dough into a ball and then into a long, thin rope by rolling it backwards and forwards under your hands. Make a loose knot, stretching the dough as little as possible.

Parker House Rolls

These are made to give plenty of crust. Roll the dough to a thickness of about ½ inch. Using a pastry cutter, cut it into 3½-inch circles and brush the top surface of the circles with melted butter. Score down the center of each circle with a sharp knife and fold the circle in half down the score line. Place them on a baking sheet and gently press them down.

Yeasted Pastries

The dough for yeasted pastries is firmer than for flat breads, but it still needs to be rolled without stretching. It is then cut according to the final pastry shape required. Use a sharp knife or a dough scraper, so that the edges do not become pulled, and a ruler to obtain straight edges and similar sizes. Below are some of the more popular shapes.

Crescent

This shape is used all over the world and is probably most well known as the shape of the French croissant. Cut equilateral triangles with the sides measuring 6 inches. Use a rolling

pin from top to base of each one to slightly elongate them. Slightly pull out the corners of the base so they stick out, and then begin rolling tightly from the base to the tip. Bring the ends round to make a crescent shape and tuck the tip underneath. As the dough expands in the oven the tip should pull itself out again to lie across the top. To make a filled crescent, spread the filling over the bottom half of the triangle before rolling.

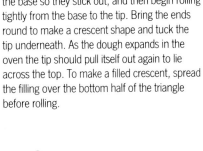

Pinwheels

Cut the dough into 6-inch squares. Cut a line from each corner to within ½ inch of the center. Put a portion of the filling in the center. Fold one bottom corner of each cut section to the center with the tips overlapping slightly. Seal by pressing down in the center.

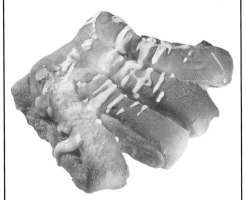

Cockscombs

Cut the dough into 8-inch-wide rectangles and spread half with a filling. Fold over

the other half and then cut the folded dough into 4-inch squares. Make three cuts in the folded side of the dough from the fold to within ½ inch of the opposite side. After laying the pastries on a floured baking sheet, gently spread out the sections.

Snails

Cut the dough into a rectangle 8 × 16 inches. Spread it evenly with filling. Roll up the dough along one long side and cut into 1-inch-thick slices. Lay these flat.

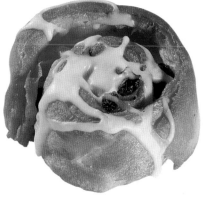

Finishes

Various toppings and glazes can improve the appearance of your bread.

Glazes give the finished loaf a shiny surface. The simplest is a plain beaten egg. You can also use egg beaten with a little water or milk.

For sweet buns you can use milk, sweetened by being warmed with a little sugar – 2 teaspoons to ⅔ cup milk.

Most loaves are glazed immediately after shaping.

The topping on a loaf adds to the appearance and also, to some extent, to the final flavor. It is sprinkled on after glazing but before slashing, so that the slashes will show up plainly. The following are ingredients that are used most frequently: poppy seeds, sesame seeds, caraway seeds, cracked wheat (on whole-wheat breads only), slivered almonds and chopped nuts (the latter two mainly on sweet breads).

THE HISTORY OF BREAD

The story of bread begins around 10,000 BC, after the last ice age. As the earth warmed up, grasses with seeds began to grow, and the nomadic hunters of the world discovered that they could harvest, dry and grind them to produce a coarse, gritty flour.

Wild wheat and barley grasses grew most abundantly in the Eastern Mediterranean. Strong, hot winds scattered the wild seeds as soon as they ripened, so that local people had to react fast, when the time was right, to gather in what they could before it blew away. Because there was no organized cultivation, the rest was left to seed itself for the following year.

By 9000 BC, the people of the Middle East had established themselves in villages near to the best wild crops, and from this time onwards, they started to select, domesticate and cultivate the wild animals and grasses around them.

The first primitive breads appeared at this time. The toasted and ground grains were first mixed with water, then kneaded into a thick paste or dough. The resulting unleavened, stone- or ash-baked hearth cakes became a staple food. Middle Eastern *lavash*, Indian *chapatis*, Mexican tortillas, Ethiopian *injera* and Scottish oatcakes all evolved. Nowadays some of these are eaten cold, but originally, because of the type and coarseness of the grain, they were really only palatable when hot. Although a few attempts were made to improve bread during the Neolithic period, such as sprouting the grain before it was toasted, soaking it in water, and simmering it, the real improvement in quality came with the development of a better grain.

In 6000 BC, the Nutufian race, living around the Persian Gulf, began to develop the first real farming methods. They dug the soil and scattered the seeds by hand, instead of leaving it to the wind. They threshed their grain by driving animals over it, and winnowed it by throwing handfuls into the air, a process which continued in Europe until the nineteenth century. In the hope of better harvests and more palatable bread, the Natufians also developed new strains of wheat.

At around the same time, fermented liquids were discovered, perhaps because someone left some honey-sweetened water by a fire. This was the beginning of yeast, and its inclusion in wheat-flour doughs was found to make bread rise. The ancient Egyptians, whose farming communities grew up along the Nile before 5000 BC, certainly knew about and ate leavened bread, although it was usually reserved for the rich. The majority of the people ate flat breads, made from a mixture of coarse-grained flours, and a kind of sourdough bread, known as *ta*, which was made from wheat and barley.

By 4000 BC, many countries in Europe were farming countries. Peoples from northern France and Belgium took various types of cereals and domesticated animals to Britain, where they settled, mainly in the south and southwest. New types of wheat were developed in different European countries and by the Iron Age (*c.* 1000 BC), the main types of grain were spelt and club wheat.

The first ovens in Europe were called pot ovens – domed iron pots which were placed over hot hearth-stones. Steam trapped inside them made the bread softer and, even though no leaven was added, encouraged it to rise slightly. Rotary hand querns, for grinding, first appeared in Spain and spread across Europe in the first century AD. At around the same time, Celts in Gaul began to sift their ground grain through a hair sieve, to make it finer, and also found a way of using beer as a leaven. All these developments vastly improved the quality of bread.

By about 1000 BC, the ancient Greeks had devised the first primitive mills to grind the wheat and barley which was grown all over the country. They were made from two horizontally-placed rectangular stones. The top stone had a slit through which the grain was poured, and was worked backwards and forwards using a system of pulleys. The Greeks are also reputed to have invented the donkey-powered mill. Greek bread, raised with a leaven made by soaking millet flour in grape juice, which was subsequently kneaded and left to ferment, was far closer to modern bread than its predecessors.

Despite conquering vast areas of the world, the Romans' expertise did not at first extend to baking. The staple food of the Roman soldiers was puls, or pulmentum, a thick porridge made from millet, spelt or chick-pea flour; or small cakes baked from crushed grains (still known as haver cakes in parts of England, because they were once carried in a soldier's haversack). It took a long time for them to switch to ready-made bread because at first it was so coarse and therefore heavy to carry.

However, with the Roman invention of a new type of mill, which used circular revolving millstones, flour was made finer than it had ever been before. Yeast was subsequently imported from Gaul, and Egyptian slaves were brought in to mix the two into bread. The first bakeries were established and with them greater distinctions between bread for the rich and for the poor.

The Roman aristocracy insisted upon fine, white bread, a preference which spread throughout the then known world and which has persisted until late into the twentieth century. Wheat bread was preferred to barley bread and there were all kinds of variations. The Romans probably had the first baps and croissants, and they encouraged variation by adding honey, poppy seeds and cheese to their basic bread mixture. Bread was baked and sold on the premises, and also in market stalls.

Very little has been recorded about the development of bread between the end of the Roman world and the beginning of the Medieval period. We do know that the watermill was developed in Europe during the fifth century. The first one ever to appear in British records was one in Kent, mentioned in a charter of the year AD 762. By the time the Domesday Book was written in 1086, there were 5,624 watermills in England alone.

In the sixth century AD, the Slavs in the northeast of Europe had developed the forerunner of the moldboard plow, which made it possible to bring large areas of hitherto untouched land into cultivation. And as more grain was grown and fewer people starved, the population increased.

By the time William the Conqueror invaded England in AD 1066, the growing and milling of grain in Europe had established a pattern that was to change very little in the next four hundred years. Mills were often owned by the lords of particular villages, and poor inhabitants were bound to bring their own grain to the lord's mill and pay for the privilege of having it ground. Plows, too, were not owned by individuals, but communally, so grain growing was a community project. This fairly loose arrangement was seized upon by Medieval lords and rigidly enforced so that the growing and milling of grain helped to confirm the hierarchical nature of the feudal system.

Tremendous amounts of bread were consumed by Medieval households. At the tables of the poor, bread often had to be a meal in itself, or was served with a thin pottage of vegetables and pulses. In rich households, bread was often the only accompaniment to roasted or stewed meats and was essential in the winter, when most of the meat and fish was brined, to counteract the saltiness of the diet. Despite this, very few plain bread recipes were written down. Apprentices learned them from master bakers, and young girls from their relatives at home.

The regular peasant bread in Medieval Europe was whole-wheat, often containing pieces of chaff as well as the bran and coarsely-ground grain. It was made with a mixture of grains, was dark in color, heavy in texture and probably had quite a strong flavor. In times of hardship other ingredients were added to increase the amount of flour. Pea and bean flours were common, acorns, ground root vegetables and sawdust could be found in Swiss bread, and in Scandinavia they used tree bark.

Dark whole-wheat bread had quite another use in the homes of rich Normans – namely, to make trenchers (after the French, *tranche*, meaning slice) – a custom since the time of Charlemagne. Trenchers were used as plates, and were cut from large, square loaves that had been turned during baking to give them an even shape. Stewed meat was placed on them before being eaten with the fingers. Trenchers soaked up the gravy so as to make the process as polite as possible, but were rarely eaten themselves during the course of a meal. Instead they were collected in baskets and given to the servants or dogs, or distributed to the poor.

The best-quality bread in the Medieval period was wheat bread, made with flour that had been bolted several times through wool and linen cloths to make it as white and bran-free as possible. It was demanded by the rich and longed for by the poor. The English called it wastel, from the Norman *guastel* meaning cake, and similar to wastel were pandemain, mayne bread; and manchet bread, which was made up into small, bun-sized loaves. Other breads, such as cocket, in England, were less expensive, because the flour for them was less finely ground. There was a coarse, whole-wheat type called cheat, chet, bis or treet, which was made from unbolted wheat flour; various maslin and mixed grain breads; and horse-bread, which consisted of a large proportion of pea and bean flours.

In Scandinavia there were long-keeping crispbreads and hard, round loaves that were strung on poles and hung in the rafters, while in Italy, although pasta was the staple, and bread was expensive, two special breads *were* devised in the Middle Ages, the colomba and panettone (see page 54). In the Middle East, at the same time, there was the white flour bread, *al khobz al huwmara*, and the coarse flour bread, *al khobz al khashkar*. Both were glazed with borax which was imported from Armenia.

As towns grew larger, there were more and more commercial bakers who not only made bread for sale, but also took in dough from ordinary house-holders for baking. As with all trades in Medieval London, the bakery business in England was controlled by the guilds, and there were separate guilds for white and brown bread bakers, which existed until the seventeenth century.

Bakers sent their servants and apprentices into the streets with trays of bread, ringing handbells to attract custom. Competition was fierce, with the result that price cutting and reduction in the size of loaves were common practices. In 1277, the first full version of the Assize of Bread was therefore drawn up, to establish sizes and weights according to the quality of the bread. The laws were complicated and it was small wonder that one of the commonest crimes of all in Medieval England was selling underweight bread. For this, and the crime of stealing another baker's dough, the offender's punishment was to be dragged on a sled through the dirtiest streets of the town with a loaf tied around his neck. After a second offence he would be put in the pillory and after a third, banished from trading forever.

Paris bakers were also organizing themselves into guilds at about this time. They formed the Corporation des Boulangers, and the rights and duties of master bakers, apprentices and servants were clearly set out. The price of bread was fixed, but the size of loaves depended on the price of wheat.

During the sixteenth and seventeenth centuries bread changed very little. Rye, maslin and barley bread were still made. White wheat bread remained the food of the rich, whilst the poor made do with coarser varieties. The finest bread in English cities was still manchet, which was sometimes baked without leaven, giving it a very close texture. It was a creamy color and sometimes enriched with butter and eggs. Cheat bread was more or less the equivalent of present-day whole-wheat, and "brown bread" was the term used for the coarsest and most branny of all. In sixteenth-century France, however, there was a new kind of fine wheat bread called *le pain de chapitre* but it was not until 1650 that sifted flour became commonly available in Paris.

In Roman times, the French had been famous for using brewer's yeast as a leaven, but this method had virtually died out, and most bread was risen by the sourdough process. In 1665, however, a brewer's yeast leaven was reintroduced by the Flemish. The new bread received court honors and Marie de Medici called it *pain à la reine*. In 1668, however, the French Faculté de Médecine declared that it was made from rotten barley and therefore injurious to health. Furious arguments ensued, but in the end the lovers of good bread won, and the use of brewer's yeast was authorized in 1670. Until then, French bread had had a thin crust and a close, compact crumb. Large loaves weighing 16 pounds or more had been made at home to last the family a week. The new bread was light and airy with a hard crust, but it did not keep. Consequently, housewives not wishing to bake at home every day relied on a daily visit to the baker.

The discovery of new countries has made a great contribution to culinary history, and bread is no exception. Not only were these new lands for wheat growing, but they also provided new ingredients for bread making. At the end of the fifteenth century, Columbus discovered America and the Caribbean islands and there he found something that the native Indians called "may-ees." It was a decorative grass with huge ears. The Europeans named it maize, or sweet corn. Eaten with beans and vegetables it was the staple food of the Aztecs and Mayans, who used it to make the flat breads that the Spaniards christened tortillas. In North America and what was to become Canada, when the first harvests of the European settlers were unsuccessful, it was the American Indians who taught them to make the maize-based johnny cake (see page 123), also known as hoe cake, ash cake or corn pone.

Maize seeds were taken back to Spain and from there to the rest of southern Europe and eventually the Philippines and even China. Corn breads and the thick corn porridge called polenta, so like the Roman puls, became popular in Italy.

Maize bread was not the only new bread to be discovered. In the Bahamas lived the Taino tribes, who made flat hearth cakes from the stem pulp of the zamia plant. This discovery may have had little effect on the rest of the world, but the discovery of manioc in Cuba did. The roots of the plant were grated and peeled and the bitter juices squeezed out before the pulp was sieved, made into flat cakes and cooked. This was known as cassava bread and, surprisingly, it was very much liked by the Spanish and the French. In the sixteenth century, manioc (a source of tapioca) was taken to Africa by the Portuguese where it became a principal food.

In return, wheat was taken to the New World. A colony founded by Sir

Walter Raleigh planted the first crop on Roanoke Island, off North Carolina; the Pilgrim fathers planted wheat and rye beside the local corn; and Bartholomew Gosnold, the discoverer of Cape Cod, grew wheat on Elizabeth Island, Massachusetts, in 1602. Many acres of virgin land were put under the plow, but nevertheless it was two hundred years before wheat bread ceased to be a luxury. The first watermill, however, was erected in 1634 and the prosperity and importance of New York was established at this time through its being the center of the grain trade in the East. Meanwhile, both French and English were settling in Canada, and in southern Africa, in 1652, the Dutch, led by Jan van Riebeek, established a supply port at the Cape from which the voortrekkers set out to establish farms and wheatlands.

The eighteenth century saw the improvement of agricultural methods throughout the whole of Europe and in the newly-settled areas of America. Jethro Tull invented the seed drill and a four-coultered plow, whilst Thomas Coke brought in his threshing machine. In England a four year crop rotation system was devised, whilst Holland vastly improved Europe's grain yields with a seven year system. Steam-powered mills were introduced in both Britain and America to cope with the increasingly abundant crops. Wheat flour became more available everywhere. The people had more bread, and, as a result, the population of Europe increased by 48 million to 188 million between 1750 and 1800.

In France, bread making was reaching perfection. Brewer's yeast was replaced by a special baking yeast, imported from Holland and Austria, and there was a great deal of research and discussion into what made a good loaf. In 1778 the basic ingredients and methods were agreed and the Ecole de Boulangerie was established in Paris in 1780, although it lasted for only thirteen years. By then nearly every baker was a master of his craft.

There were several really poor harvests in England towards the end of the eighteenth century but, although wheat became scarce, it did not lose its popularity. In times of great shortage the government

● *Harvesting, Palouse, Washington state*

sponsored a "standard loaf" made of coarse, dark wheat flour, containing a large proportion of bran; but the people wanted white bread and the result was bread doctored with chalk, alum, beanmeal and even bonemeal. Even the poorest demanded white bread, and in 1795 the recently introduced poor relief system was calculated on its price.

During the nineteenth century, agricultural methods continued to increase wheat yields in both Britain and North America. By this time, land in Australia was being farmed – the climate of the southwest, in particular, being ideally suited to the growing of wheat.

The reaping machine was invented by a Scots preacher called the Reverend Patrick Bell. While the British resented change to a method of harvesting that had been the same since the first wheat was planted, the Americans thought it a great idea and eventually used one patented in their own country. John Deere of Illinois invented a lightweight plow, and a binding machine was introduced, first in America, and later perfected in Britain. Australian farmers came up with the idea of a combine harvester that would cut and thresh in one go.

New types of wheat were also being developed, such as Red Fife, a good, hard, bread-making wheat that was taken west by the pioneers; and Maquis wheat, which could be sown in the spring and cropped early.

America became the world's largest grain producer – the new railways ensured transport across the country – and in 1884 Canada actually exported wheat back to Britain. Despite all the developments, however, there was widespread adulteration of bread by bakers, and soaring costs. It was these factors that induced two British writers to encourage every housewife to bake their own.

William Cobbett produced his *Cottage Economy* in 1823, giving instructions on all aspects of country housekeeping and smallholding. "How wasteful," he says, "how shameful, for a laborer's wife to go the the baker's shop; and how negligent, how criminally careless of the welfare of his family, must the laborer be, who permits so scandalous a use of the proceeds of his labor." But in praise of home-baked bread: "Here is cut and come again. Here is bread always for the table. Bread to carry afield; always a hunch of bread to put into the hand of a hungry child."

Eliza Acton wrote her *English Bread Book* in 1857 because she disliked the unhygienic conditions in commercial bakeries and the fact that bread was still adulterated.

In America, Fannie Farmer wrote *The Original Boston Cooking School Book* in 1896, into which she put twenty pages of bread recipes. "The study of bread making," she said, 'is of no slight importance and deserves more attention than it receives."

But no matter how housewives were urged to bake their own bread, more and more was being made commercially and the process became increasingly mechanized. The first kneading machine was invented in the late nineteenth century, but in both Britain and Europe it was disregarded until after the upheavals of the First World War, during which bread was rationed and was made of whatever grains there were available. Also at the end of the nineteenth century, the first roller mills were introduced.

Between the two World Wars, the Chorleywood baking process (involving the addition of improvers to the flour and intensive mechanical kneading) was devised in England. This method could produce uniform, mass-produced bread, and large-scale bakeries in many parts of the world use a similar process today.

Nowadays, sophisticated city supermarkets stock a large range of breads in addition to the ubiquitous white-sliced loaf. However, commercialization takes little account of the amazing variety of local shapes and flavors to be found all around the world. This book aims to bring just such regional diversity to a wider audience.

FRANCE

Bread is extremely important in the French diet, as the main accompaniment to every meal – from a simple salad to a rich blanquette or ragout. Where the British choose potatoes, the Chinese rice and the Italians pasta, the French will have bread.
Bread is dunked into hot chocolate, covered in nourishing soup, used to mop up gravies and sauces, and is, of course, eaten with ripe local cheese.
French families shop for bread daily, and the joy of this is that there is at least one craftsman baker to be found in every village to satisfy the demand.

Boulangeries were traditionally opened six days a week, closing on Mondays, but now they often stagger their working days so that there is always at least one local shop open every day. Each shop sells a vast selection of different shapes and sizes of loaves, including some specific to the locality.

France has been famous for its bread since Roman times when, unusually for the age, it was risen with brewer's yeast. With the fall of Rome, however, refinements slipped, and the common French diet reverted to a cereal porridge, supplemented occasionally by bread made in the home. This bread was either unleavened or started by a sourdough method, and typically made from a mixture of coarsely ground and unsieved grains including rye, wheat, buckwheat, barley and oats.

By the eleventh century, however, bread had become a mainstay of the French diet. The bread of the ordinary people was still very coarse, often made from mixed cereals, but, as in the rest of Europe, finer wheaten breads were produced for the rich. Many windmills and watermills were built at this time and communal bakehouses were set up in every village, where bread prepared at home could be taken for baking.

Using the sourdough method to make all types of bread, generally called *pain au levain*, was common practice throughout France. One of the most famous breads, from the thirteenth century to the Revolution, was the *pain de gonesse* – a fine wheat bread, highly praised by Henry IV and later by Marie de Medici. Both brown and white types were sold in the Paris markets. In the fifteenth and sixteenth centuries there were *pain de chailli*, a quality white bread; *pain coquille*, a mixed grain middle quality bread; and *pain bis*, which was the cheapest and coarsest. Throughout this time, and much later, there were strong regional differences regarding the types of grains used.

In 1665, brewer's yeast was introduced to France by the Flemish. Although the Faculté de Médecine said that it was harmful to health, it was finally authorized in 1670, and changed the bread making and tastes of France. Later, a proper baking yeast was imported from Holland and Austria, and it was eventually made in France in 1874. *Pain au levain*, however, was only gradually super-seded by *pain au levure* (yeasted bread) and even now there are some loaves which must be baked by the sourdough process in order to maintain their character and flavor.

Until the eighteenth century most French loaves were round, but around 1770 long shapes began to appear. At first these were pointed cylinders, like a bloomer, but they developed into the long thin loaves that are now called French sticks, or baguettes. Towards the end of the eighteenth century, much research went into the best methods of baking, and the short-lived Ecole de Boulangerie was set up in Paris. At this time, the main ingredients of bread and the approved method of baking it were agreed. Bread was made by craftsmen bakers, in small bakeries, in wood-fired brick ovens. Little or none was made at home.

The government levied a bread tax in 1880 which, unwittingly, varied the scope of the French baker. The finer the flour used and the purer the loaf (that is, without the addition of grains other than wheat), the higher the tax. The ingenious French bakers, however, used this legislation as a means to improve their product and make money. They decided to interpret "lack of purity" as a license to add not different grains to their wheat flour, but different ingredients altogether. These included milk, butter and eggs, and resulted in the production of rich doughs. These delicious, but admittedly impure, breads and rolls could be sold at a high price and yet at a low tax.

At the end of the nineteenth century, the first kneading machines were introduced, but they did not come into full use until after the First World War. To start with, they were used with discretion, and bread in France in the 1930s was better than it had ever been, often made with a mixture of sourdough, yeast and fine wheat flour. During the Second World War, bread had to be made from wholegrain flour – a mixture of every cereal available: maize, rye, barley, beans and rice, besides wheat.

With the recovery of normal life in the 1950s, the theme was "good bread for all," and there was a strict control on its price. However, in the 1960s,

● *A gentleman with morning paper and baguette, exchanging a word with a friend in St. Maxime, near Aix-en-Provence*

over-use of the kneading machines resulted in a great number of voluminous loaves without much substance. Bakers were urged to think again and combine the best of the old methods with the best of the new.

Today, French bread is once again of excellent quality, with the bread-making process usually part mechanical and part manual. Besides the well known crusty white breads, there are many special regional breads which were revived during the 1980s. In any one boulangerie you can expect to find at least twenty-five different types of bread.

The main bread-making flour is home-grown wheat, produced mainly in the Plaines de Beauce, le Bassin Parisien and la Région du Nord. French wheat is softer than the bread-making wheat used in most other countries. It may be used alone or mixed with a small percentage of imported hard wheats. Rye bread, *pain de seigle*, is made from rye alone or from a varying mixture of rye and wheat. Other grains are only used very rarely. The idea that white bread is the best bread has held fast in France. When, in the 1970s and 80s, the rest of us were turning to health foods by the score, the French held out, and today *le pain complet* (whole-wheat bread) accounts for only 2 percent of all bread sold. A leaflet by the Centre d'Information des Farines et du Pain states: "the *pain complet* is richer, without doubt, in vitamins and minerals, but it contains a good deal of fiber, which is diges-ted less well. It is best not to eat it every day."

French bread, as we have come to know it, is made only from flour, yeast (or sourdough), water and salt. Why then, can't we all achieve that crackling crust, the creamy-colored, well-aerated crumb, the aroma of the brick oven and the flavor of sweet wheat? The answer is in the flour and the baking. The flour is softer than that used for bread in most other parts of the world, and it has a very special sweet flavor. It is unbleached and without chemical improvers.

In the bakery, which is usually behind the boulangerie, the dough is mixed and put into a kneading machine for 10 to 15 minutes, with a rest period of about 3 minutes in the middle. It is then given the first rising, called *la fermentation en cuve* (in a vat). This rising is quite a long one, producing a strong, elastic dough, and is considered very important for the aroma. The dough is divided into loaf-sized pieces. This process is rapid and usually mechanical, producing loaves of a standard weight. Each piece then gets a further rising time, before being shaped. In the smaller bakeries this is done by hand and in the large ones, by machine. This is called *la tourne* (the turning). Once shaped, the loaves are put into linen-lined baskets, or laid on linen worktops, for the second rising period called *l'apprêt*. Some are put into pans to make the shape equivalent to the English sliced loaf, and called *pain moulé*. However, in France this is not very popular and this sort of bread is commonly used for making bread crumbs. After the second rising, the loaves are three times their original size.

Just before putting the loaves into the oven the baker *signe son pain* (signs his bread), by slashing the tops. Besides giving a pleasing appearance to the loaves, this releases gases built up during baking and helps to produce a good crust.

Meanwhile, the ovens are heated to 500°F and steam is injected into them. The loaves are put in either by hand, using a wooden shovel, or on a system of linen conveyor belts. The steam continues to enter the oven for the first 10 to 15 minutes of baking time. This enables the bread to expand to its fullest capacity without being hindered by a hard crust. It also forms a starch on the surface of the loaves which becomes crackly, golden and shiny when the steam is turned off.

The finished loaves are handled with extreme care. When they first come out of the oven, they are left to cool for a while before being taken in a large basket to be stacked upright on the shelves, ready for sale.

French bread is baked every day and sometimes as often as three times a day. It is always eaten fresh, nearly always without butter, and any left over is toasted or put into soup on the second day.

The baguette is difficult to reproduce completely successfully outside France, but this recipe comes very near. This is the loaf synonymous with French bread all over the world. Treat it just like the genuine article: eat it fresh, as soon as it has cooled.

The Baguette

To make two 14-inch baguettes:
¾ ounce fresh yeast or ¾ tablespoon dried
1½ cups warm water
1½ teaspoons salt
3½ cups (14 ounces) plain cake flour
½ cup (2 ounces) all-purpose flour

Dissolve the yeast in a little of the water and leave to stand – five minutes for fresh yeast and 15 for dried. Dissolve the salt in the rest of the water. Combine the two types of flour in a bowl. Make a well in the center and pour in the yeast mixture. Mix in a little of the flour from the sides of the bowl and then add the salt water. Mix everything to a dough and knead it on a floured board. Cover it with a clean cloth and leave it in a warm place for 1 hour to rise.

Heat the oven to 400°F. Knead the dough again and divide it in half. Form each one into a roll about 14 inches long. Place them on floured sheets and leave them for 20 minutes.

Make four long diagonal slits down each loaf, using a razor blade or very sharp knife. Brush the loaves well with cold water. Just before you place the loaves in the oven, put a small basin of water on the

• *Outside a Paris bakery*

• *Loaves and croissants in Brittany*

• *Easy shopping in the Dordogne*

bottom shelf. Bake the loaves for 1 hour, brushing the surfaces well with more cold water every 15 minutes. This seems like a very long baking time, but regular brushing with water will prevent the loaves from drying out or burning. If they look as if they are going to color too quickly, cover them with aluminum foil.

When the loaves are done, lift them on to wire racks to cool. Eat them slightly warm or as soon as they are cool, and certainly on the day that you make them.

This basic dough is made into many different shapes, some standard throughout France and others particular to a region, town or even shop where a *boulanger* has a specialty. The same dough can taste different depending on the size and shape of the finished loaf.

The *flûte* is a longer and thinner version of a baguette, and the *ficelle*, meaning "string," even thinner. The *opéra* or restaurant is shorter and fatter; the *petit Parisien*, shorter, fatter and usually softer in the middle; the *pain d'Alsacienne* like a short bloomer with lengthways scores; and the *pain Espagnol* similar, with very pointed ends. It is said that the *epi* was made for the person who, sent out to buy the loaf, was tempted to break off and eat the crusty end before reaching home. Cut to resemble an ear of wheat (see page 19), it has many such crusty knobs for pulling off – so everyone can have a share. Like several other breads, the *epi* has been made, over the years, for both pagan and Christian festivals. Other examples include the *couronne*, formed into a wreath, and the *couronne sartoise*, formed into a spiralled horseshoe. The palette is like an oval paddle; the *pain collier* like a horse collar; the *tabatière* like an open snuff box; and the *champignon* like a mushroom.

The *pain de campagne*, however, is the most popular of the specialty breads, and it can be found all over France, in small bakeries and in hypermarkets. It is made with wheat flour or a mixture of wheat and rye, using the sourdough method which makes it moist, pleasantly acidic and long keeping. The *pain de campagne* is usually round with cross cuts on the top that divide it in six sections – in other words, a *miche* (see page 16). Sometimes it was made almost as big as a cartwheel, in order to last a family for a week. Cartloads of such loaves were taken each week to outlying districts and left at the side of the road for families to collect.

The most popular of the enriched breads, brought about by the taxes of the nineteenth century, is the *pain Viennois*, which looks like a baguette, and is semi-sweet with a fluffy-textured crumb. The dough is enriched with malted flour, sugar and milk powder.

The *petits pains*, literally "small breads," are shaped rather like outsize rolls, some with diagonal slashes and others with one slash lengthways. They are made of white wheat flour (*petits pains ordinaire*), with rye flour or with a

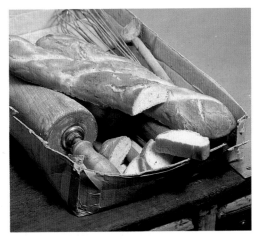

● *The Baguette*

mixture, and the dough can be plain or enriched with milk, eggs or butter.

The following recipe is for semi-sweet rolls made with milk and egg. In the area around Paris they are called fougasses, which can be confusing since this is also the name of a different bread, made in Normandy.

Petits Pains au Lait

To make sixteen buns:

1 ounce fresh yeast or 1 tablespoon dried
1 cup warm milk, plus 2 tablespoons
4 cups (1 pound) all-purpose flour
1 teaspoon salt
5 tablespoons sugar
1 egg
¼ cup (½ stick) butter, softened

Dissolve the yeast in a little of the warm milk and leave to stand – five minutes for fresh yeast and 15 for dried. Place the flour in a bowl and toss in the salt and 3 tablespoons sugar. Make a well in the center, pour in the yeast and the remaining milk and add the egg. Mix everything to a dough and knead it on a floured board until it is smooth. Knead in the butter. Place the dough in a bowl, cover it with a cloth and leave in a warm place for 1 hour.

Heat the oven to 400°F. Knead the dough again and divide it in sixteen equal pieces. Form them into round rolls and place them on a floured baking sheet. Leave the buns to rise for 20 minutes and bake them for 15 minutes. Cool them on a wire rack.

To glaze the fougasses, dissolve 2 tablespoons sugar in 2 tablespoons milk and brush over the hot buns.

A visit to the *boulangerie* on the way to school is a treat for many French children, and bakers in different areas bake certain small rolls for them. These rolls are eaten with chocolate during the first break of the day. To give the right blend of bread and semi-soft chocolate, the rolls can be split open and left with pieces of chocolate in them near a heater, or even sat upon for a short time! Some bakers actually bake the chocolate inside the rolls and this really is the most delicious combination. When eaten, they are still warm, the chocolate is soft, but not runny enough to be messy. Even after cooling, when the chocolate has solidified again, they still make an excellent sweet snack. You can even serve them as a dessert with cream.

Petits Pains au Chocolat

To make eight buns:

½ quantity basic bread dough (see page 12), made with milk, or dough as for Petit Pains au Lait

One 7-ounce bar of plain chocolate that can be broken into 8 rectangles

Make up the dough and leave it to rise in the usual way. Preheat the oven to 400°F.

Knead the dough on a floured board, divide it in eight pieces and roll each one into a rectangle about 4 × 6 inches. Break the chocolate into eight rectangles. Lay a piece of chocolate on one of the rolled pieces of dough. Fold over the ends of the dough and then the sides, to enclose the chocolate completely.

Place the finished parcel, with the seams of the dough underneath, on a floured baking sheet. Continue to make the rest of the buns in the same way.

Leave the buns to rise for 20 minutes. Bake them for 15 minutes or until they are golden-brown. Cool them on a wire rack and eat them warm or cold.

Flat, flavored breads are popular in France. They are ideal snacks and, when accompanied by a salad, make a complete meal. The *forron* is the simplest of all these. It comes from the Dauphiné region of southeast France and is made of an oil-enriched dough pressed into a tart pan and topped with cream cheese made from either cow's or goat's milk. Walnuts and onions are used to top another flat bread called *le sale de bugey.*

When making a savory tart, French housewives often use a bread dough in place of pastry. They may well buy the dough ready-made from the local baker and knead in a little oil themselves.

The following two recipes are examples of tarts made with bread bases: one with a quiche Lorraine filling and the other with a simple béchamel sauce flavored with Gruyère cheese. They are very simple to make and lift out of the pans so easily that you will never want to make a pastry tart again. Both are best eaten warm, with a salad.

Tarte Lorraine

To make one 10-inch-diameter tart:

½ quantity basic bread dough (see page 12), plus 2 tablespoons olive oil, risen for 1 hour

2 slices bacon

1 small onion

1 tablespoon butter

1 egg

1 egg yolk

½ cup milk, plus 2 tablespoons light cream

1 ounce Cheddar or Gruyère cheese, grated

Preheat the oven to 400°F. Dice the bacon and thinly slice the onion. Cook them in a frying pan in the butter until the onion is golden and the bacon is just cooked through.

Knead the dough on a floured board and roll it out to line a 10-inch-diameter tart pan. Prick it in several places with a fork. Spread the bacon and onion over the dough. Beat together the egg, egg yolk, milk, cream and cheese. Pour them over the bacon and onion. Leave the tart for 20 minutes. You will find that the edges of the dough begin to rise and the filling forms a wide well in the middle.

Bake the tart for 25 minutes, or until the edges are golden-brown. Push the loaf out of the pan and serve.

Cheese and Tomato Tart

To make one 10-inch-diameter tart:

½ quantity basic bread dough (see page 12), plus 2 tablespoons olive oil, risen for 1 hour

2 tablespoons butter

1 small onion, thinly sliced

2 tablespoons all-purpose flour

1¼ cups milk

4 ounces Gruyère cheese, grated

3 ripe tomatoes

Line a 10-inch tart pan as for Tarte Lorraine above. In a saucepan, over medium heat, gently cook the onion in the butter until it turns golden. Stir in the flour and milk and cook, stirring, until you have a thick sauce. Take the pan from the heat and beat in the cheese. Cool the sauce and pour it over the dough that lines the tart pan. Slice the tomatoes and lay the slices on top. Leave to rise and bake as for Tarte Lorraine.

In Normandy there is a *fougasse* containing eggs and butter, which is rolled into a rectangle with leaf shapes incised into it. Cheese or anchovies are scattered over the top, and it is folded in half to make a shape that resembles a bagpipe.

The *pissaladière* is the Niçoise equivalent of the pizza, made with oil-enriched dough, rolled flat and topped with anchovies and in some cases a fresh tomato salad. Anchovies are also used a lot in Provence and the following recipe comes from that area. It is not a flat bread, but a round dome of moist, flavorsome dough made using a sourdough leaven. It is wonderful with butter (although not traditionally served with it) and also with tomato soup or a stew.

La Pompe aux Anchois

To make one 1-pound loaf:

½ quantity basic bread dough (see page 12), put into a large bowl, covered with plastic wrap and kept in a warm place for 2 days

Two 1¾-ounce cans anchovy fillets

¼ cup (½ stick) butter, softened

2 eggs, beaten

2 cups (8 ounces) all-purpose flour

Take five of the anchovy fillets, cut them in half lengthways and then into pieces about 5 inches long. Crush the remaining fillets to a paste.

With the fermented dough still in the bowl, knead in the crushed anchovies, the butter and then the eggs, a little at a time. At first it will look impossible for all the egg to be absorbed, but this will happen after about 10 minutes and you will be left with a smooth, very soft dough. Knead in the flour and then turn the dough on to a floured work surface for a final kneading to make it smooth and elastic. Return the dough to the bowl, cover it and leave it in a warm place for 1 hour or until it has doubled in size.

Preheat the oven to 400°F. Knead the dough again, form it into a ball and place on a floured baking sheet. Put the pieces of anchovy on top, pressing down lightly. Leave the dough in a warm place to rise for 20 minutes.

Bake the loaf for 25 minutes, or until it is golden-brown and sounds hollow when tapped. Cool on a wire rack.

The richest of all breads in France is the brioche, made with white flour, eggs and large amounts of butter. The crumb is light, moist and truly golden in color, and the crust is thin and crisp. A brioche is best when it is still warm from the oven, but it will keep well in a plastic bag and also makes excellent toast.

Brioches are made in the traditional fluted pan, narrower at the base than

● *La Pompe aux Anchois*

● *A plain brioche*

at the top, with a standard capacity of about 3 cups. They can also be made in ordinary round cake pans, loaf pans, ring molds, *gugelhupf* molds or small dariole molds. Brioche dough is put into the refrigerator to chill for at least 30 minutes and preferably eight hours. This firms the butter and makes the dough easier to handle.

Brioche

To make three large or eighteen small loaves:

1 ounce fresh yeast or 1 tablespoon dried
1/3 cup warm water
4 cups (1 pound) all-purpose flour
1 tablespoon sugar
1 teaspoon salt
4 eggs
1 cup (2 sticks) butter, softened
1 egg yolk, beaten with 1 teaspoon water
(for Cheese Brioche, add 4 ounces Gruyère cheese, grated)

Dissolve the yeast in the warm water and leave it to stand – five minutes for fresh yeast, and 15 for dried. Place the flour in a bowl and toss in the sugar and salt. Make a well in the center. Pour in the yeast mixture and break in the eggs. Mix everything to a dough and knead it in the bowl for about 5 minutes. Turn it on to a floured board and knead it until it is smooth. Punch it out flat and dot it with one third of the butter. Knead this well in. Repeat this twice, with the remaining butter. This process may well take 20 minutes or so. When you have finished you should be able to form it into a ball and coat it with flour. Place the dough in a bowl, cover it and leave it in a warm place for 1 hour.

Punch the dough down and knead it again. Return it to the bowl and chill it for at least 30 minutes. At this point the dough can be left in the refrigerator for up to eight hours, in fact the longer you leave it, the more workable it becomes.

Preheat the oven to 400°F. Grease any pans that are not non-stick. Knead the dough again, lightly. If you are making a cheese brioche, knead in the grated cheese at this point. Divide the dough into the right number of portions for your pans. To shape a brioche, divide each piece again in portions of about two thirds and one third. Put the larger piece into the pan and make a hole in the center. Shape the smaller piece into a plug and insert it in the hole so that it makes a small round, sitting on top of the first piece.

Leave the brioche for 30 minutes, or until the base has risen to the edge of the pan. Brush with egg and water glaze. Bake the large brioches for 25 minutes and the small ones for 10 minutes. They should be golden-brown. Turn them on to wire racks to cool.

A fresh brioche can be served with jelly or other preserves to accompany tea or coffee, or with pâtés or hors d'oeuvre. The tops of the small ones can easily be pulled away, giving space for a sweet or savory filling.

Brioche dough can also be used for wrapping other ingredients such as beef for boeuf-en-croûte, a salmon filling for a koulibiaca, or a spicy garlic sausage. For these recipes you can halve the amount of butter to make the dough more workable, if preferred.

Sausage Brioche

To make one 14-inch-long loaf:

Brioche dough (see above) made with 2 cups (8 ounces) all-purpose flour, risen and chilled
12 ounces French garlic sausage, in one piece, skinned if necessary
egg and water glaze, as for Brioche

Preheat the oven to 375°F. Roll the dough into a rectangle, large enough to cover the sausage completely. Lay the sausage on top. Fold the dough over the sausage. Place the brioche on a floured baking sheet with the seam on the underside. Leave it to rise for 20 minutes and brush with the glaze.

Bake the brioche for 30 to 35 minutes, or until golden-brown. Serve hot, or cool on a wire rack.

Cheese Brioche Braid

To make one 15-inch-long braid:

Brioche dough (see above) made with 4 cups (1 pound) flour, risen and chilled
6 ounces Gruyère cheese
egg and water glaze, as for Brioche

Preheat the oven to 400°F. Divide the dough in three pieces. Roll them into sausage shapes about 1½ inches thick and then flatten them. Cut the cheese into thin sticks and lay a line of sticks down the center of each piece of dough. Bring the edges of the dough together to reform the sausage shapes. Braid them (see page 18). Lay the braid on a floured baking sheet, let it rise for 20 minutes and brush it with the glaze.

Bake the braid for 30 minutes, or until it is golden-brown. Cool it on a wire rack and serve it warm or cold.

Croissants came to France from Austria, but in many countries they are deemed typically French. When croissants are expertly made they can be a delight, slightly crisp on the outside and soft and buttery in the middle. There are sadly, however, many very poor imitations on the market. Well made, and rich but not sweet, croissants are good at any time of day. They have come to typify the continental breakfast, and are excellent with morning coffee.

Croissants are most often made quite plain, but various fillings can be rolled up inside them such as marzipan, apple purée, mixtures of nuts and honey, dried fruits or candied citrus peel or, for a savory bake, grated cheese.

They are not difficult to make, but the ten-minute chilling periods make them fairly time consuming. They are made in this way in order to keep the butter firm and the dough therefore easier to handle. In France, many bakers have special chilling cabinets for croissants, which change temperature at measured intervals. Hard wheat flour is best for making successful croissants, so the French use imported flours.

● *Croissants*

and water. Mix everything to a dough and knead it on a floured work surface until it is smooth. Return the dough to the bowl, cover it with plastic wrap and put it into the refrigerator for approximately 1 hour.

Preheat the oven to 400°F. Put the remaining butter in between two pieces of plastic wrap and bang it with a rolling pin until it is a flat rectangle about 5 × 9 inches. Knead the dough again and roll it into a rectangle of about 10 × 18 inches. Lay the rectangle of butter in the center of the rectangle of dough. Fold over the ends of the dough and then the sides. Roll this parcel lengthways into a rectangle and then fold it in three. Wrap the folded dough in plastic wrap and put it in the refrigerator for 10 minutes. Repeat this rolling and chilling process three more times.

After chilling for the final time, roll the dough into a square ¼-inch thick. Cut it into 6-inch equilateral triangles and form them into crescent shapes (see page 21).

Lay the crescents on floured baking sheets and leave them to rise for about 30 minutes. Glaze the croissants before baking, by brushing them with the beaten egg. Bake them for approximately 15 minutes, or until they are golden-brown. Cool them on wire racks and serve them warm.

Croissants

To make about twenty croissants:
¾ cup warm water
1 cup warm milk
1 ounce fresh yeast or 1 tablespoon dried
5 cups (1 pound 4 ounces) all-purpose flour
2 tablespoons sugar
1 teaspoon salt
1¼ cups (2½ sticks) butter, chilled
1 egg, beaten

Mix together the water and milk. Dissolve the yeast in a little of the mixture and leave to stand – five minutes for fresh yeast and 15 for dried.

Place the flour in a bowl and toss in the sugar and salt. Rub in ¼ cup (½ stick) of the butter. Make a well in the center and pour in the yeast mixture plus the remainder of the milk

The French make many different kinds of sweet breads and yeasted cakes. There is the small oval *empereur*, the *cassadière corse* – like a large croissant with cherries in the center – and in Alsace, a migrant from Austria, the *gugelhupf* (see page 45). There is the *solilemme*, a rich, egg bread made in a brioche or *gugelhupf* mold and the simple Breton *kouing-aman* which consists of a basic dough into which are kneaded butter and sugar.

Walnuts and prunes are favorite ingredients of many sweet breads. The *pain aux noix* from Périgord-Noir is a sweet milk dough containing chopped walnuts. Raisins, walnuts, butter, eggs, sugar and lemon rind are all ingredients in small buns traditionally served at funerals in Corsica. For festivals and christenings in the area around Lyons there are *pognons aux peurniaux*, brioche-shaped loaves made from basic dough into which are kneaded prunes, eggs, sugar and butter.

The richest and most delicious of all these sweet fruit breads is the *birewecke*, made at Christmas time in Alsace. Large pieces of dried fruit, soaked in kirsch, together with chopped nuts, peel and raisins, are kneaded into a basic bread dough. When you look at the amazing amount of fruit in comparison with the small amount of bread dough, you may be alarmed, but keep mixing with your hand inside the bowl and eventually everything will come together. The *birewecke* is not the most attractive of loaves, but if you like large pieces of dried fruit packed tightly together with nuts, you will love it. You will see that there is no sugar in the recipe. The dried fruits give plenty of natural sweetness.

Birewecke

To make two 7-inch-diameter loaves:

6 ounces dried pears
2 ounces dried apple rings
4 ounces prunes
4 ounces dried figs
2 ounces candied citrus peel, chopped
3 ounces raisins
⅓ cup kirsch
½ quantity bread dough (see page 12), kneaded and risen for 30 minutes
4 ounces walnuts, chopped
2 ounces almonds, chopped
2 ounces hazelnuts, chopped
¼ teaspoon ground cloves
2 teaspoons ground cinnamon
grated rind 1 lemon
1 egg yolk, beaten with 2 tablespoons water

Place the pears, apple rings, prunes and figs in a saucepan and just cover them with water. Bring them to the boil, simmer them for 5 minutes and cool them for 10 minutes in the liquid. Drain and cut the fruit into large pieces, pitting the prunes. Place them all in a bowl with the candied citrus peel and raisins. Pour the kirsch over them and leave them overnight.

Place the bread dough in a mixing bowl and knead in the fruits and all the remaining ingredients except the beaten egg. This will take some time. Aim at getting everything evenly mixed. Leave the dough in the bowl in a warm place for 1½ hours for it to begin to rise. With this large amount of fruit in the dough it will not double in size.

Preheat the oven to 400°F.

Knead the dough again and form it into two round loaves. Place them on floured baking sheets and leave them to rise for 30 minutes. Brush them with the egg yolk and water glaze. Bake them for 30 minutes or until a skewer inserted in the center comes out clean. Lift the loaves on to wire racks to cool.

There are very few unleavened or baking-powder risen breads in France. One, called *la foncée*, is made in Normandy. It consists of flour mixed with eggs, butter and heavy cream, glazed with egg yolks and baked in a flat round. It is very similar to some types of flat bread made in Scandinavia.

A bread very similar to the English gingerbread and parkin is *pain d'epice*, which is made around Reims, Dijon and Orléans. The large amount of honey produces a very sweet bread with a delicious chewy texture. It is more of a sweetmeat than a bread and very good for picnics and lunch-boxes.

Pain d'Epice

To make one 10-inch-square loaf:

4 cups (1 pound) rye flour
1 teaspoon baking soda
¾ cup honey
⅔ cup sugar
2 ounces slivered almonds
2 ounces candied citrus peel, finely chopped
1 teaspoon ground cinnamon
1 teaspoon ground cloves
½ teaspoon ground aniseed
¼ teaspoon ground nutmeg
grated rind ½ lemon
¼ cup milk, heated with 2 tablespoons sugar

Place the flour in a bowl. Heat the honey to a pouring consistency, skim it if necessary and pour it over the flour. Mix the two together to make a stiff paste. Form the paste into a ball in the bowl, cover it with a clean, dry cloth and leave it for 1 hour.

Preheat the oven to 350°F. Knead all the remaining ingredients into the flour and honey paste and then knead on a floured work surface until you have an even mixture. Roll out the dough to a 10-inch square about 1-inch thick and lay it on a floured baking sheet.

Bake for 35 minutes or until the top is brown, but not dark brown, and a skewer inserted in the center comes out clean. Lift the bread on to a wire rack to cool.

GERMANY AND AUSTRIA

Since the time rye was first planted in central Europe, in around 2000 BC, bread has been a staple food of the German peoples, and it is now linked inextricably with the economy, religion and folklore of the area.

Austria has traditionally sat, politically, between East and West, and for several centuries was part of the much larger Austro-Hungarian Empire – which included present day Austria and Hungary, and the countries which became Czechoslovakia and Yugoslavia, as well as part of Romania.

Long famous for its baking, it could well have supplied enough recipes for a chapter on its own – its sweet yeast cakes providing a frivolous contrast to the plainer breads of its neighbor Germany.

GERMANY

In Germany, the word *Brot* (bread) refers only to wheat or rye bread. Breads made of other grains such as oats, maize or barley, are called after the grains themselves, for example *Maisbrot* (maize-bread).

The history of bread in Germany is similar to that in other parts of Europe. It gradually developed from hard, hearth-baked flat cakes to risen loaves. It differs, however, from more Western breads, in that the sourdough method of rising has remained popular ever since it was first introduced from the Middle East, via Greece, in about 800 BC.

During the Middle Ages, as in other countries, there was a distinction between the white bread for the rich and the dark for the poor, and rural bakers were forbidden by law to make anything but the dark rye loaves. In the years of poor harvest many holy men and women are said to have travelled through the country distributing bread to the poor. Two of these, Saint Antonius von Padua and Elizabeth von Thiringen, who went to Germany in the famine of 1226, became patron saints both of bakers and the hungry.

Baking very quickly transferred from the home to the communal bakehouse and village baker. Most villages consisted of small houses, built close together for protection against enemies. There was no room for an oven in every house and, besides, there was a restriction on fuel. Bread was either home-mixed and baked in a central oven, or it was bought direct from the owner of the oven, the local baker.

The same Medieval-style communal ovens were used well into the twentieth century and the bread from each village had its own characteristic qualities, the result not only of local recipes but of the individual effect of each oven. Called *Holzofen-bauernbrot* (wood-oven farm-bread) it was made from various grades of rye flour, either used alone or mixed with wheat flour, and was always raised with a sourdough starter.

Sourdough bread, wherever it is baked, has a thick crust, a spongy crumb, and a characteristic sour-sweet flavor. It is excellent spread thickly with butter or eaten with German cheeses, pickles and smoked sausage. There are many different recipes, using a variety of starters and mixtures of fine and coarse rye and wheat flours. They are simple to make, but the rising times are long, and necessitate a little forward planning.

The first recipe below, for *feines gesauertes roggenbrot*, is one of the simplest, using only rye flour. It is dark in color with a strong flavor. Sausages, strong cheeses and pickles are the best accompaniments for this type of bread.

The second recipe, *schwarzbrot*, is not really *schwarz* (black) at all, but a rich golden brown color with a sweet flavor and light texture. You either love or hate caraway seeds, so leave them out if you prefer. Because it is not as tangy as the *Roggenbrot*, *Schwarzbrot* can be served with mild cheese or sweet preserves.

● *Traditional German breads on sale*

Feines Gesauertes Roggenbrot

To make one 2-pound loaf:

¼ *rye sourdough starter (see page 11)*

4 cups (1 pound) whole rye flour

1¼ cups warm water or warm buttermilk

2 teaspoons salt

To make this fine sourdough rye loaf, first place the starter in a small bowl. Mix in ½ cup of the flour and ¾ cup of the water or buttermilk. Sprinkle on 2 tablespoons more of the flour and leave the mixture for 12 hours in a warm place to make a risen, bubbling sponge.

In a large bowl, mix together the remaining flour and the salt. Add the starter and the rest of the water or buttermilk. On a floured surface, knead the mixture thoroughly for about 15 minutes, so that the dough becomes smooth. Shape it into a long loaf, place it on a floured baking sheet and leave it in a warm place to rise for 2 to 3 hours or until a finger pressed lightly into it leaves a dent.

Preheat the oven to 400°F. Bake the loaf for 1 hour, or until it is dark brown and sounds hollow when tapped. This sounds rather a long baking time, but if you take the loaf out after the normal time of about 40 minutes you will find that the middle is still soggy.

After 1 hour, the crust will be fairly thick but the middle will have a soft, moist crumb.

After baking, cool the loaf on a wire rack.

Schwarzbrot

To make two 2-pound loaves:

4 cups (1 pound) whole-wheat flour

4 cups (1 pound) rye flour

¼ *rye sourdough starter (see page 11)*

1¾ cups, plus 2 tablespoons, warm water

1 tablespoon salt

2 tablespoons caraway seeds, optional

2 medium potatoes, peeled, cooked and mashed

For this black bread, mix the two types of flour together. Take 2 cups of the mixed flour and, in a large bowl, mix it into the starter together with ½ cup, plus 2 tablespoons, of the water. Cover the mixture with a clean, dry cloth and leave it in a warm, draft-free place for 12 hours. When you look at it again it should be bubbling.

Stir in the remaining water, the caraway seeds and half the remaining flour. Mix in the potatoes and finally the salt and the rest of the flour. Knead the dough well. It will be very lumpy at first, but after 10 to 15 minutes should become silky smooth. Return it to the bowl and make a cross-cut in the top. Cover it with a clean, dry cloth and leave it for 4 hours in a warm place until it has expanded. It should have approximately doubled in size.

Oil two 2-pound bread pans. Knead the dough again and divide it between the pans. Cover the loaves and leave them for 1 hour in a warm place so they rise to the level of the top of the pans.

Preheat the oven to 400°F. Bake the loaves for 45 minutes, or until the tops are golden-brown and they sound hollow when tapped. Transfer the loaves to wire racks and brush the tops with water while they are still hot, to give them a soft crust.

● *A choice of scored and floured brown and white rolls at a bread shop in Wangen, Germany*

The sourdough process has been adapted to commercial use and is used for most rye, rye mixture and whole-wheat loaves. There are about two hundred types of bread produced commercially in Germany, so it would be impossible to describe them all. There are also many specialty breads such as the pumpernickel types, as well as small rolls and crackers.

The German everyday bread is the *Landbrot*, sometimes called the *berliner Landbrot*. It has a dark crust and a light-brown crumb, and is usually made entirely from rye flour. *Landbrot* is a *Krustenbrot* or crusty bread. *Krustenbrot* is baked on trays at high temperatures for a relatively short time. The surfaces can be left plain, or are floured, scattered with grains, or slashed, and the loaves can be round, oval or long. There is a large selection of *Krustenbrot*, made with mixtures of wheat and rye – *Roggenmischbrot* (those with more rye than wheat) and *Weizenmischbrot* (those with more wheat than rye). A relatively new addition to these commercially-baked crusty mixed breads is the *Zwiebelbrot* or onion bread, for which chopped cooked onions are mixed into the dough. Onions are often used in the home as a starter for sourdough

(see page 11) and their flavor goes well with the sour flavor of rye bread. Caraway seeds are another favorite addition. There are also crusty loaves made with white flour, called *Weizenbrot*, but all such wheaten loaves are risen with yeast instead of using the sourdough process.

There are also loaves baked in pans – the standard, long rectangle shape with a risen, crusty top. These include white, mixed and whole-wheat loaves and specialties such as the *Grahambrot* (using the American graham flour), the fiber-rich, sweetly aromatic *Schluterbrot*, and the mixed-flour *paderborner Brot* which has a pattern of holes on its browned top.

The other large category of breads consists of those that are baked in steam chambers at low temperatures for up to twenty hours. The dough is completely enclosed in pans, round or square, to give little or no crust and the bread is consequently called *Kastenbrot*, box-bread. Very often whole grains are used in addition to whole-wheat flour, together with a sourdough starter. The result is a rich, dark, moist bread with a sour-sweet flavor. It can be cut into thin slices and keeps for a long time. The bread is often sold ready-sliced in vacuum packs and probably the best known in other countries is pumpernickel. There are, however, many other varieties such as *Sonnenblumenbrot*, made completely with rye flour with the addition of sunflower seeds; *Leinsamenbrot* with linseeds; *Kümmelbrot* with caraway seeds; and *Fünfcornbrot* made with five different types of grain.

Then, of course, there is the vast array of *Kleinegebäck*, literally meaning 'little-bakes' – plain or rye flour bread rolls decorated and shaped in many ways. Most *Kleinegebäck* are made from white wheat flour, but those with the enchanting name of *Roggelchen* (little-rye), are made completely from rye flour. There are regional specialties from all over Germany; they can be long or round, braids, knots or crescents. Some are plain, some have a pattern slashed in the top, some are glazed, and some are scattered with poppy, caraway or sesame seeds or with salt.

The most well-known of the *Kleinegebäck* outside Germany is the pretzel, although few people realize that they are made from bread dough. Fresh and homemade they are absolutely delicious.

There are two ways of cooking pretzels. If they are poached before baking they will remain slim and after cooking they will be very crisp with an outside that is glossy and smooth. Pretzels cooked in this way make excellent snacks and are good with dips. If you leave out the poaching, pretzels will rise more and take on the texture of very crisp bread. They are excellent eaten with soup or cheese. Both types of pretzels should be eaten on the day that they are made as they soon lose their initial crispness.

● *Salzbrezeln*

Salzbrezeln

To make about sixteen pretzels:

½ ounce fresh yeast or 2 teaspoons dried

pinch of sugar

¾ cup, plus 2 tablespoons, warm water

4 cups (1 pound) all-purpose flour

1 teaspoon fine salt

1½ tablespoons butter, softened

½ cup, plus 2 tablespoons, milk

2 tablespoons coarse salt

1 egg, beaten

In a small bowl, dissolve the yeast and a pinch of sugar in the water. Leave in a warm place until it begins to froth. Place the flour and the fine salt in a bowl. Make a well in the center and pour in the yeast mixture. Stir to draw in a little flour from the edges of the bowl. Cover and leave for 10 minutes in a warm place, until the yeast begins to foam again.

Warm the butter and milk together so that the butter melts. Pour them into the well in the flour and mix well. Knead the mixture in the bowl (see page 13) until the dough no longer sticks to the sides. Cover the dough and leave it to rise in a warm place for 1 hour or until it doubles in size.

Knead the dough on a floured work surface for 10 minutes. Cut it in 16 pieces.

To shape the pretzels, first roll each piece backwards and forwards

39

under your hands to the thickness of a pencil and about 12 inches long, tapering at the ends. Place one piece sideways along the work surface. Bring the ends towards you to make a horseshoe shape. Lift up the ends and cross them over. Press them lightly backwards on to the curve of the horseshoe.

Lay the shaped pretzel on a floured baking sheet and shape the rest in the same way. Cover the pretzels with a clean, dry cloth and leave them to rise for approximately 10 minutes, or until they are beginning to rise and look rounded.

Preheat the oven to 450°F.

For very simply baked pretzels, brush them with beaten egg after rising and salt them (see below). Place them in the oven, reduce the heat to 400°F and bake them for 20 minutes, or until they are golden-brown.

Cool them on a wire rack.

To poach the pretzels before baking, fill a saucepan with 12½ cups of water, add 2 tablespoons of salt and bring it to a boil. Cover your work surface with a double layer of paper towels. Place the pretzels, two at a time, in the boiling water and leave them for 15 seconds. Remove them with a slotted spoon and drain them on the paper towels. You will find that they are very easy to handle as the poaching process makes the dough firm and almost impossible to damage. Lay them on floured baking sheets, brush them with beaten egg and salt them (see below). Bake as above: put the pretzels into the oven, reduce the temperature to 400°F and bake them for 20 minutes, or until they are golden-brown.

Cool them on a wire rack.

To salt pretzels, either 1) scatter them with coarse salt after brushing them with the beaten egg; or 2) after brushing with the egg, make a slit in the knot of the pretzel with a sharp knife. Fill the slit with about ¼ teaspoon coarse salt and leave the rest of the pretzel plain.

Besides all these plainer, everyday breads, there are white wheat flour breads made into special shapes for special occasions. They are called *Gebildbrote* or picture breads. These are descendants of the ritual and sacrificial breads made in pagan times, whose meanings have been long since forgotten. You can find horns, stars and suns, fish, serpents, flowers, sheaves of wheat and whole scenes – such as one depicting the Garden of Eden. If you have ever tried to shape dough and found it rising in all directions but the right one, you will appreciate just how much skill it takes to achieve so much detail.

Bread has always been important at German weddings. A bridegroom at one time passed bread in front of the church altar, signifying his commitment to feed and care for his bride and his future family. A bride carried a wheat-sheaf instead of flowers – the tightly-packed wheat ears showing her wish for their lasting relationship to be as close as the grains in the ear. Even today,

bread braids decorate the Church at weddings and the first things taken into the house of a newly married couple are bread and salt, with the words "*Brot und Salz sollen nie in eurem Hause fehlen*" (bread and salt shall not fail in your house).

Godparents still give their godchildren bread, sometimes in the shape of people, or sometimes baked with small coins inside, for luck. For harvest festivals, crowns of bread are made. At Easter time you may find bread in the shape of a hare with a colored egg under its tail. For St. Nicholas' Day (December 6th) and Christmas there is bread in the shape of St. Nicholas himself or made into wreaths or stars.

There is also the stollen, a rich fruit bread dusted with confectioners' sugar. I have no German relations or connections, but I always make a stollen at Christmas. It is rich and sweet, but not as much so as, say, the traditional English fruit cake. Whereas it takes several days after the Christmas dinner to think about fruit cake, a slice of stollen after apples and cheese makes an excellent snack for supper on Christmas night.

If you want to make it in advance, the stollen freezes well and will simply defrost itself at room temperature during Christmas Day. Fresh or recently thawed, it will keep for up to four days at room temperature, wrapped in aluminum foil or in a plastic bag.

Dresdner Stollen

To make one 14-inch loaf:

2 ounces seedless raisins

2 ounces currants

2 ounces mixed candied citrus peel

1 ounce candied angelica, diced

2 ounces glacé cherries, halved

4 tablespoons rum

¾ ounces fresh yeast or ¾ tablespoon dried

¼ cup, plus 2 tablespoons, sugar

1½ tablespoons warm water

4 cups (1 pound) all-purpose flour

1½ ounces slivered almonds

½ cup milk

¼ teaspoon pure almond extract

grated rind ½ lemon

½ teaspoon salt

1 egg, beaten

½ cup, plus 2 tablespoons (1¼ sticks), butter, ¾ stick diced and softened, ½ stick melted

2 tablespoons confectioners' sugar

● *Dresdner Stollen*

Place the fruits in a bowl with the rum, and soak them for at least 1 hour.

In a small bowl, stir the yeast and 1 teaspoon of the sugar into the water. Leave this five minutes for fresh yeast and 15 for dried.

Sprinkle 1½ tablespoons of the flour into the fruit together with the almonds. Stir until the flour is completely absorbed.

Warm the milk until it is lukewarm and stir in the remaining sugar until it has dissolved. Stir in the almond extract and lemon rind.

Place all but ¼ cup of the flour in a large bowl with the salt and make a well in the center. Pour in the yeast mixture and stir in a little of the flour from the edges of the well. Add the egg and the milk and sugar mixture. Beat in the softened butter. Mix everything to a dough, turn it on to a floured work surface and knead it, using the rest of the flour, for 15 minutes or until it is no longer sticky. Knead in the fruit and almonds, 4 tablespoons at a time. Clean and dry the bowl and brush the inside with 1 tablespoon of the melted butter. Brush the top of the dough with another 2 teaspoons of the melted butter and place it in the bowl. Cover the dough with a clean cloth and leave it for 2 hours, or until it has doubled in size.

Punch down the dough and let it rest for 10 minutes. Roll it out into a rectangle 8 × 12 inches. Brush it with the remaining melted butter. Bring one long side to the center of the rectangle and press it down lightly. Fold the other long side across it, overlapping the center seam by about 1 inch. Press the edge gently to keep it in place. With floured hands, taper the ends of the loaf slightly and push the sides gently together to mound it in the center. The finished loaf should be about 3½ inches wide and 14 inches long.

Place the loaf on a floured baking sheet and brush it with any remaining melted butter. Leave it in a warm place for 1 hour or until it has doubled in size.

Preheat oven to 375°F.

Bake the stollen for 45 minutes, or until it is golden and crusty. Cool it on a wire rack. Just before serving the stollen, sift the confectioners' sugar over the top.

Bread plays an important part in almost every meal in Germany. Breakfast may be hot crisp rolls served with butter and fruit preserves, with eggs or, particularly in northern Germany, with thin slices of cheese or cold meats. At 9 or 10 o'clock there may be a *zweites Frühstuck* (second breakfast). The main meal is often eaten in the middle of the day and bread may accompany a stew or a soup. In the afternoon there is *Kaffee* (afternoon coffee) with yeasted cakes or small sandwiches. In the evening there is *Abendbrot* or supper (literally translated as bread of the evening). This will consist of dark breads as open sandwiches or simply accompanying cheeses, meats and pickles.

Bread can also be made into a complete meal. In country districts cubes of cheese are put into bread mixtures. The onion cake below, based on a white bread dough, is traditionally eaten with new wine. It is absolutely huge, wonderfully tasty, risen and golden and perfect for picnics and informal lunch parties.

Zwiebelkuchen

To make one 10-inch cake:

1 ounce fresh yeast or 1 tablespoon dried
1 cup warm water
pinch of sugar
2 teaspoons salt
4 cups (1 pound) all-purpose flour
¾ cup (1½ sticks) butter or lard
3 egg yolks, beaten
2 pounds onions, finely chopped
7 ounces lean bacon, finely chopped
3 eggs, beaten
½ cup sour cream
½ teaspoon caraway seeds, optional, or to taste

In a small bowl, dissolve the yeast in half the water, add the sugar and leave it five minutes for fresh yeast and 15 for dried. Dissolve the salt in the remaining water. Place the flour in a large bowl, make a well in the center and pour in the yeast. Mix in a little of the flour from the edges of the bowl, add the salt water and mix in a little more flour. Melt ½ cup (1 stick) of the butter or lard and put it into the well together with the egg yolks. Mix to make a dough and knead it in the bowl (see page 13) until it is smooth. Cut a cross in the top, cover the dough with a clean, dry cloth and leave it in a warm place for 1 hour, or until it has doubled in size.

Over low heat, fry the onions in the remaining butter or lard until they are transparent. Add three quarters of the bacon and continue to fry it gently until it is cooked through.

Preheat the oven to 375°F.

Knead the dough again. Roll it into a round 12 inches across and lay it on a floured baking sheet. Fold over 1 inch all the way round to make a raised rim about ¾ inch high. Leave the dough to rise for approximately 10 minutes.

Beat the eggs with the sour cream. Put the onions and bacon on top of the round of dough and pour the egg mixture over them. Sprinkle with the remaining bacon and the caraway seeds. Bake the cake for 30 minutes or uuntil the filling is set and the edges are golden.

AUSTRIA

Austria is the land of afternoon coffee and sweet yeasted cakes. The Viennese in particular have loved bread and pastries for over five hundred years and it is said that the country's sweet tooth developed in the eleventh and twelfth centuries when returning Crusaders stopped in Vienna, bringing with them spices and sugar cane from the East.

In 1488, Vienna gave its name to the Vienna roll, a small plain bread roll made with a dough enriched with milk and butter. Emperor Frederick V ordered a batch of rolls which were to be stamped with his likeness to be distributed to poor and needy children. The rolls were originally called *Kaiser-semmeln* (emperor rolls) but, when the portrait of the emperor was dropped, they became plain Vienna rolls. Today they are usually made round, with the top slashed in four sections.

The golden age of Vienna began in the early seventeenth century, the Baroque era, when the eating habits of the rich became more than extravagant. Many different baking guilds existed at that time, each specializing in a particular delicacy. There were the sugar bakers, chocolate makers, marzipan makers, cake bakers and sweet bakers; and the bread bakers were divided into ordinary bread bakers, roll bakers and luxury bakers.

One of the favorite shapes into which sweet yeasted cakes and breads were molded was the crescent. On Christmas Day 1217 the bakers of Vienna paid homage to Duke Leopold of Babenburg with an offering of crescent-shaped rolls and again in Vienna in 1683, crescent rolls said to be in the shape of the Mohammedan crescent were baked to celebrate the victory over the Turks. Crescents are easy to make (see page 21) and the ones below, made with rich but unsweetened dough, have a surprise of sweet dried fruits and peel in the center. These are literally "crescents to accompany coffee."

Kaffeekipfeln

To make about 20 crescents:

1 ounce fresh yeast or 1 tablespoon dried

¾ cup warm milk

¾ cup, plus 2 tablespoons (1¾ sticks), butter, cut into small pieces

4 cups (1 pound) all-purpose flour

pinch of salt

2 egg yolks

2 tablespoons heavy cream

1 egg, lightly beaten

Filling:

3 ounces walnuts, chopped

3 ounces raisins

3 ounces candied citrus peel, finely chopped

⅛ teaspoon ground ginger

Mix the yeast with half the milk and leave it to stand – five minutes for fresh yeast and 15 for dried. Rub the butter into the flour as though you were making pastry. Add the salt, the egg yolks, cream, yeast mixture and the remaining milk. Mix everything to a stiff dough and knead it for a few minutes.

● *Immature wheat fields*

● *Gugelhupf*

Roll the dough into a rectangle, three times as long as it is wide and fold the short sides across to fold it in three. Repeat the rolling and folding four times, each time having the length of the rolling pin going across the fold. After the final fold, put the dough on to a floured board or baking sheet. Cover it and leave it in a warm place for about 1 hour or until it doubles in size. Knock it back by kneading the dough again. Roll it out to about ¼ inch thick and cut it into 6-inch equilateral triangles.

Mix all the filling ingredients together. Shape the triangles as on page 21 and place about 2 teaspoons of the filling at the center of the base of each one. Roll the triangles into crescent shapes (see page 21, again) and lay them on floured baking sheets and leave them to rise for 20 to 30 minutes or until they have risen by about half as much again.

Preheat the oven to 400°F. Brush the crescents with the beaten egg and bake them for 20 minutes or until they are golden-brown.

The *Gugelhupf* (also called *gugelhopf* and *kugelhopf* in other countries) is another Viennese specialty. It is a sweet yeasted cake baked in a fluted, spiral-patterned mold. If you do not have such a mold, an ordinary ring mold will do quite well. These type of yeasted cakes have a close texture, rather like a cross between bread and sponge cake. They are sweet but not over-sweet and excellent with tea or coffee in the afternoon or in the middle of the morning. Try to eat a *Gugelhupf* on the same day that it is made as they tend to go stale very quickly. When first baked they are a dream, light in the center and crisp on the outside.

The first recipe below is plain and simple, very much like that made by the actress Katherina Schratt for her lover, Emperor Franz Joseph I, who called at her house at 4:30 every afternoon when he knew the *Gugelhupf* would be coming out of the oven. (*Gugelhupf*, incidentally, was a favorite with Marie Antoinette, whose mother, Maria Theresa, was Austrian.)

For a richer *Gugelhupf*, try making a *Pattzerl-gugelhupf*. The same basic *Gugelhupf* mixture is first cut in slices which are spread with a sweet filling. When the slices are layered in the mold they produce a marbled sweetness throughout. Instead of the nut filling in the recipe that follows, you can use a sweet preserve, or a purée of cooked fruit.

The name *Pattzerlgugelhupf* comes from the *pattzerln*, or slices, into which the dough is cut.

Gugelhupf

To make one 8-inch Gugelhupf:

1 ounce fresh yeast or 1 tablespoon dried
½ cup, plus 2 tablespoons, warm milk
¾ cup sugar
3 cups (12 ounces) all-purpose flour
½ cup (1 stick) butter
1 egg
2 egg yolks
pinch of salt
3 ounces golden raisins
2 ounces slivered almonds
2 tablespoons superfine sugar, or vanilla sugar, if available

Mix the yeast with the milk, 1 teaspoon of the sugar and ¾ cup of the flour. Leave the mixture for 20 minutes to make a frothy sponge.

Cream together the butter, the rest of the sugar, the egg and egg yolks. Place the rest of the flour in a large bowl with the salt and ⅔ of the golden raisins. Make a well in the center. Add the yeast sponge and the butter and egg mixture.

Mix everything to a dough and knead it on a floured work surface for about 10 minutes, or until it is smooth and elastic. Return it to the bowl, cover it with a clean, dry cloth and leave it to rise in a warm place until it has doubled in size (about 1½ hours).

Preheat the oven to 400°F.

Butter an 8-inch *Gugelhupf* mold and sprinkle it with the remaining golden raisins, the almonds and a little flour. Knead the dough again and put it into the mold (see page 19). Leave it to rise for 1 hour, or until it almost reaches the rim of the mold.

Bake the *Gugelhupf* for 40 minutes, or until a skewer comes out clean when pushed into the center.

Turn the *Gugelhupf* on to a wire rack, sprinkle it with superfine or vanilla sugar and leave it to cool before you cut it.

● *A bread stall at Linz Market, Austria*

Pattzerlgugelhupf

To make one 8-inch Pattzerlgugelhupf:

1 ounce fresh yeast or 1 tablespoon dried

¼ cup, plus 2 tablespoons, warm milk

4 cups (12 ounces) all-purpose flour

½ cup sugar

1 teaspoon salt

2 eggs, beaten

2 tablespoons rum

grated rind ½ lemon

¼ cup, plus 2 tablespoons (¾ stick), unsalted butter, in small pieces

2 tablespoons confectioners' sugar, sifted

Filling:

3 ounces walnuts, finely chopped

¼ teaspoon ground ginger

grated rind ½ lemon

2 tablespoons milk

2 tablespoons sugar

1 tablespoon butter

2 tablespoons rum

In a small bowl, dissolve the yeast in the milk. Leave it to stand – five minutes for fresh yeast and 15 for dried. Place the flour, sugar and salt in a bowl and toss them with your fingertips to mix them. Make a well in the center and add the yeast, eggs, rum and lemon rind. Mix everything to a dough. Turn it on to a floured work surface and knead it vigorously for 10 minutes. Punch it down. Place one third of the butter pieces over the surface and knead them in. Do this twice more. Put the dough into a bowl and make a cross-cut in the top. Cover it and leave it to rise in a warm place until it has doubled in size, about 1½ hours.

To make the filling, mix the walnuts with the ginger and lemon rind. Warm the milk, add the sugar and butter and stir until they have dissolved. Pour the mixture over the walnuts. Cool to lukewarm and add the rum.

Butter an 8-inch *Gugelhupf* mold and dust it with flour. On a floured surface, roll the dough into a thick sausage shape, about 3 inches in diameter. Slice it in pieces about ⅜ inch thick. Divide the filling between the slices, spreading it out and pressing it well down into the dough. Cover the bottom of the mold with the slices, filling side up. Add another layer of slices, arranging them across the gaps

in the first layer. The top layer should be put in with the filling side down. Cover the dough with a clean, dry cloth and leave it for about 1 hour, or until the dough has almost risen to the rim of the mold.

Preheat the oven to 350°F. Bake the *Gugelhupf* for 45 to 50 minutes or until the dough has slightly shrunk away from the sides of the mold and the top is browned. Leave the *Gugelhupf* to cool in the mold for a few minutes. Turn it on to a wire rack and dust it with confectioners' sugar.

The following two recipes use an ordinary white bread dough, made with milk, into which are kneaded butter or lard and sugar. They are basic, no-nonsense recipes, the kind any housewife appreciates, and wonderful for feeding a hungry family after a day out in the open air. The *Kletzenbrot*, dried fruit buns, are folded packets of light dough round a rich fruit and nut filling. These kind of recipes are intended to make use of whatever is in the cupboard so if, for example, you do not have any pears or prunes, try whole dried apricots.

Kletzenbrot

To make sixteen buns:

½ recipe basic bread dough (see page 12) made with milk instead of water

¼ cup (½ stick) butter or lard, softened

2 tablespoons sugar

Filling:

12 ounces dried pears or prunes

4 ounces walnuts or hazelnuts, finely chopped

¼ cup sugar

1 egg, beaten

After mixing and kneading the dough for the first time, press it down flat. Spread it with half the butter or lard and sprinkle it with half the sugar. Knead these in well and then repeat with the remaining butter and sugar. Place the dough in a bowl, make a cross-cut in the top, cover it and leave it in a warm place for 1½ hours to double in size.

Soak the fruits in water to cover for 1½ hours. Drain and chop them finely, stoning the prunes. Use a food processor for a fine, even mix, if you like. Mix in the nuts, sugar and egg.

Knead the dough. Cut it in sixteen pieces and roll each piece into a thin (about 1 inch thick) 5- to 6-inch square. Place a portion of the filling on each square. Wet the edges of the dough and fold them over the filling. Turn the buns over so the seams are underneath. Place them on a floured baking sheet and leave them to rise for 30 minutes.

Preheat the oven to 350°F.

Bake the buns for 30 minutes until they are puffed up and golden-brown.

Zwetschkenfleck

To make one 13-inch tart:

½ recipe basic bread dough (see page 12) made with milk instead of water

¼ cup (½ stick) butter or lard, softened

2 tablespoons sugar

Topping:

2 pounds gooseberries or other fruit such as rhubarb, plums, red or white currants, black currants or blackberries

1 cup sugar

Prepare the dough as for the *Kletzenbrot* and leave it to rise for 1½ hours or until it has doubled in size. Preheat the oven to 400°F.

Knead the dough and roll it into a thin 15-inch square. Place it on a floured baking sheet and turn in 1 inch all round to make a thickened edge.

Plums should be stoned without being cut right through, and placed stalk end down on the dough, tightly packed. Cut rhubarb in ¾-inch lengths and put them end up on the dough. Gooseberries should be placed end up but the currants and blackberries can simply be scattered over the top. Sprinkle the fruit with sugar. Leave the tart to rise in a warm place for 20 minutes. The dough should rise slightly round the fruit to hold it in place.

Bake the tart for 25 to 30 minutes, or until the fruit is cooked and the edges are risen and golden.

This fruit tart is wonderful – golden and puffy round the edges and moist, sweet and juicy in the middle. Again, make it with any fruit in season. It being springtime when I first made it, I used rhubarb which gave the whole center a rosy pink tinge. Another very popular filling, however, are gooseberries – sweetened to taste.

● *Zwetschkenfleck*

47

ITALY

From its borders with Austria, Switzerland and France, to its southern tip – surrounded by the Tyrrhenian and Ionian seas and the islands of Sicily and Sardinia – Italy is a country of distinct regions. Each has its own culinary traditions and styles that have not blurred even to the present day. Think of Italian food and you think of pasta, herbs, vegetables, seafood, cheese, smoked ham and pizza. Pizza is the only bread-based Italian specialty that has become famous worldwide. It would be easy to imagine that bread has taken a poor second place to pasta all over Italy for hundreds of years, but this really is not so.

Bread has been so important that there is a saying in the country: "*Senza il pane tutto diventa orfano*" (without bread, one is deprived of everything). A generous, loving and warm-hearted person is described as "*buono come il pane*" (as good as bread), but someone who takes advantage of his fellows is "*uno che mangia pane a ufo*" (someone who eats another's bread but never gives in return). Young children in Italy are told to finish up their bread, or their job in the next life will be to go around picking up all the small pieces that other children have thrown away.

Bread has been made in Italy since ancient times. The cooking of early Italy was influenced by Greek and Etruscan ideas, developed and improved by the Romans. It is said that the Romans themselves were never excellent bakers. In early times their staple dish was called puls or pulmentum, a kind of porridge made from coarsely-ground millet, spelt (a primitive wheat) or chickpea flour. Each Roman soldier was given a ration of about two pounds of this grain which he roasted on a hot stone and then mixed with water. The resulting porridge was either eaten as gruel or made into small, flat hearth-cakes. In early Roman houses, the process was much the same.

The Greeks influenced the Romans in the baking of bread as we know it today, for it was Greek slaves who worked in the first bakeries, set up in around 170 BC, using wheat which was grown in Sicily and Sardinia and imported from Egypt. Even though wealthy Roman ladies could afford to buy the best white flour to powder their faces, white wheat bread remained out of reach for all but the rich and, as in all European countries, this state of affairs remained the same until at least the seventeenth century.

Italy was one of the first Western countries to plant and use maize, and in the eighteenth and nineteenth centuries, polenta (a maize dish very similar to the early Roman gruel) took the place of bread in northern Italy. However, good though it might be as an occasional alternative to wheat or rye bread, its general consumption caused bad outbreaks of pellagra and wheat once more became the staple grain. Polenta is still widely eaten in northern Italy, but as part of a mixed and balanced diet which includes other grain products.

During the 1950s and '60s there was a plethora in Italy, as in other European countries, of white, commercially-baked, nondescript bread, but regional specialties did not disappear and have, over the past twenty years, been undergoing a revival. This was helped by the Confraternita Amanti del Pane (the Brotherhood of Breadlovers) who formed in 1971 in order to promote real bread. In 1983, a museum of bread was opened in a thirteenth-century building in Bassa Lombardia, which displays one hundred varieties of grain and many different bread shapes from all the regions and villages of Italy.

There are said to exist a thousand or more different bread shapes in the country, some only to be found in a certain region or even in only one baker's shop in a small village. Much Italian bread is now made by small family bakers. In a large town or city the baker's shop is called a *panetteria* and it will sell standard loaves, the specialties of the town or region plus cakes and pies, pizzas and brioches. In the villages, the baker's shop is known as the *forno*. Very often the *forno* will look from the outside like an ordinary house, but as you enter, there will be a wooden counter, racks of loaves and a large brick oven which takes up one wall. Village women still take their cakes, pies, roasts and stews to the *forno* to be cooked in the oven after the bread has been removed to the shelves.

Most Italian bread is made from white wheat flour. Despite the shift towards whole-wheat breads in some European countries, *pane integrale* (whole-wheat) still has the stigma of "bread for the poor" and it makes up only 2 percent of total consumption. When made, it is usually shaped like a sandwich loaf or made into rolls.

Yeast is the main leavening for bread in Italy and it is still called *lievito di birra* (brewer's yeast), from the yeast that was imported by the Romans from Gaul, where it was used to make beer. Dried yeast is also available and occasionally a piece of dough is kept moistened with water and used as a starter for the next batch. This *lievito naturale* (natural leavening, or sourdough) is only used when the distinct sourdough flavor is required, such as in this rich cheese bread which is made at Easter time.

Although the process is lengthy, like all sourdough breads it really takes very little work time, apart from the adding of the final ingredients. Forward planning, however, is essential. The bread is light-textured, moist and yellow-colored with a golden crust, rather like a savory panettone (see page 54). The cheese flavor is strong, but not overpowering and, especially when the loaf is fresh, the slices need no butter.

The dough is very soft, even after the final kneading, so handle it lightly. It will rise only to the top of the pan while it is left to stand, but more as it bakes.

● *Carte da Musica, Sardinia*

Crescia di Pasqua con Formaggio

To make one 2-pound loaf:

4 cups (1 pound) all-purpose flour
¾ ounce fresh yeast or ¾ tablespoon dried
⅔ cup warm water
½ cup warm milk
3 tablespoons butter, softened
1 teaspoon salt
2 eggs, beaten
2 ounces Parmesan cheese, grated
4 ounces Gruyère cheese, grated

Make this Easter bread with cheese over two days. On the first day, make the sourdough. Place 1 cup of the flour in a bowl. Dissolve one third of the yeast in the water and leave to stand – five minutes for fresh yeast and 15 for dried. Gradually stir it into the flour. Stir in half the milk to make a creamy-textured batter. Cover it and leave it in a warm place for 24 hours.

On the second day, place 2 cups of the flour in a large mixing bowl and make a well in the center. Add the sourdough and mix it into the flour, gradually taking flour from the sides of the well. The dough will be very moist at first but should soon become dry and spongy. Form the dough into a ball and leave it in the bowl. Cover it with plastic wrap, to prevent a crust from forming on the top, and leave it for 12 hours.

Dissolve the rest of the yeast in the remaining milk. While the dough is still in the bowl, knead in the yeast mixture (see page 13). The dough will be very wet and slippery at first, but the liquid will gradually work itself in to make the dough smooth. Knead in the butter, in small pieces, together with the salt, and then the eggs, in exactly the same way as you did the yeast mixture. This will take about 15 minutes. Knead in the cheeses and then a further ½ cup of flour. Turn the dough on to a floured work surface and, using the remaining flour, knead it until it is smooth. It will still be very soft and quite difficult to shape. Place the dough in a greased, 2-pound bread pan and leave it in a warm place to rise until it reaches the top of the pan (about 1 hour).

Preheat the oven to 400°F. Bake the loaf for 40 minutes, or until it is golden-brown and risen.

Although bread shapes and types are highly regional, there are some that are made nationally. The two best known are the *biova* and the *michetta*. The *biova* came originally from Piedmont. It is cylindrical, with pointed ends, very crusty and so highly-leavened that the inside is almost hollow. The smaller version, the *biovetta*, is still popular mainly in the north. The *michetta*, which came from Milan, is a small roll, also extremely light and crusty, delicious to eat, but with very short keeping qualities. It is said that it should be eaten within an hour of coming out of the oven.

Focaccia bread also seems to be made in every region of Italy, mainly in country districts. Focaccia is a flat bread that is made with a white flour dough which may or may not be enriched with a little olive oil. It has a topping of

• *Bread baked in wood-fired ovens*

● *Focaccia (see page 52)*

coarse salt and olive oil. The oil on top gently seeps into the top layer of the bread, making it moist and springy. Traditionally, Focaccia bread was baked in large copper baking pans in a brick oven.

Toppings for focaccia bread vary. The oil and coarse salt are compulsory. The other ingredients may be as simple as a sprinkling of basil or oregano leaves, but can also consist of olives, onions, prosciutto ham, a local cheese, anchovies or pieces of salami, alone or in any combination, but all in moderation. The same ingredients can also be kneaded into the bread. There are many local specialties and it is easy to devise your own. For the recipe below, the blue cheese topping is the more traditional, the herb and cheese topping is the result of my own saunter round the herb garden and experimenting.

Focaccia

To make one 10-inch-square loaf:

4 cups (1 pound) all-purpose flour

1 ounce fresh yeast or 1 tablespoon dried

1¼ cups warm water

2 teaspoons fine salt

2 tablespoons olive oil

Onion and Blue Cheese Topping:

2 medium onions

2 tablespoons coarse salt

1 tablespoon chopped fresh sage leaves, or 1 teaspoon crumbled dried sage

4 ounces soft blue cheese

4 tablespoons olive oil

Herb and Cheese Topping:

5 tablespoons freshly chopped mixed herbs (about half of it parsley)

1 clove garlic, finely chopped

2 teaspoons coarse salt

4 ounces Provolone or Gruyère cheese, grated

¼ cup olive oil

Place the flour in a bowl and make a well in the center. Sprinkle the yeast into half the water – leave it five minutes for fresh yeast and 15 for dried. Pour the yeast mixture into the flour and mix in a little of the flour from the edges of the well. Dissolve the salt in the remaining water and mix it into the flour, together with the olive oil. Mix everything to a dough, knead it well and leave it in a warm place for up to 1 hour to double in size.

If you are using the onion and blue cheese topping, thinly slice the onions and place them in a bowl with all but 2 teaspoons of the coarse salt. Just before returning to the dough, drain the onions, rinse them with cold water, drain them again and dry them on paper towels.

Preheat the oven to 400°F. Knead the dough again, roll it out into a 10-inch square and place it on a floured baking sheet.

For the onion and blue cheese topping, arrange the drained onion slices evenly over the dough. Sprinkle it with the remaining salt and the sage. Cut the cheese into small dice and scatter them over the onions. Drizzle the olive oil over the top.

For the herb and cheese topping, scatter the herbs evenly over the surface of the dough. Sprinkle over the garlic, then the salt. Cover the herbs with the grated cheese and drizzle the olive oil over the top.

Leave the dough in a warm place for about 20 minutes, or until it has risen and thickened. Bake the loaf for 30 minutes. Eat it warm or turn it on to a wire rack to cool.

In some regions, the focaccia dough is divided and the two pieces rolled out and baked with a filling in between. In a village near Genoa, for example, it is filled with formagetta, a local soft cheese. In other areas it is made into a *tortino*, or vegetable pie, which can be a meal in itself or which can be an accompaniment to cheese or cold meats or fish. It is excellent for picnics. Rolled very thinly the bread dough becomes light, rich and crisp with a moist layer of filling.

Chicory, zucchini, artichokes, French beans, eggplant or cardoons are all used in *tortino* fillings, plus pine nuts, almonds, cheese or eggs.

Tortino con Spinaci e Olive

To make one 10-inch round filled loaf:

4 cups (1 pound) all-purpose flour

1 ounce fresh yeast or 1 tablespoon dried

1¼ cups warm water

2 teaspoons salt

⅓ cup (¾ stick) butter, softened

1 egg, beaten

Filling:

12 ounces fresh spinach, washed and tough stems removed

1 small onion

12 black olives

2 tablespoons butter

2 ounces pine nuts

4 tablespoons chopped fresh parsley

Place the flour in a bowl and make a well in the center. Sprinkle the yeast over half the water. Leave it to stand – five minutes for fresh yeast and 15 for dried. Pour the yeast into the well and mix in a little flour from the edges. Dissolve the salt in the remaining water, pour it into the well and mix everything to a dough.

Knead the dough on a floured surface, punch it down and spread it with one third of the butter. Knead in the butter and repeat the process two times more. Return the dough to the bowl, cover it and leave it in a warm place to double in size, for about 1 hour.

Finely chop the spinach and onion. Halve the olives and remove the pits. Melt the butter in a frying pan over high heat. Add the onion and cook it, stirring, for 1 minute. Add the spinach, lower the heat to medium and cook until the spinach has wilted and softened. Add the pine nuts and stir until they begin to brown. Take the pan from the heat and mix in the olives and parsley. Leave to cool.

Preheat the oven to 400°F.

Knead the dough again and divide it into two equal pieces. Roll each of them into 10-inch rounds. Lay one round on a floured baking sheet and spread it with all the filling. Lay the other dough round on top and pinch the edges together to seal them. Brush with the beaten egg.

Leave the loaf in a warm place for 20 minutes. Bake it for 30 minutes, or until the top is golden-brown and the loaf sounds hollow when tapped.

Eat the *tortino* warm or cool it on a wire rack.

● *Tortino con Spinaci e Olive*

53

The breads of Italy are so many and varied that it is best to go on a gastronomic tour to discover them all. Italy has northern borders with France, Switzerland, Austria and Slovenia.

The northernmost region and also the smallest, Valle d'Aosta, has borders with both France and Switzerland. It is a mountainous area, and bread and hearty soups form a large part of the diet. The bread here is, unusually for Italy, made from a mixture of wheat and rye flour and the soups themselves often contain bread, particularly one called *Valpellinentze* whose other ingredients are cabbage and the local fontina cheese.

The area of Valle d'Aosta borders on the region that is called Piemonte, or Piedmont. The town of Torino or Turin, in the center of this region, has given to the world one of Italy's most famous types of bread, *Grissini*, or bread sticks, which Napoleon called "*les petits batons de Turin*." The ones bought in other areas of Italy, and those that are exported, are factory made, but around Turin you can still buy handmade *grissini*, long and irregular in shape, lightly dusted with flour and with a crisp, crumbly texture. In Piedmont they are often served with *bagna cauda*, a rich anchovy dip that is accompanied by raw vegetables.

Tucked away to the south of Piedmont is the small, coastal region of Liguria in the center of which is the city of Genoa. Liguria boasts an excellent focaccia bread and the best toppings are either made with the local soft cheese or with olive pulp left from the first pressing of oil. A special, sweet bread, called *pan dolce*, comes from Genoa. It is a shallow dome shape with a triangle cut into the top, and its mixture includes dried and candied fruits, nuts and spices. Traditionally it is served at Christmas, brought to the table with a sprig of bay on top and cut by the youngest member of the family.

Next to Piedmont in the east, bordering on Switzerland, is Lombardy, famous for its dairy products, rice and polenta. Lombardy has its own bread stick. Called the *francesina*, it is much larger than the *grissini*, weighing about 4 ounces. The dough is only partly leavened and so it has a hard crust and compact crumb. In addition to this, Lombardy has given Italy one of its richest and most delicious breads, the panettone.

Go to Milan, the main city of Lombardy, and you will find the panettone in every food shop. They are sold in restaurants and cafés and even at the windows of trains. The exact shape of the panettone varies according to the baker. Some are made in cylindrical pans, a practice that only began in the 1920s, others are baked in the traditional round pans that are wider and flatter, but there will always be a dome-shaped top, said to resemble the cupolas of Lombardy churches.

There is a delightful story which explains the origins of the panettone. The name comes from *pan de Tonio*, Tony's bread. Tony was a baker who lived in the fifteenth century in the Milanese quarter of Borogo delle Grazie. He was poor, but he had a beautiful daughter by the name of Adalgisa. A young man of rich and noble family, one Ughetto della Tela, fell in love with Adalgisa but, old-fashioned values being what they were, was not allowed to marry one so poor and of such humble birth. Ughetto knew that his own family valued wealth above everything, so just before Christmas he sold his hunting falcons to buy the finest flour, eggs and butter. These he gave to Tony to make traditional cakes, but he added in some ideas of his own – plump golden raisins and lemons with which to make candied citrus peel. Tony set

to work and produced the best cakes that Milan had ever seen. His fame and fortune were made and Ughetto's family allowed him to marry the daughter of the once poor baker.

The panettone is still tremendously popular and the two main producers, Motta and Alemagna, make over 53 million pounds every year, with a good proportion of this sold around Christmas time. No wonder, for the panettone is a culinary delight, rich and golden-yellow in the middle and with a thin, crisp brown crust. It is sweet, but not over-sweet with just enough candied citrus peel and golden raisins to make it interesting. Although few are made at home, the recipe is not too difficult and well worth attempting.

The panettone is equally good with mid-morning coffee or after-dinner drinks. Serve it cut into wedges.

Panettone

To make one 8-inch round loaf:

1½ ounces fresh yeast or 1½ tablespoons dried
3 tablespoons warm water
6 egg yolks
½ teaspoon pure vanilla extract
grated rind ½ lemon
½ teaspoon salt
¼ cup superfine sugar
3 cups (12 ounces) all-purpose flour
butter, ⅔ cup (1¼ sticks) softened, 2 tablespoons (¼ stick) melted
2 ounces candied citrus peel, chopped
2 ounces golden raisins
2 ounces raisins

In a large mixing bowl, mix the yeast with the water and leave it in a warm place – five minutes for fresh yeast and 15 for dried. Stir in the egg yolks, vanilla extract, lemon rind and sugar.

Using your hand, mix in 2 cups of the flour, one third at a time, adding the salt as you do so. Gather the dough into a ball, but keep it in the bowl. Knead in the butter, in small pieces, about one third at a time. Knead in ½ cup more flour, a little at a time, still keeping the dough in the bowl. Take the dough out of the bowl and knead it for a short time on a work surface, using as much of the remaining flour as necessary to make it smooth and elastic. Shape it into a ball, put it into a large, clean bowl and sprinkle the surface with a little flour. Cover it and leave it in a warm place for about one hour, or until it has doubled in size.

Preheat the oven to 400°F.

Butter an 8-inch cake pan.

Punch down the dough and knead in the candied citrus peel, and all the raisins. Do this quickly so that the dough does not discolor. Shape the dough into a ball and place it in the cake pan. There should be a gap of about 1 inch all round. Leave the dough for 30 minutes, or until it has doubled in size. Brush the top with half the melted butter. Bake for 10 minutes and then brush with the remaining butter. Reduce the oven temperature to 350°F and return the loaf to the oven for a further 30 to 35 minutes, or until the top is golden-brown and crisp and a skewer stuck in the center comes out clean.

Cool the panettone on a wire rack.

At Easter time, a similar mixture to that for panettone, without golden raisins but with the addition of toasted almonds, is baked in the shape of a dove and called a colomba. The custom goes back to 1176 when two doves landed near the Milanese army standards during the battle of Legano. The Milanese saw this as a sign of protection, and their forces of the Lombard League went on to defeat the army of the Holy Roman Emperor, Frederick Barbarossa. The colomba has been baked ever since to commemorate the event.

Also at this time of year, on St. George's Day, in April, a flat, round brioche called a *pan di miglio*, is served in Milan. It is made from yeast-leavened wheat and cornstarch, butter, egg yolks and sugar, and is flavored with vanilla. Its accompaniments are cream, sugar and a garnish of elderflower.

The region of Trentino-Alto Adige to the north of Lombardy has one long border with Austria. It is really two small regions fused together. The cooking of Trentino is influenced by that of Lombardy, but Alto-Adige takes its styles and its names from Austria. There are two main types of bread in the area, *Schuttelbrot* and *Schlagbrot*, and both are made from a mixture of wheat and the rye that is grown in the local valleys. *Schuttelbrot* takes the form of large, round loaves, which are so hard that they can only be eaten if they are soaked in one of the many local soups. *Schlagbrot*, on the other hand, is soft and light.

Bread forms the basis of the local dumplings called *Canderli*. The bread is soaked in milk and mixed with eggs, flour, smoked pork fat, onion and herbs. The dumplings are the size of an orange and are cooked in soup or served with melted butter and herbs or with gravy. A variation of this is the *Schwarzplentene* which are made from rye and buckwheat bread and served with sauerkraut and tomato sauce. Leftover bread is also made into a sweet pudding with figs.

Another specialty of the area is *Krapfen*, or doughnuts. In Trentino-Alto Adige they are, typically, round and contain a blob of jelly in the center. In other parts of Italy they are fried, but in Alto Adige they are baked.

● *Sticks and Coburgs for sale, Rome*

Moving on to Veneto, in which are the cities of Venice, Verona, and Padua, the bread specialties are sweet and frivolous. On New Year's Eve in Venice, you may be served with the *vaneziana*, a large, sweet bun, made with a dough similar to that of the panettone (above), without fruits, nuts or peel, but flavored simply with orange and lemon rind and with a top covered with white sugar crystals. Also from Venice is the *fugassa*, or *fugazza*, a kind of sweet focaccia. It is raised with baking soda and contains butter, milk, rum and lemon peel. From Vicenza comes the *focaccia Vicentina*, which is made with a similar dough, baked in dove shapes with a hard-cooked egg in the center. Verona has its own Christmas cake, the *pan doro*, or golden bread, so called because of its color. Risen with yeast and enriched with butter and eggs, it is baked in a star-shape and covered with confectioners' sugar. Even the local bread pudding is a luxurious one. Instead of being soaked in milk, as it is in other Italian regions, the stale bread is soaked in wine and mixed with eggs, spices, candied citrus peel, nuts and sometimes slivers of bitter chocolate. It is known as *torta di pane ubriaca*, drunken cake.

Emilia-Romagna, the region that lies centrally in the north, boasts sausages, pasta, parma hams, wheat, butter and cheeses and the richest style of cooking in Italy. Bologna, the chief city, is known as *Bologna la grassa* (the fat). The area around the city of Ferrara, particularly the small town of Porto Garibaldi, is well known for its excellent bread. The local loaves are rounded, with the crust drawn up in four points at the top, forming a crown.

Everywhere bread is enriched with, or fried in, butter or lard. The local flat bread in Modena is known as *stria* and it is brushed or dotted with lard before being baked in a hot oven.

Piadini were once called "the national dish of the Romagnoli." They are small pieces of dough enriched with pork fat, rolled round and flat. They were once cooked on an earthenware disc called a *testo*, but now a cast-iron pan or griddle is used. The rounds of dough are cooked quickly over a high heat until they are slightly charred; smoked pork fat, salami or local cheese is laid on one half while the other half is folded over to make a substantial, easy to eat snack. Once the food of peasants, *piadini* have become fashionable in modern bars.

Gnocchi fritti from Modena, and *crescentine* from Bologna are the deep fried specialties. *Gnocchi fritti* are made with bread dough, again enriched with rendered pork fat, that are cut in diamond shapes and deep fried either in more pork fat or in olive oil. They are eaten hot with salami, ham, or cheese. *Crescentine* are enriched with lard or pork crackling and sometimes pieces of prosciutto ham. They are cut in rounds or diamond shapes and can be either baked or deep fried.

On New Year's Eve around the city of Ferraro, the traditional dessert is the *pan pepato di cioccolato*. *Pan pepato*, also called *pampepato*, is a sweet Brioche-type bread which originated in the Middle Ages and which contains pepper as a flavoring. The Ferrarese *pan pepato* is flavored with butter, cocoa powder, honey, spices, almonds and lemon peel, and is covered with chocolate icing and sprinkles.

Pan pepato was once eaten at any time between the week before Christmas and Twelfth Night and the bakers of Ferraro would send the cakes as presents to local rulers and also to the Pope.

South of Emilia-Romagna lies Tuscany, where the cooking must be amongst the healthiest in all Italy. It relies on the best of fresh ingredients cooked extremely simply. Admittedly this was the home of the Medicis, whose banquets were anything but simple, and also the headquarters of the first cooking academy, the Compagnia del Paiolo (the Company of the Cauldron), whose twelve members each had to produce an elaborate dish of their own invention at every meeting. For the ordinary people, however, "simple and good" has always been the principle of their cooking, and bread, vegetables and fresh fruit, or simply bread and soup have traditionally formed the substantial part of a meal.

The favorite Tuscan bread is *pan sciocco*, which is unsalted because the Tuscans believe that salt interferes with the flavor of other foods. It accompanies most meals and goes particularly well with delicacies such as salty ewe's-milk cheeses and salami made from wild boar. Tuscan soups, typically rich with vegetables and herbs, are always ladled over *pan sciocco*.

Another Tuscan bread dish is *panzanella*, a salad based on bread, vegetables and anchovies. In the traditional version, two-day old *pan sciocco* is soaked in water, squeezed and mixed with sweet peppers, cucumber, tomato and onion in a dressing of oil, vinegar, crushed anchovies and capers. In more modern versions, the bread is made into croutons before being added to the same ingredients.

Pane di rosmarino, rosemary bread, is served at Easter time. In Florence the dough is made into small rolls and elsewhere in Tuscany into long or round loaves. The bread is subtly flavored by simmering raisins in oil with a rosemary sprig. The rosemary flavors both oil and raisins, enabling it to gently permeate the bread, which is soft and moist in the center with a thin shiny-brown crust. It is a semi-sweet bread and can be eaten with or without butter.

Rosemary Bread

To make one large loaf or sixteen rolls:

basic bread dough (see page 12) made with 4 cups (1 pound) all-purpose flour
2 rosemary sprigs
6 ounces raisins
4 tablespoons olive oil
1 teaspoon salt
1 tablespoon superfine sugar
2 tablespoons sugar, dissolved in warm water

Gently simmer the raisins and rosemary in the oil for 10 minutes, without allowing the raisins to brown or harden. Discard the rosemary. After the dough has been kneaded for the first time, gradually knead in the cooled oil and raisins, the salt and the superfine sugar. Place the dough in a bowl, cover it and leave it to rise for 30 minutes.

Preheat the oven to 400°F. Knead the dough again and either shape it into one loaf or into sixteen rolls. Place them on a floured baking sheet and leave them for 20 minutes. Bake the loaf for 30 to 35 minutes and the rolls for 20 minutes, brushing the tops with the sweetened water halfway through. Cool on wire racks.

From Tuscany we come to the regions around Rome, which are Latium, Umbria and the Marches. Here the cooking is plain but hearty. Since Roman times, the best loved foods have been bread, cheese and vegetables. One of the most popular breads in the area today is the *ciriola*, a roll that is made with a highly-leavened dough so that it is light and airy inside with a crisp, golden crust. A specialty of Rome itself are *maritozzi*, sweet rolls containing pine nuts, golden raisins and candied citrus peel, and coated with confectioners' sugar.

All over central Italy, the standard loaf is the *pagnotta*. It is round with a double cross slashed in the top and weighs anything from 1 to 2½ pounds. It was once traditionally sliced by the man of the house at table. He held it in the crook of his arm, moving the knife toward himself across the bread.

An ancient Roman inscription on a wall in Fara, in Sabina, makes reference to a *crustulum*, an oil-soaked cake that was given out by the authorities to the townspeople on important civil or religious feast days, mainly during December and January. The *bruschetta*, served today in Latium, Umbria and Tuscany, is a direct descendant. The *bruschetta* is a coarse, flat bun, soaked in olive oil, flavored with garlic and toasted, preferably over hot coals. Once the food of the poor, the *bruschetta* is now a popular snack in cafés and bars.

Another Roman favorite is the *crostini alla provatura*, where slices of bread topped with provatura cheese are put into the oven for the cheese to melt and cover the bread completely.

On the middle of the eastern Italian coast is Abruzzi, where pasta and polenta complement the seafood, pork, lamb and vegetables. The favorite bread here is the *spaccatina*, a round flat loaf with a deep cut in the center, its top brushed thickly with lard, rendered pork fat or olive oil.

Passing through the small region of Molise, we come to Campania and the city of Naples, home of the pizza that has spread across the world, changing almost beyond recognition as it turns up in specialty restaurants and frozen food cabinets.

In Campania, as in other regions of southern Italy, cooks know how to make simple, cheap ingredients into robust and colorful dishes. Plain bread is made into garlands and shapes of fruit, flowers or religious symbols and given simple flavorings, such as the pepper in the following recipe. These pepper wreaths are beautiful to look at besides being rich and crisp. They also keep for a long time. In Campania they would be made with freshly-made lard. If you don't fancy using the commercial kind, or if you are a vegetarian, use butter instead. The unusally low cooking temperature gives the wreaths their crispness.

Taralli a Sugna e Pepe

To make eight small wreaths:

basic bread dough (see page 12) made with 4 cups (1 pound) all-purpose flour with 1 teaspoon freshly-ground black pepper added to the flour before mixing

⅔ cup lard, softened and in small pieces

1 teaspoon salt

Flatten out the dough and dot it with one third of the pieces of lard and sprinkle on the salt. Knead these in. Repeat twice, with the remaining lard.

Knead the dough again on a floured board, and divide it in sixteen pieces. Roll each one into a long sausage shape about ⅜ inch thick. Take two pieces of dough. Starting from the centers, twist them together. Bring the ends together and join them in a circle.

Lay the wreath on a floured baking sheet, and make the others in the same way. Leave them in a warm place for 1 hour.

Preheat the oven to 350°F.

Bake the wreaths for 40 minutes, or until they are golden-brown and crisp. Cool them on a wire rack.

● *Pizza Napoletana*

57

So what about the pizza? Where did it come from and what are its real ingredients. The name pizza actually means a pie and is also, to confuse matters, used to refer to fruit tarts and some cakes. However, the pizza, as we know it, goes back to Roman times, when it was a thin, flat bread, baked on a hot stone, with a topping of olive oil, herbs and sometimes honey. When tomatoes arrived from the New World, the small, sweet varieties were found to grow so well in the southern Italian sun that they were used in almost every dish. Huge batches were stewed down in cauldrons to make a thick purée that has been poured over meats and poultry, used as the basis of soup and, inevitably, spread over Italian flat bread. It was not until the eighteenth century that the present day pizza was developed around Naples. Despite the menus that you may read in world-wide pizza restaurants, the authentic topping should be a simple one: tomato sauce, mozzarella cheese, and either basil or oregano – red, white and green, the colors of the Italian flag.

The dough for the pizza base is a plain bread dough made with all-purpose flour, yeast and water. I always add a little olive oil which adds to the crispness of the edges. If I were in Naples, however, I might very well go to buy the basic dough from the local *forno*.

Basic Pizza Dough

To make one 10-inch pizza or four 7-inch pizzas:

2 cups (8 ounces) all-purpose flour
½ ounce fresh yeast or 2 teaspoons dried
⅔ cup warm water
1 teaspoon salt
1 tablespoon olive oil

Make up the dough as for the basic bread dough on page 12, adding the olive oil with the salt water. Knead it and leave it to rise in the usual way.

To make the base for a large pizza, roll the dough into a large round, about 11 inches in diameter, then fold over ½ inch all the way round. To make individual pizzas, divide the dough in four and roll each piece thinly to a diameter of about 8 inches.

Pizzas can be baked in special pizza plates or pans, but you will always get the crispest texture and the best degree of rising by laying the pizza on a floured baking sheet.

Pizzas should always be eaten hot, straight from the oven. Not only is the base at its crispest, but the mozzarella cheese is perfect when melted.

The tomato sauce for a pizza topping can be made while the dough is rising. You can also make it in advance and store it in a covered container in the refrigerator for up to three days. The onions and garlic are optional.

Tomato Sauce for Pizza

Enough for one 10-inch pizza:

1 pound ripe red tomatoes
2 tablespoons olive oil
1 small onion, finely chopped
1 clove garlic, finely chopped

Scald, skin and chop the tomatoes. Gently soften the onions and garlic in the oil in a frying pan over low heat. Add the tomatoes and simmer, stirring frequently, for 50 minutes, or until you have a thick purée.
Leave it to cool.

Pizza Napoletana

Pizza dough, as above
tomato sauce, as above
6 ounces mozzarella cheese, thinly sliced
1 teaspoon chopped basil or about 15 whole oregano leaves

Roll the dough into a circle and fold the edge as above. Lay it on a floured sheet. Spread the tomato sauce over the top. Lay the slices of mozzarella over the tomato sauce and scatter the herbs over that. Leave the pizza in a warm place for 20 minutes to rise.
Preheat the oven to 400°F. Bake the pizza for 15 to 20 minutes or until the edges are crisp, but not browned, and the cheese has melted.

Sardiniara

Pizza dough, as above
tomato sauce, as above
12 black olives, halved and pitted
Two 1¾-ounce cans anchovy fillets

This is a pizza with an anchovy topping which really comes from the small northern region of Liguria. It is rich and delicious.
Prepare the pizza base and spread it with tomato sauce. Put the olive halves on top. Cut the anchovy fillets in half lengthways and again crossways. Lay the pieces, haphazard fashion, over the top of the tomato sauce. Leave it to rise and bake as above.

● *Harvested grain field*

The calzone is a pizza which is made into a package and deep fried. The simplest filling for a calzone is a slice of prosciutto ham topped with thin slices of mozzarella cheese. Others have ricotta, diced mozzarella and grated parmesan or pecorino cheese, and sometimes beaten egg mixed together with the ham or, as an alternative, salami, in thin strips. The following recipe is the perfect combination. You still have the melting slices of mozzarella and whole pieces of ham, but underneath is a soft bed of ricotta and parmesan. The calzone should be eaten while it is hot and crisp and, accompanied only by a green salad, it makes a very substantial meal.

In Italy, the calzone is fried in olive oil. In most other countries, this would be a very expensive exercise. Olive oil also has a low burning temperature and flash-point. I have therefore used sunflower oil, which is cheaper and more tolerant of high temperatures.

Calzone

To make four 8-inch calzones:

basic pizza dough (see page 58) made with 2 cups (8 ounces) all-purpose flour
sunflower oil for frying

Filling:

4 ounces ricotta cheese
1 ounce parmesan cheese, grated
4 thin slices prosciutto ham
4 ounces mozzarella cheese, cut in 8 slices

Cut the dough in four pieces and roll each one into a round about 8 inches in diameter. Lay them flat on the work surface. Mix together the ricotta and parmesan cheeses.

Take one dough round and spread one quarter of the ricotta mixture over half of it, leaving about ½ inch round the edge. Lay a slice of ham on top and two slices of mozzarella on top of that. Fold over the other half of the dough and seal the edges. Lay the calzone on a floured baking sheet while you make the others in the same way.

For frying, choose a saucepan or casserole that will easily take the calzone lying flat. An oval-shaped one is ideal. Add sunflower oil to the depth of about 1½ inches and heat it over high heat.

Fry the first calzone in the oil until the underside is golden-brown, about 1½ minutes. Turn it over and brown the other side. Lift out the calzone with a slotted spoon and place it in a shallow dish lined with paper towels.

Cook the others in the same way and serve them hot, as soon as possible.

The other regions of the south, with a similar, colorful, sunblessed cuisine to Campania, are Apulia, Basilicata and Calabria. All over the area, the traditional loaves are large.

The local bread of the Apulia region is called *schiacciata*. It is made by the sourdough method of keeping back a batch of the previous week's baking, and each round loaf weighs up to 4½ pounds. Home baking is still popular in Apulia. Once a housewife has shaped her loaf she marks it with her own particular brand, called a *marca di pane*, which may show the family crest or initials. Some of the old wooden brands are so beautiful that they are now family heirlooms or collectors' items. The loaves are then taken to the local *forno* for baking.

Bread in Basilicata was also traditionally made at home and taken to the *forno*, but now it is mostly bought. The traditional loaf, made from coarse wheat flour, is called a *panella* and it can be as large as a cartwheel. One loaf would at one time last a family all week.

There are also two offshore islands, Sicily and Sardinia. The cookery of Sicily was learned from the Greeks and that of Sardinia from the Phoenicians. After each absorbed a little more from the Arabs, they influenced the Romans and so the whole of Italy. Both islands, throughout the Roman period, supplied the mainland with wheat.

The typical Sicilian bread is large and cartwheel-shaped, and traditionally it was made in the home and baked in the small, dome-shaped oven that was built near the fireplace in most Sicilian kitchens. There are also lozenge-shaped loaves, sandwich rolls and flat buns, and a flat, unleavened bread that is soaked in oil and served with salt fish. As Sicily is so close to Campania, it is not surprising that pizzas are popular on the island. The pizzas of Sicily are called *sfinciuni*, and they are sold in bakers' shops and also from the carts of itinerant salesmen. There are two types. One is a round of dough, thicker than that for *pizza napoletana*, covered with the local cacciacavallo cheese, tomatoes, onions, anchovies, breadcrumbs and oil. The second, called *sfinciuni di San Vito*, consists of a stuffing of minced pork, local sausage and breadcrumbs, sandwiched between two thin sheets of dough.

Other traditional loaves are the *vasteddi*, of which there are two types: the *vasteddi maritati*, or married *vasteddi*, which has a filling of meat and cheese, and the *vasteddi schietti*, which is plainer. I have not been able to find an original recipe for either but they sounded so good that I wanted to have a try. From the description, I have worked out the following ingredients for *vasteddi maritati*. I didn't have any pork spleen, so I used a lean pork chop instead. It is a wonderful loaf for a picnic and the special touch is the topping of cumin seeds that gives the bread an inbuilt spice.

Vasteddi Maritati

To make one 8-inch round:

basic bread dough (see page 12) made with 4 cups (1 pound) all-purpose flour, plus 2 tablespoons olive oil
1 lean loin pork chop
3 tablespoons olive oil
2 slices bacon
4 ounces ricotta cheese
8 thin slices Italian salami
2 teaspoons cumin seeds

Make the bread dough and leave it, covered, in a warm place for 1 hour. Cut the pork chop in thin strips and fry them quickly in the olive oil until they are just cooked through. Remove them. Cook the bacon slices in the oil until they are only just done. Remove them and cut off any rinds.

Preheat the oven to 400°F. Knead the bread dough on a floured board, divide it in two equal pieces and roll one to a round of 8 inches in diameter. Lay one piece on a floured baking sheet. Spread the ricotta cheese over the top, leaving an edge of about ½ inch. Lay the pork strips on top of the cheese, then the salami and finally the whole bacon slices. Lay the second round of dough on top and press the edges together to secure them. Scatter the cumin seeds over the top and press them down slightly.

Leave the loaf in a warm place for 30 minutes and then bake it for 40 minutes, or until it is risen and golden. Cool it on a wire rack.

Sardinia is a rolling island of low hills whose lamb, beef, pork and vegetables are made into plain but hearty meals, often accompanied by bread. Sardinia boasts the largest loaf in Italy, the *civraxiu*, which can weigh as much as 9 pounds. It is a specialty of Cagliari, the capital of the island, and is made with semolina rather than finely-milled flour.

The tradition in Sardinia is that the women make the bread while the men cook the meat. The meat specialty is the *caraxiu* – whole kid, lamb or piglet cooked in a deep enclosed pit with aromatic woods and herbs. To go with this succulent, flavorsome meat, the women make *carte da musica*, or sheets of music. They are in fact thin, round sheets of flat bread, about 12 inches in diameter, with the proper name of *pane carasau*. When cooked they crackle into lined patterns like the ruled staffs of music paper. Delicious with roasted meats, they are also highly portable and have been taken as the herdsman's lunch for centuries.

Bread is so important in Sardinia that huge, decorative loaves are baked for festivals and important occasions. There are flowers and garlands for weddings and special shapes for Easter, Christmas and harvest-time.

● *Vasteddi Maritati*

SPAIN AND PORTUGAL

Bread has long been held in the greatest of esteem in the Spanish peninsula and the art and skill of the baker have always been recognized.
The Romans praised Spanish bread, describing it as white, fine-textured, full of flavor and aroma. Conquering Arabs, in the tenth century, improved the country's agriculture by building waterwheels and channeling water into the fields. Wheat growing flourished, thus ensuring that bread would always be one of Spain's important foods. Wheat is the main product of La Mancha in central Spain, where the old windmills made famous by Cervantes' "Don Quixote" have been preserved as honored relics of the past.

SPAIN

Spanish bread today, at least that made in the country, is similar in nature to the bread of Roman times – crusty on the outside and soft and sweet-tasting inside. There are variations as to ingredients and methods of baking, but the essential character of the loaf is the same throughout Spain – rich, crusty and white. From the plain peasant bread to the sweet panettone, Spain offers a wealth of treats for the bread-lover.

Common throughout Spain is the rounded cushion-shaped loaf made by tucking the edges of the kneaded dough underneath and baking on an open tray, but there are also regional variations. In the North, tear-shaped loaves are popular, while in Andalusia you will find oblong loaves which are slashed along the top. The size of loaves also varies, depending on who they are intended to feed.

The time spent "working the yeast" coupled with the usual rising time, gives this bread a rich, sweet flavor. It has a crispy crust and soft crumb and stays fresh for up to two days.

Spanish Peasant Bread

To make two large loaves:

12 cups (3 pounds) all-purpose flour
3¾ cups warm water
3 tablespoons milk
1½ ounces fresh yeast or 1½ tablespoons dried
1½ tablespoons salt

Place the flour in a bowl, reserving one handful. If it is a cold day, warm it slightly by setting it near a radiator or on top of a stove with the oven switched on.

Pour ½ cup of the water into a small bowl, add the milk and sprinkle in the yeast. Leave fresh yeast for five minutes and dried for 15 minutes. Make a well in the flour. First stir the mixture, and then pour it into the flour – but do not mix it in. Scatter the reserved handful of flour over the top.

Leave the flour and yeast in a warm, draft-free place to stand for one hour. After this time the yeast should be bubbling well.

Using your hand, begin to draw the flour into the yeast from the edges of the well. When the center feels dry, sprinkle in the salt. Now gradually add the remaining water, still bringing flour from the edges of the bowl to the center. When all the water has been added, continue kneading until the dough begins to feel smooth.

Turn the dough on to a floured work surface and knead it well for about ten minutes until it feels soft, very workable and not at all sticky. Form it into a round cushion shape, tucking the sides underneath, and return it to the bowl, rounded side up. Cover the bowl with a clean, dry cloth and leave it in a warm place for 1 hour for the dough to double in size.

Preheat the oven to 400°F. Knead the dough again and divide it into two. Form each piece into a round cushion shape as before, folding the sides underneath to obtain a smooth, rounded top. Place the loaves on floured baking sheets and bake them for 40 to 45 minutes, or until they are lightly browned and sound hollow when tapped. Cool them on wire racks.

● *Broa (left) and Spanish peasant bread (right)*

63

Bread appears with nearly every meal in Spain. Potatoes are seldom used and rice is only popular in mixed dishes like paella. Bread is the filling part of the meal and is essential for mopping up the rich sauces and gravies which are a part of many Spanish dishes.

Castilian bread has a harder crust and is said to be ideal for scooping and mopping up the succulent *cocido madrileno*, a mixed meat, chicken and vegetable stew. Pieces of bread are also put on the plate to be mashed with the fattier pieces of meat. Typical of Aragon are chilindron sauces, made with tomatoes, onions, garlic, serrano ham and toasted sweet peppers, to accompany meat and vegetables, and always mopped up with a thick crust of Aragonese bread. From Madrid and the Basque areas comes *olla podrida*, containing five kinds of meat and spiced sausage and a mixture of vegetables and dried beans. Its only accompaniments are bread and red wine.

La pringa, a bread snack served in tapas bars, probably has its origins in the eating of bread with rich stews. It consists of a mixture of salted and fresh meats, cooked together for a long time and mashed to a paste which is then spread into half-cooked rolls before they are returned to the oven. The result is a delicious combination of hot, crusty bread and spiced, salty meats.

● *Panaderia in Madrid*

Add the onion and garlic and soften them. Stir in the paprika and cayenne pepper and cook them for 1 minute, stirring. Mix in the diced sausage. Add the meats and coat them in the mixture. Pour in the stock and bring it to a boil. Cover and simmer gently for 2½ hours or until the meats are very tender and the stock has almost evaporated.

Take out the meats and the cubes of sausage. Dice the meats, removing the bones from the pork belly. In Spanish kitchens, the meats are probably mashed and pounded by hand, which you may do if you wish. However, it works equally well if you put the meats and sausage into a food processor and work them to a coarse paste.

Meanwhile, make the bread dough and let it rise in the usual way. Preheat the oven to 400°F. Form the dough into twenty small, round buns. Lay them on floured baking sheets and leave them for 20 minutes to rise. Bake them for 10 minutes. Take them out of the oven and, with a sharp knife, quickly slit each one almost in half crossways. Fill the buns with the meat paste and close them up again. Return them to the oven for a further 10 minutes.

They are delicious eaten hot, straight from the oven, but are also excellent cold.

La Pringa

To make twenty buns:

1 pound fresh pork belly
1 pound collar of bacon, in one piece
3 tablespoons olive oil
1 large onion, thinly sliced
1 clove garlic, finely chopped
1 tablespoon paprika
1 teaspoon cayenne pepper
4 ounces chorizo sausage, in one piece
2½ cups stock
half quantity of Spanish Peasant Bread dough, page 63

Cut the rinds from the pork and bacon and remove the strip of fat from the underside of the pork (reserve it if you are making the *Broas de Torresmos de Souzel* (see page 69). Cut the sausage into ⅝-inch dice.

Heat the oil in a large, flameproof casserole over low heat.

Bread is also an essential ingredient of many dishes in Spain. One of the simplest is the simple *pa amb tomatec* (bread and tomatoes) from Catalonia. Thick slices of fresh bread are rubbed with a cut tomato until they turn pink. They are then given a light sprinkling of olive oil, are topped with tomato slices and served either alone or with serrano ham.

Migas are small cubes of fried bread that are eaten as a snack or as a separate course of a meal. Cubes of bread are soaked overnight in a wet, salted cloth and then fried until crisp in garlic-flavored oil.

Pounded bread and bread cubes are essential ingredients of the cold soup from Andalusia called *gazpacho* and also the hot, garlic soup from Cadiz called *a ajo*. From La Mancha, the huge, dry plateau in Castile in central Spain, comes *pastel de queso y bacon* (cheese and bacon cake). It is made with the local sheep's milk cheese, bread, milk, eggs and bacon.

Spain also has its sweet breads, and the most well known is the *roscon de Reyes*, produced at home and by local bakers for Reyes, the day of the Three Kings, on January 6th. Spanish children do not have a Santa Claus on December 25th; their presents are brought by the Three Kings on the night of January 5th. January the 6th is a holiday on which to visit relations and exchange presents. The celebratory cake is the *roscon de Reyes* in which a bean was traditionally hidden. The person who received the bean in their portion was to be king for the day. Nowadays, instead of the bean, a small charm or coin is put in. It is said to bring good luck although, in some families,

● *Harvesting grain by hand in Old Castile, Spain*

the tradition is that the person who gets it has to pay for the *roscon*!

The *roscon de Reyes* is a rich, sweet, yeasted cake, baked in a ring and decorated with slivered almonds and candied citrus peel. Commercially-baked ones come in a variety of sizes and some are filled with cream or a sweet filling. Many contain a variety of novelties, rather like a box of crackers. This recipe appeared in the *Gourmetour*, a gorgeous, colorful magazine about Spain, its food and wine, which is sent to food writers.

Roscon de Reyes

To make one 10-inch ring:

1 ounce fresh yeast or 1 tablespoon dried
¼ cup warm milk
1 cup sugar
4 cups (1 pound) all-purpose flour
3 whole eggs
1 egg, separated
1 teaspoon salt
1 tablespoon dark rum
1 tablespoon orange-flower water
grated rind ½ orange
grated rind ½ lemon
½ cup (1 stick) butter, softened
2 ounces slivered almonds
2 ounces candied fruit, bought in the piece and cut in thin slivers

In a small bowl, sprinkle the yeast over the milk and leave it to stand – five minutes for fresh yeast, 15 for dried. Add 1 teaspoon of sugar and gradually sprinkle in enough flour to make a soft dough – about 2 ounces. Place the dough in a bowl, cover it and leave it in a warm place for about 40 minutes, to double in size.

Place the remaining flour in a large bowl and make a well in the center. Beat the eggs and egg yolk together and pour them into the well. Add the sugar, salt, rum, orange-flower water and grated orange and lemon rinds. Using a wooden spoon, gradually work the flour into the well and beat until everything is well mixed.

Place the ball of yeast dough in the mixture and, using your hands, gradually knead the two together until you have a smooth, soft dough. Knead it lightly on a floured work surface until it is no longer sticky. Divide the dough in four. Flatten each piece out slightly and put one quarter of the butter in the center of each piece. Work it into the dough and then knead all the pieces together again. Place the dough in a clean bowl and leave it in a warm place for 1 hour to double in size.

Preheat the oven to 350°F. Knead the dough again and put a trinket or coin (nothing plastic that will melt) into it. Form the dough into a cushion shape. Push the rounded handle of a wooden spoon down through the center and gently pull the dough into a ring-shape. Either lay the ring on a floured baking sheet and fill the center with a core of aluminum foil, or put it into a 10-inch-diameter ring mold.

Leave the dough in a warm place for 30 minutes. Brush the top with the egg white and scatter it with the slivered almonds and candied fruit. Bake the cake for 40 minutes or until it is golden-brown on top and cooked through. Turn it on to a wire rack to cool.

● *Coca de Trampo Mallorcina*

THE BALEARICS

The Balearics are the islands off the coast of Spain which include Mallorca and Minorca. Their plain bread is similar to that from Spain and one of the specialties is the *coca de trampo*. *Trampo* is the word used for a mixture of aromatic vegetables, such as onions, tomatoes and sweet peppers. The *coca* is a flat bread with a rich topping, similar to a pizza. The base for the *coca* is made with a quantity of basic bread dough into which olive oil is kneaded. The result is bread with a pastry-like texture. Crisp and flaky on the outside it is soft and creamy in the middle. The rich vegetable topping melts into the base to give it flavor and additional softness. It makes a wonderful vegetarian meal.

Following, is another recipe that can be made with the basic Spanish Peasant Bread dough. The addition of the olive oil makes the cooked dough very rich. The inside is soft and creamy, especially where the vegetable juices have soaked in, and the outside is crisp. Served with a green salad and sprinkled with diced cheese, it makes a delicious, substantial meal.

This is a variation on a recipe from *Las Mejoras Tapas, Ceñas Frias y Platos Combinados*, by Gloria Rossi Callizo.

● *Market stall, Barcelos, Portugal*

Coca de Trampo Mallorcina

To make one 12-inch loaf:

Trampo:

1 pound tomatoes
3 tablespoons olive oil
1 sweet green pepper
1 sweet red pepper
1 large onion
1 clove garlic, finely chopped
3 tablespoons chopped parsley

Base:

⅓ recipe Spanish Peasant Bread dough (see page 63)
½ cup, plus 2 tablespoons, olive oil

Scald, skin and chop the tomatoes. Heat the oil in a saucepan over low heat. Mix in the tomatoes, cover and simmer them until they have cooked to a thick purée. Cool them.

Preheat the oven to 350°F.

Let the bread dough rise in the usual way. Knead it on a floured board and then gradually work in the olive oil, tablespoon by tablespoon. This looks impossible at first, but if you have patience, all the oil will eventually be absorbed. Each time you add oil, pull the dough out flat, sprinke 1 to 2 tablespoons of it in the center and then bring the edges together without letting any oil escape. When you begin kneading, the outside of the dough will be very oily and there will be oil on your work surface, but keep kneading until the dough feels smooth again. The more oil you have added, the longer you will have to knead, but eventually the dough *will* take it all.

Lightly flour the work surface and a rolling pin, and roll the dough into a 12-inch round. Lay it on a floured baking sheet and let it rest for about 5 minutes.

Spread the puréed tomatoes over the surface of the dough, leaving an edge of about 1 inch all round.

Cut the peppers in long, thin strips and halve and thinly slice the onion. Arrange them over the tomatoes. Sprinkle the finely-chopped garlic and then the parsley over the peppers and onion and finally dribble the remaining oil over the top.

Bake the *coca de trampo Mallorcina* for 40 to 45 minutes, or until the edges are browned and feel crisp, and the vegetables are cooked. Serve it hot.

PORTUGAL

Bread is just as important in Portugal as it is in Spain. Here, too, the village bakers take pride in their work and besides baking bread for sale, they also bake loaves made by local villagers for their personal consumption. Portuguese bread has a thick crust and is moist and chewy on the inside. Besides the wheat breads, there is also this corn bread, called *broa*.

Baked in a round, it remains fairly flat and has a crisp outside and crumbly middle and a strong, characteristic corn flavor. It is traditionally used to dip into the gravies of rich stews. It is also served with *caldo verde*, a kale, potato and spicy sausage soup, and with a mixed dish of peas and sausage which is typically topped with eggs.

● *Broa*

Broa

To make one 9-inch round loaf:

2¼ cups (9 ounces) fine cornmeal
1½ teaspoons salt
1 teaspoon sugar
1 cup boiling water
2 tablespoons olive oil
½ ounce fresh or 2 teaspoons dried yeast
3 tablespoons lukewarm water
1 cup (4 ounces) all-purpose flour

Place 1½ cups of the cornmeal in a mixing bowl with the salt and sugar. Add the boiling water and stir vigorously until the mixture is smooth. Beat in the oil and leave the mixture to cool.

Sprinkle the yeast over the warm water and leave it to begin to work – 5 minutes for fresh yeast and 15 minutes for dried. Stir it into the cornmeal mixture. Beginning with a wooden spoon and finishing with your hand, gradually add the remaining cornmeal and the flour to the mixture. Form the dough into a ball and knead it. Place it in a bowl, cover it with a clean, dry cloth and leave it in a warm place for 1 hour to rise.

Preheat the oven to 350°F.

Lightly oil an 8-inch-diameter flan pan. Knead the dough again and pat it into a round the size of the pan. Put it in the pan and leave it in a warm place for 30 minutes.

Bake the loaf for 40 minutes, or until the top is golden and crisp. Turn it on to a wire rack to cool.

This Portuguese recipe can be made with the plain Spanish bread dough (see page 63). It is known as crackling cake, and the result is a rich, dark brown, sweet and spicy bread that should be eaten on its own, without butter, accompanied by coffee, hot chocolate or tea. It is taken from *Cozinha Regional Portuguese* by Maria Odette Cortes Valente, published in 1976.

The best pork fat to use is that which can be found under a pork belly in a layer about ¼ inch thick. It can be peeled away easily in one piece.

Broas de Torresmos de Souzel

To make one 2-pound loaf:

basic Spanish Peasant Bread dough (see page 63) made with 2 cups (8 ounces) flour
8 ounces pork fat
1 tablespoon olive oil
2 cups (8 ounces) all-purpose flour
1⅓ cups sugar
2 eggs, beaten
1 teaspoon ground cinnamon
1 teaspoon ground aniseed
¼ cup brandy
1 egg yolk, lightly beaten

● *Communal oven, Mertola, Portugal*

ake the dough and leave it in a bowl, covered with a clean, dry cloth, for 1 hour or until it has doubled in size.

Cut the pork fat into small dice. Heat the oil in a large frying pan over low heat. Put in the diced fat and fry it gently, stirring frequently, until the cubes are brown and most of the fat has been rendered from them. Stir in the flour and keep stirring until it browns slightly. Take the pan from the heat and beat in all but two teaspoons of the sugar, with the beaten eggs, spices and brandy. Cool the mixture to lukewarm.

Preheat the oven to 400°F. On a lightly-floured work surface, knead the spiced mixture into the risen dough about one eighth at a time, working each portion in well before adding the next. The dough will feel light and spongy and immensely workable.

Oil a 2-pound loaf pan and lightly press the dough into it. Cover it and leave it in a warm place for 30 minutes or until the dough has risen about ⅜ inch above the rim of the pan. Brush the top of the loaf with the egg yolk and sprinkle it with the remaining sugar.

Bake the loaf for 40 minutes and test to see if the loaf is done by inserting a thin skewer into the center. The top will be dark brown.

An ancient festival takes place at harvest time in the town of Tomar, in central Portugal. It is called the Festival of Tabuleiros. *Tabuleiros* means "tray," the word used to describe the tall crown of bread that is decorated with wheat ears and flowers. Each must be as tall as the young girl who wears it on her head in the procession. The girls are accompanied by a male relative or fiancé who helps to steady the crown. Following behind are musicians, standard bearers and soldiers, oxen with gilded horns and wine carts. In the evening the oxen are slaughtered and there is a blessing of bread, meat and wine in front of the local Church. Then the seventeen best tabuleiros are chosen. On the next day, the food is distributed to the poor and there are donkey cart races, bull fights, dancing and fireworks.

Sweet bread is also popular in Portugal. This is a plain, sweet bread, traditionally baked in spiral shapes, called *caracois*, or, with currants added, in braids called *tranca a tricana*. When cooked, the lighter parts of the crust are golden-yellow and the inside has the texture of a dense, rich Madeira cake. Eat it as a mid-morning or afternoon snack, with coffee, hot chocolate or tea.

● *Tomar Festival, Portugal*

Massa Sovada

To make two 8-inch-diameter loaves:
1 ounce fresh or 1 tablespoon dried yeast
4 tablespoons warm water
6 cups (1 pound 8 ounces) all-purpose flour
1 cup sugar
1 teaspoon salt
¾ cup, plus 2 tablespoons, warm milk
3 eggs
½ cup (1 stick) unsalted butter, softened and cut in small pieces

In a small bowl, sprinkle the yeast over the water. Leave fresh yeast for 5 minutes and dried for 15 minutes.

Place 4 cups of the flour in a large bowl and toss in the sugar and salt with your fingertips. Make a well in the center and pour in the yeast mixture and the milk. Add the eggs whole, as though you were making batter. Gradually beat in flour from the edges of the well until everything is well mixed.

Beat in the butter and then the remaining flour, about ¼ cup at a time. Continue beating until you have a soft dough that can be gathered into a ball. Turn the dough on to a floured work surface and knead it until it feels smooth and elastic. Place it in a lightly-greased bowl and cover it with a clean, dry cloth. Leave it in a warm place for one hour to double in size.

Preheat the oven to 350°F.

Flour two 9-inch-diameter pie plates.

Knead the dough again and divide it in two. To make the *caracois*, form each piece into a sausage shape about 1½ inches in diameter and spiral it round inside one of the pie plates.

For the *tranca a tricana*, knead in 1 ounce currants after the butter and second amount of flour have been added. Divide the dough in two as before and then each piece in three. Roll these three pieces into sausage shapes and form them into a braid (see page 18). Lay the braids on floured baking sheets.

Bake the loaves for 40 to 45 minutes or until they are risen and golden brown. Cool them on wire racks.

● *Massa Sovada*

SWITZERLAND AND THE NETHERLANDS

Switzerland and The Netherlands may be two of the smaller countries in Europe, but each has its own definite style of cooking, albeit taking in influences from bordering countries. The Netherlands is one of the so-called Low Countries, with a long sea coast and borders with Belgium and Germany. Switzerland, in contrast, is completely land-locked, with high mountains and borders with France, Germany, Austria and Italy.

SWITZERLAND

Switzerland is well-known for its sausages and cured meats and its rich milk, which goes into butter, cheese and chocolate. Swiss bread also benefits from these dairy products and they are added in different proportions to give loaves and rolls in a wide variety of shapes, sizes, flavors and textures. There are over two hundred types of bread in Switzerland, some known and baked nationally and some produced only in certain cantons. You will also find croissants and brioches from France and *Gugelhupf* from Austria, all as good as they are in their countries of origin.

Baking in Switzerland goes back thousands of years. Sourdough leaven was first used around 3000 BC and the first commercial bakeries were established just before the Roman occupation. In the early Middle Ages, baking guilds were set up – bakers baked bread for sale and also took in loaves from other people for baking. At that time bread was made of flour of varying grades, and in years of poor harvest, chestnuts, acorns, root vegetables and even sawdust were mixed with whatever coarsely-ground flour was available.

In the sixteenth century, there were three basic sorts of bread, white bread for the very rich, half-white bread for the wealthy and what was known as *Graubrot* (gray bread) or *Ruchbrot* (notorious bread) for the majority of people. The main grain for this everyday bread was rye, mixed at different times with spelt, wheat, barley or oats.

Wherever you go in Switzerland today you will notice a wide variety of bread shapes and many of these have ancient origins, both practical and symbolic. The small, ring-shaped breads and rolls go back to the time when small loaves were strung on poles and stored across the rafters. The braid is said to have originated in the ancient custom whereby the newly widowed would cut off their hair as a sacrifice to their dead husband. Some bread shapes were once fertility or harvest symbols, and there are many different versions of the cross, which was symbolic even before Christianity.

Today, there are *Normalbrot* (everyday bread), *Spezialbrot* (enriched, sweetened, flavored, etc.), *Kleinbrote* (rolls), *Gebildbrote* (which are the wonderfully elaborate picture breads) and the *Kantonsbrote*, the specialties of each individual canton.

This braided bread, following, comes into the category of *Spezialbrot*. It is enriched with milk, butter and egg to make a bread that is sweet and soft on the inside with a thin, crisp crust. The Swiss braid can be made with four lengths of dough joined together at the top, but the following technique makes for a neater finish.

● *Alpine pastures*

Schweizer Zupfe

To make one braid:
1 ounce fresh yeast or 1 tablespoon dried
1¼ cups warm milk
4 cups (1 pound) all-purpose flour
2 teaspoons salt
¼ cup, plus 2 tablespoons (¾ stick), butter, softened
1 egg, beaten
2 tablespoons kirsch (optional)
1 egg, beaten, for glaze

Dissolve the yeast in a little of the milk. Leave this to stand – five minutes for fresh yeast and 15 for dried. Place the flour and salt in a bowl. Make a well in the center and pour in the yeast mixture and the remaining milk. Add the butter and one beaten egg and any kirsch. Mix everything to a dough and knead it on a floured work surface. Return the dough to the bowl, cover it and leave it for 1 hour, or until it has doubled in size.

Preheat the oven to 400°F. Punch down the dough and knead it again. Divide it in two pieces and roll each piece into a sausage-shape, about 1 inch in diameter. Lay one piece on the work surface in a straight line. Lay the other piece across it horizontally, to make a cross with equal-length arms. Take the top part of the first piece and fold it down towards you and slightly to the right (as if at four o'clock). Fold the right-hand side of the horizontal piece left over the piece you have just folded down (as if at five o'clock). Take the left-hand side of the horizontal piece and fold it across over two strands of dough (as if at four-thirty). Take the piece now on the far right and fold it to the left, over one strand. Then take the piece on the far left and fold it to the right over two strands. Continue folding, first over one strand, to the left, and then over two, to the right, until your strands run out. Then turn the whole loaf over and seal the ends together.

Lay the loaf on a floured baking sheet and leave it to rise for 20 minutes. Glaze it with the other beaten egg. Bake the loaf for 35 minutes, or until it is golden-brown. Cool it on a wire rack.

● *Birnbrot*

Another special bread is the *Birnbrot*, or pear bread. There are two ways of making it – the one below, which is rolled up, and another, more complicated method, in which the purée of dried fruits is mixed with rosewater and kirsch and kneaded into bread dough. This fruit dough is then divided into small loaves, each of which is encased in rich pastry before being baked.

This rolled *Birnbrot* is cut across into slices to reveal spirals of light, sweet dough wrapped around a spicy filling of fruits and nuts. *Birnbrot* is served in the afternoon, accompanied by hot chocolate.

Birnbrot

1 ounce fresh yeast or 1 tablespoon dried
¼ cup, plus 2 tablespoons, warm milk
2½ cups (10 ounces) all-purpose flour
1 egg, beaten
¼ cup (½ stick) butter, softened
¼ cup sugar
1 teaspoon salt
1 egg, beaten with 1 tablespoon milk

Filling:

8 ounces dried pears
6 ounces prunes
juice ½ lemon
¾ cup dry red wine, plus 3 tablespoons
¼ cup, plus 2 tablespoons, water
4 ounces grapes
3 ounces walnuts, chopped
¼ cup, plus 2 tablespoons, sugar
2 tablespoons kirsch
grated rind ½ lemon
¼ teaspoon ground cinnamon
¼ teaspoon ground cloves

Dissolve the yeast in the milk. Leave this to stand – five minutes for fresh yeast and 15 for dried. Place ½ cup of the flour in a large bowl and mix in the yeast mixture. Beat in the butter, the egg and the sugar. Add the salt to the remaining flour. Work the flour, about 2 ounces at a time, into the mixture in the bowl, using your fingers toward the end. Knead the dough, place

in a buttered bowl, cover it and leave it to rise for 1 hour or until it has doubled in size.

For the filling, coarsely chop the pears and remove the pits, and chop the prunes. Place them in a saucepan with the lemon juice and ¾ cup of wine, and add extra water to just cover the fruit, if necessary. Bring the fruit to the boil and simmer it for 10 minutes or until it is soft and all the liquid has been absorbed. Mash the fruit to a purée. Chop and remove any pips from the grapes. Mix them into the fruit purée together with the walnuts, sugar, kirsch, lemon rind and spices. Add the remaining wine by the tablespoon until you have a spreadable consistency.

Punch down the dough and knead it. Roll it out to a 15-inch square, about ¼ inch thick. Spread the fruit purée over the dough, leaving a space of 1 inch around the edge. Fold in the edges and then roll up the dough. Lay the roll on a floured baking sheet and prick over the surface with a fork. Leave it for 1 hour.

Preheat the oven to 350°F. Brush the roll with the egg and milk mixture and bake it for 35 minutes, or until the outer layer is crisp and golden. Cool the Birnbrot on a rack.

The *Gebildbrote*, or picture breads, are made with a plain bread dough which is intricately worked into many forms and patterns.

Switzerland's cantons each have their own special bread recipes, or *Kantonsbrote*, which have been around for centuries. Some have become larger or smaller over the years, but the basic shapes remain the same – rounds, ovals, knots, rings – with patterns and slashes and other embellishments to characterize them.

Special loaves are baked for weddings, betrothals and births. There are different *Gebildbrote* for St. Nicholas' Day, Christmas, New Year and Easter, and many old bread customs are associated with the time around Lent. St. Agatha is the patron saint of Swiss bakers and on St. Agatha's Day (February 5th) all bakers once made special ring-shaped loaves called the *Agatha-Ringe*. These were taken to the Church to be blessed in the early morning and were then hung up in the local houses as a protection against fire. There are also New Year bread customs. In St. Gallen, for example, every child who makes a lantern for the New Year procession is given a small loaf called the *Altjahrmann* (old year man).

Bread and milk were for many years the typical Swiss breakfast and sometimes midday and evening meal as well. The combination of bread and Swiss cheese is well known in the Swiss fondue, but also appears in another form. Enriched bread dough is used as the base for a tart which contains a mixture of cheese, eggs and cream. The one below is called a *Zwiebelwahe* or onion tart. With less onions it can be called a *Käsewahe* or cheese tart. It is similar to the French dough-based tarts, but butter rather than oil is used to enrich the dough. Dough tarts are usually easier to make in the long run than pastry ones. Although you have to wait for them to rise, the mixing and handling of the dough is as quick as for pastry and the tart is easier to get out of the pan.

● *Zwiebelwahe*

Zwiebelwahe

¹/₂ ounce fresh yeast or 2 teaspoons dried

¹/₂ cup, plus 2 tablespoons, warm water

1 teaspoon salt

4 cups (8 ounces) all-purpose flour

¹/₄ cup (¹/₂ stick) butter

Filling:

2 tablespoons butter

2 medium onions, finely chopped

¹/₂ teaspoon paprika

8 ounces Emmenthal cheese (or use Gruyère, or half and half)

2 eggs

¹/₂ cup, plus 2 tablespoons, light cream

¹/₄ teaspoon ground nutmeg

Dissolve the yeast in half the water and the salt in the other half. Place the flour in a bowl. Make a well in the center and add the yeast mixture. Stir in a little flour from the edges of the bowl and add the salt water and the butter, Mix everything to a dough and knead it on a floured work surface. Return it to the bowl, cover it and leave it for 1 hour, or until it has doubled in size.

For the filling, soften the onions in the butter over low heat, stir in the paprika and let the mixture cool. Grate the cheese. Beat the eggs with the cream and nutmeg.

Preheat the oven to 400°F.

Knead the dough and roll it in a round to fit a 10-inch tart pan. Place it in the pan, then cover it with half the cheese and then the onions. Pour in the egg and cream mixture and top everything with the remaining cheese. Leave the tart for 20 minutes in a warm place and then bake for 20 minutes, or until the top of the filling is golden.

Take the tart from the pan as soon as it is cooked and preferably serve it hot or at least while it is still warm.

THE NETHERLANDS

The character of food in Holland has remained unchanged for hundreds of years. The people of Holland have the longest life-expectancy in Europe, a fact almost certainly brought about by their taste in food and, latterly, by their interest in a healthy lifestyle.

The best of ingredients, cooked well and served simply, make up most Dutch meals. Dutch bread too, is wholesome and unfussy. There are very few intricate shapes, but it is of excellent quality. Most is made from white or whole-wheat flour, or a mixture, and most loaves are baked in open rectangular pans and have either a plain rounded top, or one divided by a lengthways slash down the center. Most everyday breads are made with a basic bread dough (see page 12) and some are enriched with milk, butter and eggs. There are also wholegrain breads, similar to the German pumpernickel but with a sweeter flavor.

The first three recipes below were given to me by a Dutch friend, now living in England. The *wir Brood* (white bread) is a rich, golden bread, with a thin, crisp brown crust and a crumbly texture like a cross between ordinary bread and Madeira cake. It is semi-sweet and goes as well with cheese, cold meats and pickles as it does with jelly and preserves.

Wir Brood

To make a 2-pound loaf:

1 ounce fresh yeast or 1 tablespoon dried
1¼ cups warm milk
4 cups (1 pound) all-purpose flour
2 teaspoons salt
3 tablespoons superfine sugar
2 egg yolks
¼ cup, plus 2 tablespoons (¾ stick), butter, softened

Dissolve the yeast in a little of the milk. Leave this to stand – five minutes for fresh yeast and 15 for dried. Place the flour in a bowl and toss in the salt and sugar. Make a well in the center, add the yeast mixture and mix in a little of the flour from the sides of the well. Add the remaining milk, the egg yolks and butter. Mix everything to a dough and knead it on a floured work surface. Return the dough to the bowl, cover it and leave it in a warm place for 1 hour, or until it has doubled in size.

Preheat the oven to 400°F. Oil a 2-pound loaf pan. Punch down the dough and knead it again. Form it into a cylinder shape and put it into the pan. Leave it in a warm place to rise for 20 minutes. Just before placing the loaf in the oven, make a deep slash lengthways down the center. Bake the loaf for 35 minutes or until it is golden-brown and sounds hollow when tapped.

The *bruin Brood* (brown bread), made with a mixture of whole-wheat and white flours, is also soft-textured, but is not as rich as the white one. It is an excellent everyday bread. The milk can be replaced wholly or, in part, by water, and you can vary the proportions of the flours. You could use all whole-wheat flour and the recipe also works well if you would rather make a simple white bread instead, using all all-purpose flour.

Bruin Brood

To make one 2-pound loaf:

¾ ounce fresh yeast or 3 teaspoons dried
1¼ cups warm milk
3 cups (12 ounces) whole-wheat flour
1 cup (4 ounces) all-purpose flour
2 teaspoons salt
1 tablespoon butter

Dissolve the yeast in a little of the milk. Leave this to stand – five minutes for fresh yeast and 15 for dried. Place the two types of flour in a bowl with the salt. Toss them together. Make a well in the center and pour in the yeast mixture. Mix in a little of the flour from the edges of the well and then add the butter and the remaining milk. Mix everything to a dough and knead it on a floured work surface. Return the dough to the bowl, cover it and leave it in a warm place for 1 hour or until it has doubled in size. Knead it again, form it into a ball and place it on a floured baking sheet. Leave it in a warm place for 20 minutes. Knead and leave to rise again in the same way.

Preheat the oven to 400°F. Knead the dough yet again and roll it out to an elongated triangle. To make a rectangle to fit into a 2-pound loaf pan, fold in the corners. Place the loaf in the oiled pan and leave it to rise for a further 20 minutes. Bake the loaf for 40 minutes or until it sounds hollow when tapped. Cool it on a wire rack.

The Dutch are, in the main, very healthy eaters, so this sugarbread from Friesland must be eaten only as a treat. It is rather like a large English Chelsea bun, both in texture and flavor. The sugar melts as it cooks and makes soft, sweet patches in the dough as well as giving it a moist texture. Eat it plain or with butter. Don't be alarmed if the top becomes very dark, this is the effect of the melted sugar. You might have to give your bread pans a good soaking after making sugarbread, as the syrup can run out and set on the edges. Nevertheless, it is well worth it.

Fries Suikerbrood

To make one 2-pound loaf:

basic bread dough (see page 12) made with 4 cups (1 pound) all-purpose flour

10 ounces sugar cubes

Make the dough and leave it to rise for 1 hour. Preheat the oven to 400°F. Place the sugar cubes in a plastic bag and bang them with a rolling pin until they are broken into coarse lumps.

Knead the dough and then gradually knead in the sugar. Form the dough into a cylinder shape and put it in an oiled 2-pound bread pan. Leave the loaf in a warm place to rise for 20 minutes.

Bake the loaf for 35 minutes, or until the top is a deep golden-brown.

I found the following recipe in Countess Morphy's book, *Recipes of all Nations*, which was published in, I believe, the 1930s. She says: "This is one of the great national Dutch cakes or 'sweet' breads. The best are made at Deventer by the famous firm of Verkade." The final note is: "Should it be a little hard, keep it in the bread pan with other breads before using." The outer crust is hard, but the inside is pleasantly chewy, very spicy and sweet. In many ways this could be described as a true gingerbread. Serve it plain or with butter.

Boterhamkoek

To make one 2-pound loaf:

4 cups (1 pound) all-purpose flour

½ cup dark brown sugar

2 teaspoons anise seeds

1 teaspoon ground cinnamon

1 teaspoon ground ginger

½ teaspoon ground nutmeg

3 teaspoons baking powder

2 cups corn syrup

½ cup, plus 2 tablespoons, milk

Preheat the oven to 325°F. Place the flour, sugar, spices and baking powder in a bowl and toss them together with your fingers. Make a well in the center and pour in the syrup. Using a wooden spoon, begin to beat the syrup into the flour. Beat in the milk, a little at a time, to make a soft, dropping consistency. You will probably find fingers more efficient than a spoon by the end.

Place the mixture in a greased 2-pound bread pan and smooth the top. Bake the loaf for 1 hour, or until a skewer stuck into the center comes out clean.

Turn it out of the pan and cool it on a wire rack.

● *Fries Suikerbrood*

● *Boterhamkoek*

GREAT BRITAIN

*The British Isles have a temperate climate, ideally suited to the growing of grain.
Wheat and barley flourish in the warmer south while the cooler, shorter summers of the
northern and upland areas are ideal for growing oats and rye.
In Britain, bread is occasionally regarded as an accompaniment to a meal, but more
commonly it is a meal in itself. Originally the bannock (a rough mixture of ground grain
and water, baked on a hot stone) was the staple food; now you have only to look at the
sandwich lunches of office workers to realize that old habits die hard.*

The United Kingdom is made up of four countries – England, Northern Ireland, Scotland and Wales. However, these countries have breads and cooking methods in common, ranging from the simple, griddle-cooked oatcake, to rich buns and loaves full of butter, sugar and dried fruits. Looking at them, you can trace the history of bread-making in all four countries.

Usable grain first came to Britain around 4000 BC. It was ground in a quern and mixed with water to make a kind of porridge. Sometimes this was formed into cakes and baked on a hot stone, but this first bread was fairly unpalatable. Gradually the grain improved and stone-baked cakes became the major part of the diet all over the country. The bakestone was eventually superseded by the cast-iron griddle, but the principle was the same. The griddle has remained in British households ever since. It hung over Saxon, medieval and sixteenth-century fires, beside the cooking pot and the spit, and was eventually placed on iron ranges and ovens. Mine is constantly in use on a wood-burning stove during the winter and frequently on an electric ring in the summer. If guests arrive unexpectedly, out comes the griddle for scones, oatcakes, muffins or singin' Hinnie (see page 82).

The masters of this type of cooking have to be the Scots. Their oatcakes and bannocks are world famous, and rightly so. In her book, *The Scots Kitchen*, published in 1930, F. Marion McNeill lists over twelve types of bannocks and oatcakes. The bannocks are made from a mixture of flours, including barley and maslin (where wheat and rye are grown together). Oatcakes, she says, were made for all occasions, including special ones for Beltane (May Eve) and other Celtic festivals, and a cross-shaped one for Christmas. There was even a special one to give to teething children.

Here are two recipes, one for oatcakes, which are thin and crisp, and another for bannocks, which are softer. The baking soda is a modern addition which did not arrive until the mid-nineteenth century. It gives a lighter texture.

● *Aerial view of wheat harvesting*

Place the lard and water in a saucepan and set them over low heat for the lard to melt. Cool them to lukewarm. In a bowl, mix together the oatmeal, baking soda and salt. Make a well in the center and pour in the melted lard and water. Mix everything to a dough.

Place the dough on a floured work surface and knead it lightly. With a rolling pin, flatten it into a round about ¼ inch thick. Trim the edges to neaten them and cut the round in eight wedges. These are called farls.

Heat a lightly-greased griddle over medium heat and bake the cakes until they begin to curl up at the edges but are not colored (if they begin to color, turn down the heat or move them to the sides of the griddle. Turn the oatcakes over and cook them until the underside is smooth and firm. Cool them on a wire rack.

Oatcakes

To make eight oatcakes:
2 tablespoons lard
5 tablespoons water
2 cups (8 ounces) medium oatmeal
½ teaspoon baking soda
¼ teaspoon salt

Bannocks

To make about sixteen bannocks:
1½ cups (6 ounces) fine or medium oatmeal
½ cup (2 ounces) whole-wheat or whole-barley flour
2 teaspoons baking powder
1 teaspoon salt
2 tablespoons lard or butter
½ cup, plus 2 tablespoons, milk

Place the oatmeal and flour in a mixing bowl with the baking powder and salt. Rub in the butter or lard. Make a well in the center and pour in the milk.

Mix everything to a dough and roll it out to about ¼ inch thick. With a pastry-cutter, stamp the dough into approximately sixteen 2-inch rounds.

Heat a lightly-greased griddle over low to medium heat.

Cook the bannocks for about 10 minutes each side, or until they are firm and are just beginning to brown (if they should start to brown too quickly, turn down the heat a little). Bannocks are at their tastiest when eaten warm.

The griddle was also used frequently in the north of England and Wales. When you buy oatcakes in the shops in Derbyshire, Lancashire and in some parts of Wales, you may well be surprised to find that, unlike their Scottish counterparts, they are soft and pliable. They are ideal for toasting or for frying.

Soda bread and scone mixtures, both plain and sweetened, have also been regularly baked on British griddles and some, such as the Selkirk bannock and the singin' hinnie from Northumberland, contain dried fruits. The singin' hinnie is so-called because it sizzles as it cooks. You will discover, if you make it, why there was a special implement called "singin' hinnie hands" to turn it over. The operation is quite difficult, best carried out (in the absence of singin' hinnie hands) with two fish slices.

The singin' hinnie is served hot, straight from the griddle, slit crossways, buttered and cut into wedges. It is a wonderful, easy, hot snack with which to welcome people on cold winter evenings.

Another name for the griddle is the girdle and so you get girdle cakes, also from Northumberland, which are similar to singin' hinnie but cut into small rounds.

● *The Black Country Museum bakery, Dudley*

Yeast came quite early to the British Isles. During the Iron Age the Celts discovered how to use ale barm as a leaven for bread and it was used to make bread similar to that we are used to now. This use of brewing yeast was carried on in country households well into the nineteenth century. When a housewife baked bread, she went to the neighbor who had most recently brewed the family beer, returning the favor when she had herself been brewing.

By Saxon times, there were professional bakers, but most bread was made at home. The English word "lady" comes from the Saxon word *hlaefdige*, meaning kneader of the bread, and "lord" comes from *hlaefward*, keeper of the bread. As with the stone- and griddle-baked cakes, the content and quality of the flour used at this time varied considerably, according to availability. Mostly it was coarsely ground and contained a mixture of flours – even pea and bean meal when times were hard. If you were rich, your bread may have been made from sifted flour, which had a certain proportion of the bran removed. From late Saxon times, white wheat bread was considered the best for both flavor and health. This attitude continued for centuries and all kinds of additions such as chalk, alum and even bones were put into the flour to make it whiter. The situation became so bad that first William Cobbett, in his *Cottage Economy*, 1823, and then Eliza Acton, in *The English Bread Book*, 1857, urged English housewives to make their own bread and to turn their backs upon the adulterated loaf that was produced so unhygienically in the commercial ovens of the towns.

Country bakers, of course, had always produced excellent bread, and throughout the twentieth century, baking standards improved. During the two World Wars there existed a "standard loaf." In the Second World War this contained all the wheat germ and a little of the bran with the result that, despite the general poverty and food rationing, standards of nutrition actually improved.

It was not until the 1960s that nutritional research actually proved that we had been wrong all along. Stoneground, whole-wheat flour was found to be good for us and people began to pay higher prices for what had for centuries been considered poor man's food. Since then, there have been reliable supplies of a wide range of flours; good quality yeast, both fresh and dried; ovens that heat up quickly and maintain an even temperature; and good storage facilities, plus the many bakers and shops which make bread. For home bakers, there are health food stores and specialty food stores which supply not only whole-wheat flour but rye and barley meals as well.

Much British flour, during the past century, has been roller ground, but recently many wind and water mills have been restored and produce their own brands of flour – some of it from organic wheat, of which there is an ever-increasing supply. Many of these mills are open to the public and have their own bakery and restaurant.

Even breads produced by the larger bread companies are improving. It was not so long ago that nearly all white flour in Britain was chemically bleached to make it white instead of the natural creamy color that it really

Singin' Hinnie

To make one 10-inch-flat cake:
3 cups (12 ounces) plain cake flour
1 teaspoon salt
½ teaspoon baking soda
1 teaspoon cream of tartar
6 tablespoons (¾ stick) butter
4 ounces currants
¾ cup, plus 2 tablespoons, milk

Place the flour, salt, baking soda and cream of tartar in a bowl and rub in the butter. Toss in the currants. Make a well in the center and mix in the milk. Mix everything to a dough. Knead the dough lightly and roll it into a round about 10-inches across and ¾-inch thick.

Heat a lightly-greased griddle over low heat. Place the dough on the griddle and cook until golden brown on each side and cooked through (about 15 minutes altogether). If you are using an electric burner with a concentrated circle of heat, you may find that you will need to turn it off completely for a time and let the hinnie cook on heat stored in the burner and the griddle.

Serve the hinnie hot, split and buttered.

● *Singin' Hinnie*

is. When, a few years ago, it was discovered that traces of chemicals remained in the finished loaf, it was banned. Vitamin C, too, was added for a time to facilitate rising, but even that is rarely used now. British bread is now healthier and there is a wider variety to choose from.

Before the greater availability of different grains, the differences between British breads were in their shapes. The cottage loaf, the bloomer, and the pan Loaf were all made to a similar recipe, but characterized by their shapes.

Following, are two examples of breads made from unusual grains: barley and maslin bread. The barley bread needs a little more yeast than normal, as the flour does not have the same rising ability as wheat or rye flours. barley bread is light in color, with a sweet, rich flavor. For the maslin bread, I have used all-purpose flour instead of the whole-wheat which would have been common in poorer households. The white flour makes the bread lighter. There is a good mix of flavors, with the slightly sour rye complementing the sweet barley. Both breads are made up like the basic bread dough (see page 12), so I have given the ingredients without the method.

Barley Bread

To make one 2-pound loaf:

1¹/₂ ounces fresh yeast or 1¹/₂ tablespoons dried
1¹/₄ to 1¹/₂ cups warm water (add the 1¹/₄ cups first and the rest if necessary)
4 cups (1 pound) barley meal
2 teaspoons salt

Maslin Bread

To make one 2-pound loaf:

1 ounce fresh yeast or 1 tablespoon dried
1¹/₄ to 1¹/₂ cups warm water, as above
2¹/₂ cups (10 ounces) all-purpose flour
³/₄ cup (3 ounces) barley meal
³/₄ cup, plus 1 tablespoon, rye meal

The following bread comes from Wales and it was originally adapted by Bobby Freeman from one in *Y Tyr, a'r Teulu* (meaning The House, and Domestic Economy) written in 1891. It appears in Bobby Freeman's booklet *Welsh Bread*. Caraway bread was popular in rural Wales as caraway cake was in England. The loaf is light-textured and dark brown, with a sweet, nutty flavor. If you do not like the flavor of caraway seeds you can omit them and the loaf will still be good. Serve it with fruit preserves or with cheese.

Bara Caraw

To make one 2-pound loaf:

1 ounce fresh yeast or 1 tablespoon dried
1¹/₄ to 1¹/₂ cups warm water
1¹/₂ cups (6 ounces) all-purpose flour
1¹/₂ cups (6 ounces) whole-wheat flour
1 cup (4 ounces) rolled oats
1 teaspoon salt
1 teaspoon caraway seeds
¹/₃ cup dark brown sugar

In a small bowl, sprinkle the yeast over half the water. Leave this to stand – five minutes for fresh yeast and 15 for dried. Put the flours, oats, salt, caraway seeds and sugar in a mixing bowl. Make a well in the center and pour in the yeast and ¹/₂ cup, plus 2 tablespoons, of the remaining water. Mix everything to a dough, adding the rest of the water if necessary. Turn the dough on to a floured work surface and knead it. Return it to the bowl, cover it and leave it in a warm place for 1 hour to double in size.

Preheat the oven to 400°F. Knead the dough again and place it in a 2-pound loaf pan. Leave it to rise for 20 minutes. Bake the loaf for 40 minutes and cool it on a wire rack.

A great favorite of the English has always been bread rolls, made with yeasted wheat flour dough. I just had to include the following recipe for Kentish huffkins, small, slightly enriched rolls, made in a circular shape with an indentation in the middle. This recipe was the first that I ever had published. I always make them with whole-wheat flour, but white flour or a mixture works just as well. Looking for Scottish recipes to put into this chapter, I found baps or breakfast rolls, which are always served fresh, and sometimes warm. The flour is white but the recipe almost identical to that for huffkins.

Kentish Huffkins

To make sixteen buns:

1 ounce fresh yeast or 1 tablespoon dried
¹/₂ cup, plus 2 tablespoons, warm water
4 cups (1 pound) whole-wheat flour
2 teaspoons salt
¹/₄ cup lard
¹/₂ cup, plus 2 tablespoons, warm milk

In a small bowl, sprinkle the yeast over the water. Leave this to stand – five minutes for fresh yeast and 15 for dried. Place the flour and salt in a mixing bowl and rub in the lard. Make a well in the center and pour in the yeast mixture and the milk. Mix everything to a dough. Turn it on to a floured board and knead it until it is smooth. Return it to the bowl, cover it and leave it in a warm place for 1 hour to double in size.

Preheat the oven to 400°F.

Knead the dough again and divide it in sixteen equal pieces. Form each piece into a round bun. Push your finger through the center of each piece of dough and pull out the edges gently to form a ring. Lay the rolls on floured baking sheets and leave them in a warm place for 20 minutes to rise.

Bake them for 20 minutes until they are cooked through but only lightly brown. As they cook, the hole in the center will close to make a deep indentation. As soon as the rolls come out of the oven, wrap them in several clean, dry cloths. This keeps in the steam and gives a soft crust. Leave the rolls until they are quite cool.

Scottish Baps or Breakfast Rolls

To make sixteen baps:

ingredients as for Kentish Huffkins, using all-purpose flour

After the second kneading, divide the dough in sixteen pieces and make them into oval shapes about 3 inches long and 2 inches wide. Lay them on floured baking sheets. Brush them with a mixture of milk and water to give a glaze. If you would rather have a floury-textured surface, brush them with flour just after glazing and again after rising.

Leave the rolls for 20 minutes in a warm, draft-free place to rise. Just before they go in the oven, press your finger gently, a little way into the center of each one.

This will prevent the crusts from blistering as the rolls bake. Bake the baps for 20 minutes and cool them on wire racks.

● *Kentish Huffkins*

The recipe for rolls that follows also comes from Scotland, this time from Aberdeen. They are actually a cross between bread and flaky pastry. They are wonderful when warm and keep exceptionally well for about two days. Serve them with soups and salads or perhaps as part of a savory table at parties.

Sourdough bread, although rarely mentioned in British cookery or history books, was made throughout Britain, but not frequently. In Ireland, where yeast was less used than elsewhere, potatoes were occasionally used as a leaven. The following recipe comes from Florence Irwin's book, *The Cookin' Woman*, which was published in 1949. It makes a close-textured loaf with a nutty flavor.

Buttery Rowies

To make about 20 rolls:

1 ounce fresh yeast or 1 tablespoon dried
1½ cups warm water
4 cups (1 pound) all-purpose flour
1 tablespoon salt
1 tablespoon sugar
¾ cup (1½ sticks) butter, softened
¾ cup lard, softened

Barm Bread

To make two 2-pound loaves:

First Day:
3 medium potatoes
2½ cups water
1 cup (4 ounces) whole-wheat or all-purpose flour
Second Day:
8 cups (2 pounds) whole-wheat flour
2 teaspoons salt
½ cup, plus 2 tablespoons, warm water

In a small bowl, sprinkle the yeast over half the water and leave it to stand – five minutes for fresh yeast and 15 for dried. Place the flour, salt and sugar in a large mixing bowl and rub in 2 tablespoons of the butter. Make a well in the center, pour in the yeast mixture and the remaining water and mix everything to a dough. Knead it on a floured work surface, return it to the bowl, cover it and leave it in a warm place for 1 hour, or until it has doubled in size. Knock it back, wrap it in plastic wrap and put it in the refrigerator for 15 minutes.

Take the dough out of the refrigerator, roll it into a rectangle and dot one third each of the remaining butter and lard on two thirds of the surface. Along its shortest sides, fold the dough in three, wrap it again in plastic wrap and chill it for a further 30 minutes. Repeat this twice more. Finally, roll the dough into a rectangle about 8 × 10 inches and cut it into 2-inch squares. Lay the squares on floured baking sheets and leave them in a warm, draft-free place for 20 minutes to rise.

Preheat the oven to 400°F.

Bake the rolls for 20 minutes or until they are puffed up and golden-brown.

Cool them on wire racks.

● *Wheat field, Hampshire, England*

On the first day, boil the potatoes in their skins in the water. Drain them, reserving the water, and peel them. In a medium-sized bowl, mash the potatoes to a purée and mix in the flour and 1¼ cups of the water. Cover the mixture with plastic wrap and leave it for 24 hours.

By the next day, the potatoes and flour will have begun to ferment and the mixture will be risen with a cracked surface. When you tip the bowl you will see that the mixture has become stretchy like risen dough.

Place the flour in a large mixing bowl and add the salt. Make a well in the center and pour in the barm and the warm water. Form the mixture into a dough. Turn it on to a floured board and knead it until it is smooth. Return it to the bowl, make a cross-cut in the top, cover the dough and leave it in a warm place for 5 hours.

Preheat the oven to 400°F.

Knead the dough again and divide it in two. Form each piece into a round loaf and place them on baking sheets. Leave the loaves in a

● *Buttery Rowies*

warm draft-free place for 20 minutes to rise.

Bake the loaves for 40 minutes or until they sound hollow when tapped and the tops are golden-brown.

Ireland's specialty is soda bread, made either on a griddle or in the oven and risen with baking soda and sometimes baking powder. Soda Bread is usually made with wheat flour, either whole-wheat or white, or half and half; or with a mixture of wheat and oatmeal flour. In Ireland there are many variations. During times of famine, cornmeal was sent to Ireland from the United States, and soda breads were then made with a mixture of cornmeal and wheat flour. Flour, salt and buttermilk are the main ingredients. Originally, the buttermilk was the liquid left in the churn after the butter had been made, now you can buy commercially-prepared buttermilk which works excellently. You can also use a thin, natural yogurt, such as a goat's milk yogurt, or ordinary milk to which you add 1 teaspoon of cream of tartar per 1¼ cups.

A little fat, such as butter or lard, was added when it was available and soda breads could be sweetened with honey or sugar. Dried fruits, candied citrus peel and spices were added for Sunday tea or special occasions.

Wherever you go in Ireland today you will always be able to buy marvelous soda bread, either white or brown. Its texture and flavor varies from baker to baker as real bread should, but whenever you eat it you will be reminded of that wonderful country.

The following is a variation that can be worked upon. To change the flour, use all white or ½ white and ½ oatmeal; or ½ white, ¼ oatmeal and ¼ brown. Add ¼ cup of sugar or honey and/or up to 4 ounces of dried fruits or candied citrus peel. Bake the dough on a baking sheet or griddle.

Soda Bread

To make one 1-pound loaf:
2 cups (8 ounces) whole-wheat flour
1 teaspoon salt
1 teaspoon baking soda
½ teaspoon cream of tartar
1 tablespoon butter or lard
½ cup, plus 2 tablespoons, buttermilk

Preheat the oven to 400°F. Place the flour, salt and baking soda in a bowl and rub in the butter or lard. Make a well in the center and pour in the buttermilk. Mix everything into a dough. Turn it on to a floured board and knead it lightly.

Press or roll the dough into a round about 1½ inches thick. Lay it on a floured baking sheet. Score the top in four sections. Bake the bread for 20 minutes, or until it is just colored and sounds hollow when tapped. Cool the soda bread on a wire rack.

Varieties of soda bread are also made in Wales and often baked on the griddle. There is bake-stone bread and blanc bread, and Welsh cakes which are small and spicy. From Scotland, besides the many oatcakes, there are Highland slim cakes, made with wheat flour and enriched with butter and eggs. In England, a similar mixture is cut into rounds and baked to make scones.

● *Harvesting*

During the seventeenth century, spices, sugar and dried fruits became more readily available to the general population, along with butter, milk and eggs. As a result, more and more recipes for enriched and sweetened breads appeared. The easiest one to make was lardy cake. This required a plain bread dough, homemade lard, and any sugar, spices and dried fruits that were available. Because it called for lard, it was made mainly in the English counties where pigs were kept, and usually as a treat at the end of the day's baking. It was called lardy cake in the West Country, lardy Johns in Sussex, and dough cake in Buckinghamshire. In Suffolk there was a similar cake called fourses cake, which was eaten in the fields at harvest-time at the four o'clock break.

Lardy Cake

To make one 8-inch-square cake:

basic bread dough (see page 12) made with 2 cups (8 ounces) flour, risen for 1 hour
³⁄₄ cup lard
¹⁄₂ teaspoon ground cinnamon
¹⁄₂ teaspoon ground nutmeg
¹⁄₄ cup sugar
1¹⁄₂ ounces currants
1¹⁄₂ ounces golden raisins

Preheat the oven to 400°F. Knead the dough and roll it into an oblong about ¹⁄₂ inch thick. Spread 2 tablespoons of the lard on two-thirds of it and fold it in three. Roll it out again and spread on one quarter of the lard that is left. Sprinkle it with a quarter of the spices, sugar and fruit. Repeat the rolling, spreading and sprinkling three more times.

The last time the dough is folded, do not roll it. Put it in a greased baking or Swiss-roll pan (not on a baking sheet as some of the fat runs out during cooking). Leave the cake in a warm place for 15 minutes or until it has almost doubled in size.

Bake the cake for 40 minutes or until it is golden-brown. Cool it on a wire rack for 10 minutes and eat it warm.

From Cornwall comes saffron cake, once made only at Easter time but now available from many Cornish bakers throughout the year. Saffron was once grown in England, in Saffron Walden in Essex, but there is a story that it first arrived in the country with the Phoenicians who traded it for Cornish tin. It was certainly grown in Cornwall until the eighteenth century.

Saffron Cake

To make either two 1-pound loaves or sixteen buns:

large pinch of saffron strands
4 tablespoons boiling water
1 ounce fresh yeast or 1 tablespoon dried
³⁄₄ cup milk, warmed
4 cups (1 pound) all-purpose flour
pinch of salt
¹⁄₄ teaspoon ground nutmeg
²⁄₃ cup butter
8 ounces currants
2 ounces candied citrus peel, chopped
2 eggs, beaten

Place the saffron in a bowl and pour on boiling water. Leave it to infuse overnight.

In a small bowl sprinkle the yeast over the milk. Leave this to stand – five minutes for fresh yeast and 15 for dried. Place the flour in a mixing bowl and add the salt and nutmeg. Rub in the butter. Toss in the currants and peel. Make a well in the center. Pour in the saffron and saffron water, yeast mixture and eggs. Mix everything to a dough. Knead the dough in the bowl. Cover it and leave it in a warm place for 1 hour or until it has doubled in size.

Preheat the oven to 350°F. Knead the dough again. Either divide it in half and put it in two greased 1-pound loaf pans, or divide it into sixteen buns and place them on a floured baking sheet. Cover the loaves or buns with a cloth again and leave them in a warm place for 10 minutes, or until the loaves have risen about ¹⁄₂ inch above the top of the pans and the buns have almost doubled in size.

Bake the loaves for 1 hour and the buns for 30 minutes. Cool them on wire racks. Eat them plain or buttered.

From Wales comes bara brith and from Ireland, barn brack. Both names are a derivation of the respective country's words for speckled bread. The breads are similar, containing a variety of currants and other dried fruits, but both are included here as representatives of their various countries.

There are many recipes for bara brith, but the best are made with yeast instead of baking powder and recommend the use of tea for soaking the dried fruit. Whole-wheat flour is used in the bara brith recipe below, but all-purpose flour is also suitable.

Bara Brith

To make one 2-pound loaf:

6 ounces dark raisins

6 ounces golden raisins

⅓ cup dark brown sugar

2 cups hot black tea

1 ounce fresh yeast or 1 tablespoon dried

4 cups (1 pound) whole-wheat flour

½ teaspoon salt

½ teaspoon ground nutmeg

½ cup (1 stick) butter, plus extra for greasing

Place the dried fruits and sugar in a bowl. Pour on the tea and leave them to soak for at least 4 hours. Drain the fruits well, reserving the tea. Measure the tea. If necessary, make it up to 1¼ cups with warm water.

Pour the tea into a small bowl. Sprinkle in the yeast and leave it – five minutes for fresh yeast and 15 for dried. Place the flour, salt and mixed spice in a mixing bowl. Rub in the butter and toss in the fruits. Make a well in the center and pour in the yeast mixture. Mix everything to a moist dough and knead it in the bowl (see page 13). Cover the dough and leave it in a warm place for 1 hour to double in size.

Preheat the oven to 350°F. Grease a 2-pound loaf pan. Knead the dough again. Place it in the prepared pan. Leave it in a warm place to rise for 20 minutes. Bake the loaf for 1 hour or until a skewer stuck in the center comes out clean. Turn it on to a wire rack to cool and serve it sliced and buttered.

● *Combine harvesters in Sussex, England*

Barn Brack

To make one 2-pound loaf:

Sponge:

½ ounce fresh yeast or 2 teaspoons dried

1¼ cups warm milk

1 cup (4 ounces) all-purpose flour

Loaf:

1 egg, beaten

¼ cup (½ stick) butter, softened

2½ cups (10 ounces) all-purpose flour

¼ cup superfine sugar

4 ounces golden raisins

2 ounces currants

2 ounces candied citrus peel, chopped

1 tablespoon sugar, melted in 2 tablespoons water

To make the sponge, first place the yeast in a large mixing bowl and pour in the milk. Stir in the 1 cup of flour. Leave the mixture in a warm, draft-free place for 1 hour or until it is risen and bubbling.

Stir the egg and the butter into the sponge and then the flour, sugar, fruits and peel. Mix everything to a dough. Turn it on to a floured board and knead it until it is smooth. Return the dough to the bowl, cover it and leave it in a warm place for 1 hour.

Preheat the oven to 400°F.

Knead the dough again. To form the loaf, bring the edges to the center, turning the loaf, so the underneath becomes smooth. Turn the dough upside down and roll it out to about 1½ inches thick. Place it on a floured baking sheet and leave it in a warm place for 20 mintues to rise.

Bake the loaf for 30 minutes, or until it is golden and sounds hollow when tapped. Brush it with the sugared water and return it to the oven for 1 minute.

Cool it on a wire rack.

The most amazing enriched bread is the Scots black bun which is made of a buttery dough, packed full of dried fruits and spices, encased by a plain version of the same dough. It was traditionally served on Twelfth Night, but is now more often a Hogmanay (New Year's Eve) specialty.

Scots Black Bun

To make one 8-inch loaf:

basic bread dough (see page 12) made with 4 cups (1 pound) all-purpose flour

¾ cup (1½ sticks) butter, softened

1½ ounces slivered almonds

8 ounces dark raisins

8 ounces golden raisins

3 ounces candied citrus peel, chopped

1 teaspoon ground allspice

½ teaspoon ground cloves

1 teaspoon ground ginger

½ teaspoon ground nutmeg

Knead the dough for the first time and then knead in the butter. Place the dough in a bowl, cover it and leave it in a warm place for 1 hour or until it has doubled in size.

Preheat the oven to 350°F.

Knead the dough again, cut off about one third and reserve it. Mix the almonds, dried fruits, peel and spices together. Knead them into the larger quantity of dough, a little at a time. You will find that the dough gradually darkens in color. Form the fruit dough into a ball. Roll the smaller quantity of dough into a flat sheet. Put the ball of fruit dough into the center and bring the sides of the plain dough to the center. Pinch them together to seal them. Turn the loaf over so that it has a smooth, unbroken top.

Place the loaf on a floured baking sheet and place an 8-inch metal ring around it. Gently press the dough down so that it almost touches the sides of the ring. Prick the loaf all over with a fork, going right through the outer layer. Leave the loaf for 20 minutes to rise.

● *Scots Black Bun*

Bake the loaf for 1 hour, removing the metal ring after the first 30 minutes. The outside will be golden-brown and the loaf will sound hollow when it is tapped. Cool it on a wire rack.

Sweet yeasted buns became popular during the sixteenth century. In books of traditional recipes you will find Belvoir Castle buns from Nottingham, Cheltenham buns from Gloucestershire, Bath buns and Chester buns. London Buns are long, fat fingers of dough covered with pink or white icing, and Chelsea buns, first made by Richard Hand at the Old Chelsea Bun House in the Pimlico Road, London, are made by spreading an enriched dough with butter, spices and fruits, rolling it up and cutting it into whirled slices.

Hot cross buns, too, are still made all over Britain around Easter time. At one time, buns with a cross on them were made all through Lent. They were banned by Oliver Cromwell and brought back again at the time of the Restoration. Whole-wheat Hot cross buns are becoming more popular each year. This is the marvelous recipe that I always use, with separate short-crust-pastry crosses made for the tops.

● *Hot Cross Buns*

In a small bowl, sprinkle the yeast over half the milk. Leave this to stand – five minutes for fresh yeast and 15 for dried. In another bowl, mix the eggs and butter into the remaining milk. Place the flour in a mixing bowl and add the salt, nutmeg, currants and candied citrus peel. Make a well in the center and put in the yeast mixture, butter and egg mixture, and honey. Mix everything to a dough and knead it in the bowl (see page 13). Cover it and leave it in a warm place for 1½ hours, or until it has doubled in size.

Preheat the oven to 400°F. Knead the dough again and form it into 16 round buns. Lay them on floured baking sheets. Roll out the pastry and cut it in thin strips. Use these to make the crosses on the buns, hanging them over the dough loosely and letting them touch the baking sheets on each side. This allows for the expansion of the buns. Brush the buns with the beaten egg mixture and leave them in a warm place for 20 minutes to rise. Place a tray of hot water in the bottom of the oven to make it steamy. This gives the buns a thin, soft crust.

Bake the buns for 20 minutes, or until they are golden-brown. Cool them on wire racks and serve them split and buttered.

Hot Cross Buns

To make sixteen buns:

1 ounce fresh yeast or 1 tablespoon dried
1¼ cups warm milk
⅓ cup butter
2 eggs, beaten
4 cups (1 pound) whole-wheat flour
½ teaspoon salt
½ teaspoon ground nutmeg
6 ounces currants
2 ounces candied citrus peel, chopped
⅓ cup honey
1 egg, beaten with ¼ cup, plus 2 tablespoons, milk

Crosses:

pastry made with 1 cup flour and ½ cup shortening

Crumpets and muffins became popular in the eighteenth century and both were traditionally eaten around an open fire at teatime, toasted and dripping with butter. Muffins are made with a bread dough containing milk and butter, cooked on a griddle, toasted, split and buttered. They were originally baked in town ovens and carried on a tray on the head of the "muffin man" who rang a bell to tell customers of his imminent arrival. At one time, so many muffins were made that violence regularly broke out between rival sellers looking for trade.

Crumpets are made with a similar but more liquid mixture, rather like a thick batter. To make them you will need two crumpet rings. These are metal rings about 3½ inches in diameter and ⅝ inch deep. You only need two, as the rings are removed from the crumpets half way through cooking. You can, of course, be beginning to make two new crumpets as the first ones are finishing off.

Your homemade crumpets should not look anything like the rubbery, holey ones that you can buy in the stores; they will bubble as they cook to give the same aerated inside, but the tops and base will be slightly smoother as they are turned over during cooking. When done, they should be a light, golden-brown color. They are richer and more filling than bought crumpets and do not have anything of that unpleasant, dry, soda-like taste.

Pikelets are similar to crumpets, only smaller, and you can make them with the same mixture. The name comes from the Welsh, *Pyclid*, which was a soft griddle cake.

You can also make Scotch pancakes with the same mixture, by adding a little sugar.

Crumpets

To make eight crumpets:

½ ounce fresh yeast or 2 teaspoons dried
1¼ cups warm milk
2 cups (8 ounces) all-purpose flour
1 teaspoon salt
1 egg, beaten
2 tablespoons butter, softened, plus extra for greasing

In a small bowl, sprinkle the yeast over half the milk and leave it to stand – five minutes for fresh yeast and 15 for dried. Dissolve the butter in the remaining milk. Place the flour and salt in a mixing bowl and make a well in the center. Gradually beat in the yeast mixture, milk and butter mixture, and egg, to make a thick batter. Cover the batter and leave it to stand in a warm, draft-free place for about 45 minutes, or until it has bubbled up the sides of the bowl.

Grease a cast-iron griddle and warm it over low heat. This low heat is important as the crumpets are quite thick and have to be cooked for a relatively long time. A griddle that is too hot will make them burned on the outside and too soft in the middle.

Lightly grease the crumpet rings and place them on the griddle. Spoon two tablespoons of the batter into each ring. Cook the batter for about 3 minutes on the first side. During cooking the batter will bubble and the base and sides will become firm. The underside should cook to a light, golden brown. Remove the crumpet rings. Remember that they will be hot. They are best removed by slipping a palette knife under the edge of the ring, and then lifting it up. Turn the crumpets over and cook the second side in the same way. Clean the rings, if necessary, and start two other crumpets beside the first. Be sure to re-grease the griddle at any point during cooking that it becomes dry.

Cool the crumpets on a plate.

When you are ready to eat them, toast them lightly on each side so that the outsides become firm and dry. Eat them hot with plenty of butter.

crumpets are always best eaten on the day that you make them.

Pikelets

Make the mixture as for crumpets and heat the greased griddle over low heat. Spoon single tablespoons of the batter on to the griddle, without using the rings, and cook them for about 1½ minutes on each side. They should be oval shaped and golden-brown. Pikelets can be eaten straight away or cooled and toasted. As with crumpets, eat them on the day you make them.

Scotch Pancakes

Make as for pikelets, using the crumpet mixture but adding 2 tablespoons of sugar to the batter before leaving it to stand.

One other thing that the British Isles are famous for is their tea bread – richer than a bread but less so than a cake. Tea breads are usually baked in a loaf pan and eaten sliced and buttered at teatime. Many contain dried fruits that have been soaked in tea and quite a lot contain golden syrup.

The following recipe for brown fadge was given to me by a home economics student from Northern Ireland who was helping me with some recipe testing about ten years ago. It is her mother's recipe.

Brown fadge can be eaten plain or buttered, and if made in a round pan it can be split like a sponge cake and sandwiched back together with a thick layer of butter.

Brown Fadge

To make one 2-pound loaf:

4 cups (1 pound) plain cake flour
1 tablespoon baking powder
¼ cup superfine sugar
½ cup molasses
1 egg, beaten
1 cup milk

Preheat the oven to 350°F. Place the flour in a mixing bowl. Toss in the baking powder and sugar and make a well in the center. Put in the molasses and egg and gradually beat in flour from the sides of the well.

Place the mixture in a greased, 8-inch-diameter cake pan or 2-pound loaf pan. Bake the cake for 40 minutes or until a skewer inserted into the center comes out clean.

Turn it on to a wire rack to cool.

EASTERN EUROPE

Throughout all the political boundary drawing and re-drawing of the area, the peoples of Eastern Europe have fiercely maintained their own ethnic characters, traditions, languages and tastes in food. The bread is therefore as varied as its peoples. The main grains are wheat and rye, with some buckwheat and also maize. Dark rye bread is popular in the colder regions and light wheat bread where the climate is warmer. Besides plain breads there are many sweetened wheat breads made for everyday and for special occasions.

Bread has been the most important item of the diet in this area for centuries and it is involved in many ancient customs. In northern Russia, the coming of spring is celebrated at a pre-Lent festival called Maslenitsa. A young girl, dressed as Spring, is offered a loaf and a pot of salt, while a woman, dressed as Winter, is given a decanter of wine as a going away present. Also eaten at this festival are blinis – small yeasted buckwheat pancakes – which, fried in butter until they are golden, were eaten in pre-Christian times as the symbol of the returning sun.

Khlib i sil (bread and salt) are also traditionally given to guests in the Ukraine. Symbolically this means that even if the house cannot afford more than bread and salt, the guest is welcome to share them. In other countries, bread and salt are symbols of prosperity. In Poland, for example, they are traditionally the first gifts given to a newly married couple.

The Eastern Europeans love festivals and celebrations, and in many countries, rich, yeasted cakes are baked for such occasions. Generally these contain liberal amounts of eggs and butter, plus sugar, spices, dried fruits and sometimes nuts. A favorite Russian birthday cake, called a *krendel*, is formed in a figure-of-eight shape. The Polish have a festival bread called *babke wielkanocna*, which is made from a rich yeast dough and baked in a large *Gugelhupf* mold. This is flavored with lemon and orange rinds and contains nuts and dried fruits. In the days before reliable ovens and standard yeast, the dough for this was treated extremely gently and left to rise on feather pillows. Every housewife had her own recipe for *babke wielkanocna* which was passed down through the family like an heirloom. One of the occasions on which it was baked was Easter, the most important religious festival in Eastern Europe.

Russians, too, have an Easter cake. It is known as *kulich*, and is either baked in a round pan or in the shape of a stepped pyramid, said to represent Mount Golgotha. It is traditionally eaten with the molded cheese dessert known as *pashka*.

● *Lunchtime in Hungary*

Kulich

To make one 8-inch-diameter round or pyramid-shaped loaf:

1¼ cups milk
1 teaspoon saffron strands
1½ ounces fresh yeast or 1½ tablespoons dried
4 egg yolks
1 cup (2 sticks) butter, softened
¾ cup sugar
1 teaspoon pure vanilla extract
6 cups (1 pound 8 ounces) all-purpose flour
4 cardamom seeds, crushed
½ teaspoon salt
grated rind ½ lemon
4 ounces golden raisins
3 ounces dark raisins
3 ounces slivered almonds
1 egg, beaten

Place the milk and saffron in a saucepan. Bring them gently to a boil, stirring, so the milk turns yellow. Strain the milk and cool it to lukewarm. Pour the milk into a large mixing bowl, sprinkle over the yeast and leave it to stand – five minutes for fresh yeast and 15 for dried. Stir in the egg yolks, butter, sugar and vanilla extract. Mix the flour with the cardamom seeds, salt, lemon rind, raisins and nuts. Gradually stir these into the yeast mixture to make a dough. Turn it on to a floured work surface and knead it until it is smooth. Return it to the bowl, cover it and leave it for 1 hour, or until it has doubled in size.

Preheat the oven to 425°F.

Knead the dough again and roll it out to a thickness of about ⅝ inch. Cut a 7-inch circle of dough and lay it on a floured baking sheet. Cut a 6-inch circle and lay it on top. Continue building up circles of dough, down to a 1-inch circle, so that you have built up a pyramid shape. Alternatively, form the dough into one large, round loaf and bake it in a round pan or on a baking sheet.

Leave the loaf in a warm place to rise for 30 minutes. Brush it with the beaten egg and bake it for 5 minutes. Turn the heat to 400°F and cook it for a further 25 minutes, or until it is golden-brown and cooked through.

Cool it on a wire rack.

Everyday breads throughout Eastern Europe can be divided into three main types: dark or black breads, usually made from rye meals; unsweetened white bread; and sweetened white bread. There are also several corn breads.

The rye breads are strongly flavored. They come in a variety of shapes and sizes, such as pan loaves, enormous cartwheels, small ovals and large rounds with slashes across the top. There are pumpernickel types and lighter-textured loaves sometimes made with a mixture of flours. These dark breads are often served in thick slices and spread with plenty of butter.

In the Ukraine, dark rye breads, called *chernyi khlib*, are the most popular. The really black shiny ones come in pointed oval shapes or large rounds, and the rougher-textured dark brown ones in pan shapes or small rounds. Rye bread is also favored in the Baltic states. In Latvia there is the almost black, sour pumpernickel type and a lighter-colored, lighter-textured one. Here the bakers' shops are identified by a large gold pretzel-shaped pastry hung over the door.

Buckwheat is another type of flour that makes a dark, rich bread. The dough is totally different to that made with any other flour, because it is silky-

● *Kulich (see page 95)*

textured and contains little gluten. It is most commonly used to make blinis or pancakes, but is also used in the Baltic states and in Poland to make bread. This recipe from Poland maintains the dark color and strong flavor of buckwheat bread, but also contains a small amount of strong wheat flour to make the loaf rise and to give it a light texture. It is very crumbly and does not hang together like wheat or rye bread, so be very careful when you are taking it out of the pan. It is good buttered thickly and served with soup or salads.

Pyza z Hreczanej Maki

To make one 10-inch round, flat loaf:

1 ounce fresh yeast or 1 tablespoon dried
1½ cups warm water
4 cups (1 pound) buckwheat flour
1 cup (4 ounces) all-purpose flour
1 teaspoon salt
1 cup lard, melted

In a small bowl, sprinkle the yeast over ⅔ cup of the water. Leave this to stand – five minutes for fresh yeast and 15 for dried. Place the flours and salt in a large mixing bowl, make a well in the center and pour in the melted lard. Mix it in and add the yeast and remaining warm water. Mix everything to a dough and knead it in the bowl until it is smooth. Cover it and leave it in a warm place for 1 hour, or until it has doubled in size.

Preheat the oven to 350°F. Knead the dough again and press it into a greased 10-inch-diameter tart pan. Leave it in a warm place for 30 minutes to rise. Bake the loaf for 30 minutes or until it sounds hollow when tapped. Cool it on a wire rack.

Maize is an important crop both in Georgia and Romania. In Georgia there is a saying: "Better beans and corn bread at home than cake and wine in the land of strangers." Here, the cornmeal is mixed, uncooked, with water and salt and baked in a pottery dish. The bread is eaten hot or warm as it becomes unpleasantly hard as it cools. The corn bread in Romania, called *mamaliga*, is more like the Italian polenta. It is cooked with water first to a thick mush, turned out and cooled to a moist cake which is cut, not with a knife, but by drawing fine string through it. The corn bread from Bulgaria combines the two methods. The cornmeal is first cooked with water to a thick porridge and then baked.

Unsweetened wheat bread is usually made with unbleached white wheat flour and the variety of shapes, textures and flavors is enormous. Some types are heavy and rich and made by the sourdough method and others are light and airy and risen with yeast.

In the Ukraine you will find the *korzh*, which is large, flat and round, and the *lalach*, which is made in a variety of shapes – long and oval, a bloomer-type with squared ends, and an enormous rectangle made from four smaller loaves joined together. Then there is the *polianitsa*, a large round loaf with one deep slash.

The traditional wheat bread of Georgia was once baked in a brick-lined oven, dug into the ground, called a *tone*. The bread was made from stone-ground wheat, leavened by a sourdough starter. On baking day, a fire was lit in the bottom of the *tone*, which heated the walls. The oval-shaped loaves were not baked on trays but were literally thrown at the walls of the oven, where they stuck and gently cooked. It sounds easy, but it probably took a great deal of practice to get a throw just right.

In Armenia, the wheat breads show their Middle Eastern ancestry. There is *lavash*, thin unleavened sheets which are also baked on the walls of an oven, and *churek*, light-leavened flat breads enriched with butter and sprinkled with sesame seeds. Sprinkling them with water before baking gives them a delicious, thin, flaky crust which bubbles slightly in the oven. They are best eaten slightly warm or at least on the day of baking.

Churek

To make five large rounds:

¾ ounce fresh yeast or 3 teaspoons dried
1½ teaspoons salt
3 cups (12 ounces) all-purpose flour
¼ cup (½ stick) butter, softened
1 tablespoon sesame seeds

In a small bowl, sprinkle the yeast over half the water. Leave this to stand – five minutes for fresh yeast and 15 for dried. Dissolve the salt in the remaining water. Place the flour in a bowl and make a well in the center. Pour in the yeast mixture and salt water and add the butter. Mix everything to a dough. Turn it on to a floured work surface and knead it until it is smooth. Return it to the bowl, cover it and leave it in a warm place for 1 hour or until it has doubled in size.

Preheat the oven to 350°F.

Knead the dough again and divide it in 5 equal pieces. Roll each piece into a thin round, about 7 inches in diameter. Lay the rounds on floured baking sheets. Sprinkle each one with a little cold water and some sesame seeds. Leave the breads for 10 minutes in a warm place. Bake them for 15 to 20 minutes, or until they are a light golden-brown.

Cool them on a wire rack.

These flat breads are best eaten warm, but they will keep for several days if kept airtight, and can be heated before serving.

A similar type of flat white bread is made in other parts of Eastern Europe. There are several different kinds and many are sold in the streets on market stalls. Most commonly the breads are about 7 inches round with a grid or spiral pattern stamped in the center. Also to be found in the area are a variety of small round loaves and leaf-shaped buns.

In the Balkans, Czech Republic and Slovakia, the country bread was made with a white wheat flour and a sourdough starter, giving it a creamy color, a close texture and rich flavor. In the Balkans, this bread was called *pogaca* or farmer's bread. Traditionally, the loaves were made up into flattened 10-inch rounds, baked on a heated stone shelf and covered with a dome-shaped lid which had a special ring on top containing hot coals or wood. The finished loaves were cut crossways into long, thin slices and were often served with a fermented cream known as *kajmak*.

Caraway seeds and fennel seeds are often used to flavor bread in Eastern Europe. The following recipe comes from Hungary. The light, yeasted, white flour dough contains fennel seeds which give it a sweet, spicy flavor.

Feherkenyer

To make two small round loaves:

1 ounce fresh yeast or 1 tablespoon dried
1½ cups warm water
4 cups (1 pound) all-purpose flour
2 teaspoons sugar
2 teaspoons salt
½ teaspoon fennel seeds
1 egg and 4 tablespoons heavy cream

In a small bowl, dissolve the yeast in ½ cup of the water. Place the flour in a large mixing bowl with the sugar, salt and fennel seeds. Make a well in the center and pour in the yeast mixture and the remaining water. Mix everything to a dough. Turn it on to a floured work surface and knead it. Return it to the bowl, cover it and leave it in a warm place for 1 hour or until it has doubled in size.

Preheat the oven to 400°F. Knead the dough again and form it into two round loaves. Lay them on floured baking sheets. With a razor blade or sharp knife, make a ¼-inch-deep slash across the center of each one. Leave them in a warm place for 20 minutes to rise. For the glaze, lightly beat the egg yolk with the cream. Brush the loaves with the glaze and sprinkle them with the fennel seeds.

Bake the loaves for 35 minutes, or until they are golden-brown and sound hollow when tapped.

Sweet bread is probably served in Eastern Europe far more than cake. Besides the festive varieties mentioned earlier, there are many simpler versions which can be bought throughout the year. The Ukraine is not only famous for its wheat but also for its sugar production. It has an enormous number of sweet breads and rolls that are served mid-morning or in the afternoon, at breakfast time or suppertime – in fact, when anyone needs a snack. The *khala* are braided breads which sometimes have a scattering of poppy seeds; *zdoba* are small loaves or buns in a variety of shapes, and *perepychka* are large and flat, and scored with a ring and a striped pattern in the center. The *kalach* is bloomer-shaped; the *kruchenyk*, round with a sun pattern; and the *rizhok*, horn-shaped. Solomka are small, sweet bread sticks (like sweet *grissini*) and *bublyky* are ring-shaped rolls.

● *Kirghiz making bread, Central Siberia*

Doughnuts and rum babas are popular in Moscow as are sweet rusks made in a similar way to Scandinavian crisprolls.

The poppy seed roll is popular throughout Eastern Europe. The version below is a combination of Hungarian and Russian recipes. There is also a version from Poland where the milk is scalded before being poured, still hot, over the flour. The poppy seed filling is sweet and rich and the roll is served, cut in slices, with morning coffee.

Makos es Dios Kalacs

To make one 12-inch-long roll:

¾ ounce fresh yeast or 3 teaspoons dried

4 tablespoons warm water

½ cup warm milk

½ teaspoon pure vanilla extract

grated rind ½ lemon

2 tablespoons sugar

2 eggs, beaten

3 cups (12 ounces) all-purpose flour

1 teaspoon salt

⅓ cup butter, softened

1 egg, beaten with 1 tablespoon milk

Filling:

4 ounces poppy seeds

½ cup (1 stick) unsalted butter

¼ cup honey

2 tablespoons heavy cream

2 ounces dark raisins, chopped

2 ounces golden raisins, chopped

grated rind ½ lemon

In a large mixing bowl, sprinkle the yeast over the water and leave it to stand – five minutes for fresh yeast and 15 for dried. Add the milk, vanilla extract, lemon rind, sugar and eggs. Stir in the flour and salt and add the butter. Mix everything to a dough. Knead it in the bowl (see page 13) until it is smooth. Cover it and leave it in a warm place for 1 hour or until it has doubled in size.

Make the filling. Place the poppy seeds in a coffee grinder or blender and work them to a coarse paste. Beat together the butter and honey and beat in the cream, a little at a time. Fold in the poppy seeds, raisins, sultanas and lemon rind.

Preheat the oven to 350°F.

Knead the dough again and roll it into a rectangle about

9 × 12 inches. Spread the filling over the top, leaving a border of about ¾ inch on each long side, but spreading to the edges of the short sides. Roll up the rectangle from one long side and lay it on a floured baking sheet with the overlap underneath. Leave the roll in a warm place for 20 minutes to rise. Glaze it with the egg and milk, and bake it for 40 minutes, or until it is golden-brown. Cool it on a wire rack.

Crescent-shaped rolls are just as popular in parts of Eastern Europe as they are in Austria. From Hungary come *sorkifli*, salted crescents, made with an unsweetened dough, and sprinkled with caraway seeds and coarse salt. The Balkan *kiflici od sala*, below, are filled with walnuts and are made with suet instead of butter. As you roll the dough, the layers become paper-thin and the result is a deliciously flaky pastry rolled round a sweet, nutty filling.

Kiflici od Sala

To make about twenty crescents:

1 ounce fresh yeast or 1 tablespoon dried

½ cup warm milk

2 egg yolks

grated rind 1 lemon

3 tablespoons confectioners' sugar

4 cups (1 pound) all-purpose flour

1 teaspoon salt

1 cup vegetable shortening

Filling:

6 ounces walnuts, ground

6 ounces superfine sugar

½ teaspoon pure vanilla extract

4 tablespoons milk

Topping:

2 ounces walnuts, ground

1 egg yolk, beaten

3 tablespoons superfine sugar

In a large mixing bowl, sprinkle the yeast over the milk and leave it to stand – five minutes for fresh yeast and 15 for dried. Stir in the egg yolks, lemon rind, confectioners' sugar, 1 cup of the flour and the salt. Mix everything to a dough. Turn it on to a floured board and knead it until it is smooth. Return it to the bowl, cover it and leave it in a warm place for 30 minutes.

Mix the remaining flour with the suet. Roll the dough into a ¼-inch-thick rectangle. Sprinkle one third of the suet mixture over two thirds of the dough. Fold the dough and let it stand for 30 minutes. Repeat this twice more, giving the dough a quarter turn each time.

To make the filling, mix together the walnuts, superfine sugar and vanilla extract. Bring the milk to a boil, stir it into the walnuts and sugar and leave the mixture until it is cool.

Roll out the dough again and cut it into 6-inch triangles. Roll the triangles into crescent shapes, filling them with the walnut mixture (see page 21). Lay the crescents on floured baking sheets. Brush them with the beaten egg yolk and scatter them with the walnuts. Leave them in a warm place for 20 minutes to rise.

Preheat the oven to 425°F.

Bake the crescents for 15 minutes, or until they are golden-brown.

Lift them on to wire racks and dust them with the sugar while they are still warm.

● *A generous slice, Romania*

Remove any rind and bones from the belly of pork and dice the meat. Place it in a frying pan and set it over low heat. Cook it gently for about 30 minutes, stirring frequently, so the pieces become golden-brown and crisp. Lift them out with a perforated spoon and drain them on paper towels. Use the fat that is produced as part of the lard to be used in the recipe.

Sprinkle the yeast over half the milk and leave it for 5 minutes. Place the flour in a bowl, make a well in the center and pour in the yeast mixture and the remaining milk. Add the pork pieces and 2 egg yolks and season well. Mix everything to a dough. Turn it on to a floured work surface and knead it until it is smooth. Return it to the bowl, cover it and leave it in a warm, draft-free place for about 1 hour, or until it has doubled in size.

Preheat the oven to 425°F.

Roll out the dough to a 1-inch-thick square. Spread it with one third of the lard, fold it in half and roll it out again. Repeat this twice more, the last time rolling to a thickness of ¾ inch. Cut the dough in 2-inch squares. Place them on a floured baking sheet and cut a shallow, diamond-shaped grid pattern on top of each one.

Brush the squares with the remaining egg yolk. Leave them in a warm place for 10 minutes and bake them for 15 minutes, or until they are golden-brown and risen. Serve them hot.

You will find many savory breads in Eastern Europe. The following buns containing pork pieces are another Balkan recipe. In truth, they are more like a rich, flaky pastry than a bread, but make an excellent lunch and are ideal for picnics.

In some recipes, ½ cup of the milk can be replaced by dry white wine, which gives them extra flavor. The use of bacon was my idea, and it works extremely well. The dough can also be stamped in rounds rather than cut in squares.

Cheese is a popular ingredient in Eastern European savory breads. Rounds of flat bread layered with the local sirene cheese make up the following Bulgarian recipe. Sirene cheese is a brined goat's cheese, similar to feta, which can be used as a substitute. Serve it warm, while the cheese is still soft, and accompany it with a salad.

Pogacice sa Ovarcima

To make about sixteen flat buns:

12 ounces belly of pork or 8 ounces unsmoked bacon
½ ounce fresh yeast or 2 teaspoons dried
½ cup, plus 2 tablespoons, warm milk
2 cups (8 ounces) all-purpose flour
3 egg yolks
salt and freshly ground black pepper
½ cup lard

Tootmanik s Gotovo Testo

To make one 8 × 10-inch loaf:

basic bread dough (see page 12) made with 4 cups (1 pound) all-purpose flour
⅔ cup butter, melted
8 ounces feta cheese, crumbled
1 egg, beaten

● *Tootmanik s Gotovo Testo*

● *Khliab Raiska Ptitsa*

ake the bread dough and leave it to rise. Divide it in nine pieces and roll each piece into an 8-inch-diameter circle. Stack the circles in threes, using half the butter to brush between them. Roll each stack into a 8 × 10-inch rectangle.

Brush a 8 × 10-inch baking pan with a little of the butter. Mix the beaten egg into the cheese. Place a sheet of dough in the pan, brush it with the butter and spoon over half the egg and cheese mixture. Place another sheet of dough on top and do the same. Place the remaining sheet of dough on top and brush it with the remaining butter. Leave the loaf in a warm place for 30 minutes or until it has doubled in size.

Preheat the oven to 350°F.

Bake the loaf for 35 minutes or until it is golden-brown.

Serve the loaf warm, if possible.

irene cheese is also served in a salad with tomatoes and cucumber. It is accompanied by small bread rolls and a bowl of mixed herbs and spices called *ciubritsa*, after the local herb, similar to tarragon. Small pieces of bread are broken off, dipped into the *ciubritsa* and eaten with the salad.

In Bulgaria, *tootmanik s gotovo testo* is accompanied by a drink of tea or yogurt. Another loaf, also from Bulgaria, containing sirene cheese, is the bird of paradise bread, *khliab raiska ptitsa*, so-called because of its colorful decoration. It is a rich loaf, similar to a brioche, lightly flavored with the salty cheese. As before, I have used feta cheese as an alternative.

Khliab Raiska Ptitsa

To make one 8-inch round loaf:
1 ounce fresh yeast or 1 tablespoon dried
4 tablespoons warm water
4 cups (1 pound) all-purpose flour
2 teaspoons salt
⅓ cup plain yogurt
4 eggs
2 ounces feta cheese, crumbled

Decoration:

1 egg, beaten
3 tablespoons milk
red pepper cut in a star shape, about 1 inch across
4 triangles Munster or Edam cheese about ¼ inch thick
four 1-inch squares cooked ham, about ¼ inch thick
4 black olives, pitted

n a small bowl, sprinkle the yeast over the water. Leave this to stand – five minutes for fresh yeast and 15 for dried. Place the flour and salt in a bowl and make a well in the center. Add the yeast mixture, yogurt, eggs and feta cheese. Mix everything to a dough. Turn it on to a floured work surface and knead it until

● *At a traditional watermill, Armenia*

it is smooth. Return it to the bowl, cover it and leave for 1 hour.

Preheat the oven to 400°F. Knead the dough again and form it into an 8-inch-diameter round loaf. Make sure that the top is completely smooth. If there are any cracks, it may rise unevenly in the oven and the decoration will slide out of place. Place the loaf on a floured baking sheet. Mix the beaten egg with the milk, and brush the top of the loaf with the mixture. Place the red pepper in the center, put the cheese triangles on the four quarters of the loaf, and decorate with an olive and a piece of ham between each.

Leave the loaf in a warm place for 20 minutes to rise. Place it in the oven for 15 minutes. Turn the heat to 350°F and continue baking for a further 20 minutes, or until the loaf is golden-brown. Cool the loaf on a wire rack and serve it just warm.

Khachapuri, another cheese-filled loaf, is a Georgian specialty. It is easy to make, using a plain bread dough enriched with a little butter and Edam cheese instead of Munster. The result is an attractive, crown-shaped loaf with a wonderful soft, melted filling. It is good warm, but will keep surprisingly well for about two days.

Khachapuri

To make one 8-inch-diameter tart or 24 tartlets:

½ ounce fresh yeast or 2 teaspoons dried
½ cup, plus 2 tablespoons, warm milk
2 cups (8 ounces) all-purpose flour
1 teaspoon salt
¼ cup (½ stick) butter, softened

Filling:

1 pound Munster or Edam cheese
2 tablespoons butter, softened
1 egg, beaten
2 tablespoons chopped fresh coriander

In a small bowl, sprinkle the yeast over the milk and leave it to stand – five minutes for fresh yeast and 15 for dried. Place the flour and salt in a bowl, make a well in the center and pour in the yeast mixture. Add the butter and mix everything to a dough. Turn it on to a floured work surface and knead it until it is smooth. Return it to the bowl, cover it and leave it in a warm place for one hour, or until it has doubled in size.

To make the filling, finely grate the cheese and mix it with the butter, egg and coriander.

Preheat the oven to 350°F. Knead the dough again and roll it

into a large round, about 20 inches in diameter. Lay it over a floured, 8-inch-diameter tart pan and place the cheese mixture in the center. Gather the sides of the dough to the center, pleating them evenly as you do so. Twist the edges together in the center to seal them and to make the tart crown-shaped. Leave the tart for 20 minutes in a warm place to rise. Bake it for 40 minutes, or until it is golden-brown. Serve it warm.

To make the tartlets, roll out the dough as above and cut it in 4½-inch rounds. Place about 1½ tablespoons of the filling in the center of each round. Fold up the edges of the dough circle and pinch the corners to make a diamond shape, leaving the top of the filling uncovered. Place the tartlets on floured baking sheets and leave them in a warm place for 20 minutes. Bake them for 20 minutes and serve them warm.

Kulibiac is served in Russia on special occasions and it can also be found in Poland. It is really a large, flat pie made of yeast dough with a savory filling. The fillings vary from cabbage and mushroom to a mixture of fresh fish, including salmon, with cooked rice or semolina. So long as you keep in character, you can really make up your own filling, depending on the availability of ingredients.

Here is my special recipe for a 13-inch rectangular loaf.

Kulibiac

1 ounce fresh yeast or 1 tablespoon dried
4 tablespoons warm water
¾ cup warm milk
4 cups (1 pound) all-purpose flour
1 teaspoon salt
¼ cup (½ stick) butter, softened
2 eggs, beaten

Filling:

¾ cup long grain rice
2 cups chicken stock
¼ cup (½ stick) butter
1 medium onion, thinly sliced
4 ounces button mushrooms, thinly sliced
4 ounces green cabbage, shredded
2 eggs, hard cooked
8 ounces fresh salmon
2 tablespoons chopped fennel

● *Khachapuri*

In a large mixing bowl, sprinkle the yeast over the water. Leave this to stand – five minutes for fresh yeast and 15 for dried. Add the milk and gradually add half the flour, beating with a wooden spoon to a thick batter. Cover the mixture with a cloth and leave it in a warm place for 30 minutes, or until it is bubbling. Add the remaining flour, the salt, butter and eggs, and mix everything to a dough. Turn it on to a floured work surface and knead it until it is smooth. Return it to the bowl, cover it and leave it in a warm place for 1 hour or until it has doubled in size.

Meanwhile, prepare the filling. Put the rice and stock into a saucepan, bring them to a boil and cook them until the rice is tender and all the liquid has been absorbed. Cool the rice. Melt 2 tablespoons of the butter in a frying pan over low heat. Add the onions and cook them for 2 minutes. Raise the heat, add the mushrooms and stir them for 2 minutes or until they are cooked through. Remove the onions and mushrooms from the heat.

Cook the cabbage in boiling water for 3 minutes, or until it is just tender. Drain it. Mix it into the rice. Cut the salmon into small, thin slices. Cook them in the remaining butter over low heat until they are well cooked through but still firm. Lift them out and cool them. Meanwhile, peel and slice the eggs.

Preheat the oven to 400°F. Knead the dough on a floured work surface. Divide it into two pieces of about one third and two thirds. Roll the smaller piece into a large rectangle and lay it on a floured baking sheet. Place half the rice on top, leaving a space of about 1½ inches all round. Add half the mushrooms and onions, the eggs and then the salmon. Scatter the fennel over the salmon. Add the remaining mushrooms and onions and finally the remaining rice. Roll out the second piece of dough and use it to cover the filling completely. Seal the edges. Small pieces of dough can be used to decorate the top. Brush the top with the beaten egg and leave the kulibiac in a warm place for 20 minutes to rise.

Bake the kulibiac for 30 minutes or until it is golden brown. Serve it straight from the oven.

SCANDINAVIA AND ICELAND

The fresh foods of Scandinavia are cooked simply and taste of themselves. To go with them are a wealth of breads — from those eaten as part of the famous smörgåsbord, to crispbreads, flat breads, buns and rusks, and sweet rich breads for serving with morning coffee. The custom goes that any bread taken during a meal must be finished up, except for a small piece which should be left on the table to act as the "seed" for the next meal.

Everyday Scandinavian breads are usually made with whole-wheat flour or rye meal, which may or may not be mixed with all-purpose flour to give softness of texture and extra rising ability. Some are made of a mixture of all three flours. The grains that are most widely grown now, as for many years past, are rye, barley and oats, which are quick growing, can stand cool, damp springs and which ripen early in the long summer days. A little wheat is grown in Sweden and Denmark, but most is imported.

Rye is by far the most widely-used grain for bread and there are three grades of the flour – light, medium and rye meal (which is the equivalent to whole-wheat flour). There are many different rye breads baked all over Scandinavia, their texture and color depending on the grade of flour used and their shape and flavor depending on local tradition and taste.

Many Scandinavian breads are not made in standard loaf shapes. There are round breads with holes in the middle which come from the days when bread was made in the autumn and stored strung on poles in the rafters; there are flat rectangles and large flat wheels; flat breads risen with baking powder instead of yeast, and pumpernickel-type breads baked slowly in round, enclosed, sausage-shaped pans.

Crispbreads come from Scandinavia and originated in the days when wheat was harvested early, ground immediately and made into light breads that were unleavened and easily stored. The following recipe is typical of crispbreads throughout the whole region – the dough being made from a mixture of flours, rolled thinly and baked until it is crisp.

Many people in other countries have probably never thought of making their own crispbreads before – I certainly hadn't – but it is surprisingly easy and the results are delicious.

Crispbreads can be served with cheese, dips or patés and are good simply buttered, to accompany a salad.

● *Sweet pastry selection, Denmark*

Preheat the oven to 450°F. Pour the water into a large mixing bowl and whisk in the butter. Mix the flours and salt together. Beat them into the water and butter a little at a time, kneading in the final third with your hands. Knead the mixture on a floured surface to make it smooth.

Divide the dough in eight pieces and roll each one into a thin, 10-inch round. Lay the rounds on floured baking sheets and bake them for about 6 minutes or until they are crisp, but only lightly colored. Cool them on wire racks. You will probably not be able to get all the circles in your oven at once, so bake them in relays, cooling the trays in between.

To store the crispbreads, wrap them in twos or fours in a double layer of plastic wrap, making it as airtight as possible. Keep them in a cool, dry place. Do not freeze them or they will go soggy.

Ordinary white bread is not much eaten in Scandinavia, but where it is made, whatever shape it is, it tends to be called "French" bread. The Scandinavians are, however, very fond of enriched white breads which are served with morning or afternoon coffee. Many of these are quite plain, apart from being flavored with cardamom which is the favorite spice for sweets and pastries. *Pulla* is typical. It is a rich, golden-colored bread which rises beautifully in the oven. It is made in a variety of shapes and is particularly popular around Christmas time.

Flatbrod

To make eight 10-inch-diameter crispbreads:

1¼ cups boiling water
2 tablespoons butter
1 cup (4 ounces) plain cake flour
1 cup (4 ounces) rye meal
1 cup (4 ounces) whole-wheat flour
½ teaspoon salt

Pulla

To make three braided loaves or one wreath:

2 ounces fresh yeast or 2 tablespoons dried
½ cup warm water
½ cup sugar
8 cardamom seeds, crushed
2 cups warm milk
4 eggs, beaten
½ cup (1 stick) butter, softened
7 cups (2 pounds 4 ounces) all-purpose flour
2 teaspoons salt
beaten egg, for glaze
4 tablespoons sugar

In a large mixing bowl, sprinkle the yeast over the water and leave it to stand – five minutes for fresh yeast and 15 for dried. Stir in the milk, sugar, cardamom, eggs and butter. Mix the flour with the salt and then gradually beat it into the yeast mixture. Knead the dough in the bowl until it is smooth (see page 13). Cover it and leave it in a warm place for 1½ hours, or until it has doubled in size.

Preheat the oven to 375°F. Knead the dough again and divide it in three equal parts. Form each one into a braid (see page 18). Alternatively, make one long braid and join the ends to make the traditional wreath. You can also make the dough into a crown. Form it into a round and make a hole in the center using the rounded handle of a knife or a wooden spoon. Then, using your hands, make the hole larger. Using sharp kitchen scissors, cut two-thirds of the way into the ring from the outside at 1½-inch intervals all round the edge. Place the loaves on floured baking sheets and leave them for 20 minutes to rise. At this point they will look very flat and moist, but do not worry, they will rise considerably during baking. Brush them with the egg glaze and sprinkle them with the sugar. Bake the loaves for 25 minutes, or until they are lightly browned and sound hollow when tapped. Cool them on wire racks.

Many Christmas or mid-winter breads, like *pulla*, have for centuries been baked in the shapes of animals. This goes back to the times when animals were sacrificed to the gods at the darkest time of the year. Small farmers were very poor and often could not spare an animal so, as an alternative, they fashioned them out of dough, and offered them instead.

DENMARK

Denmark is the smallest of the Scandinavian countries, but it is also the most southerly and the greenest, with good pastures producing butter for spreading on to dark rye breads and for making rich yeasted doughs for the famous Danish pastries.

Both barley and rye are grown on the largest, most northern island, but much of the grain for Danish bread is imported. Rye bread was for many centuries the staple of the Danish diet, eaten with herring and sour milk for breakfast or made into a soup with beer and milk for the evening meal. It even formed part of an old-fashioned dessert, which was made by leaving a bowl of milk to sour on a window sill and serving it sprinkled with sugar and crumbs of sourdough rye bread.

The Swedish smörgåsbord came originally from Denmark where it is called *smørrebrød*, literally meaning buttered bread. What was originally a simple lunch of buttered bread topped with pickle and herring has become the groaning board that tourists now find. In Denmark, however, the slice of bread topped with something savory is still a popular lunch. The preferred bread is a sour rye, dark, moist and close-textured. It is well buttered, preventing the bread from becoming soggy or impregnated with other flavors. Cold meats, sliced sausage, marinated fish, seafood or cheese can all be used in the typical open sandwich and these are garnished with a range of salad vegetables and pickles.

The bread below is typical of a Danish rye bread. It is close-textured, dark and strong flavored, and is excellent for open sandwiches. Its slight sweetness contrasts well with savory and sharp flavors. Ever since I was given black bread as a child, by our Scandinavian neighbors, I have adored it and been searching for something that resembles it. This is the closest that I have come, although it is slightly lighter in color.

Rugbrod

To make two small round loaves:
1 ounce fresh yeast or 1 tablespoon dried
1½ cups warm water
2 cups (8 ounces) rye meal
3 cups (12 ounces) all-purpose flour
2 teaspoons salt
2 tablespoons caraway seeds
¼ cup molasses
3 tablespoons butter, softened

Place a little of the water in a large bowl and sprinkle over the yeast. Leave it five minutes for fresh yeast and 15 for dried. Mix together the flours, salt and caraway seeds. Add the remaining water, the molasses and the butter to the yeast and gradually add the flours, stirring at first and kneading with your hand toward the end.

Turn the dough on to a floured work surface and knead it until it is smooth. Return it to the bowl, cover it with a clean, dry cloth and leave it in a warm, draft-free place to rise for 1 hour, or until it has doubled in size.

Preheat the oven to 350°F.

Knead the dough again and divide it in two. Form each piece into a small, round loaf and lay it on a floured baking sheet. Bake them for 40 minutes or until they are brown and sound hollow when tapped. Cool them on a wire rack.

● *Danish Pastries (see page 110)*

Pumpernickel-type bread, made commercially by steaming the dough in enclosed containers for long periods, is also much used for open sandwiches and *smørrebrød*. Crispbreads and rusks, such as the Swedish ones that follow, are also popular.

The Danes are famous for their pastries, which are now made all over the world. They are called Danish pastries in the English-speaking world, *Kopenhagener* in Germany and Austria and, strangely, in Denmark they are called *Wienerbrot* or Vienna bread. The story attached to them goes some way to explain why. In the sixteenth century, a young French baker called Claudius Gelée was one day making brioches and forgot to put in the butter. He was just about to knead some into the dough when he was interrupted. Not wishing his mistake to be discovered, he folded the dough over the butter and rolled it out several times. He was surprised to find that the butter did not run all over the place when the dough was in the oven – instead, the finished pastry was light and flaky and tasty. Gelée opened his own bakery in Paris to sell his delicacies, before being invited to Florence by the Italian Mosca brothers. Subsequently they took Gelée's recipe for pasta "fogliate" or "dough in layers" to Vienna, where *they* met two Danish bakers. The Danes, in turn, learned the recipe, but added their own finishing touch – a sweet filling – thus making the Danish pastry an early example of European co-operation.

Danish Pastries

To make about thirty pastries:

1¼ cups milk
¾ cup, plus 2 tablespoons (1¾ sticks), butter, chilled
2 tablespoons sugar
1 egg
1 egg yolk
1½ ounces fresh yeast or 1½ tablespoons dried
4 cups (1 pound) all-purpose flour
½ teaspoon salt
¼ teaspoon ground cardamom

Place the milk, 2 tablespoons of the butter and the sugar in a saucepan and heat them gently, stirring until the butter has melted and the sugar dissolved. Cool them to lukewarm. Beat in the egg and egg yolk and add the yeast (dried yeast should be dissolved first). Leave to stand – five minutes for fresh yeast and fifteen for dried.

Place the flour in a bowl and toss in the salt and cardamom. Make a well in the center and pour in the yeast mixture. Mix everything to a dough. Turn it on to a floured work surface and knead it until it is smooth. Form the dough into a cube shape, put it in a plastic bag and chill it in the refrigerator for 20 minutes.

Place the remaining butter between two pieces of plastic wrap and bang it with a rolling pin into an 4 × 8-inch rectangle. Take out the dough and roll it into a rectangle measuring 8 × 16 inches. Lay the butter in the center and fold the dough over it. Roll out the dough to a rectangle ¾ inch thick. Fold the dough in three. Place it in the bag again and refrigerate for 10 minutes. Repeat this rolling, folding and chilling process three more times.

After the final chilling, roll out the dough and fold it as before. Then cut it crossways in three pieces. You can now make three different types of Danish pastry.

Fruit Snails

2 tablespoons butter, softened
2 tablespoons superfine sugar
1 teaspoon ground cinnamon
1 ounce golden raisins
⅓ recipe Danish Pastry dough, as above

Beat the sugar and cinnamon into the butter and fold in the raisins. Roll out the dough to a ¼-inch-thick rectangle and spread it evenly with the filling. Roll up the dough along one long side and cut it into 1-inch-thick slices. Lay the slices on a floured baking sheet.

Almond-filled Coxcombs

¼ cup ground almonds
¼ cup superfine sugar
1 tablespoon beaten egg
3 drops pure almond extract
⅓ recipe Danish Pastry dough, as above

In a bowl, mix together the ground almonds and sugar. Bind them together with the egg and beat in the almond extract.

Roll the dough into a long, 8-inch-wide rectangle. Spread half the width with the filling. Fold over the other half and cut the folded dough into 4-inch squares. Make three cuts in the folded side of the dough, from the fold to within ½ inch of the opposite side. Lay the pastries on a floured baking sheet and gently spread out the sections.

● *The sign of the baker, Copenhagen*

Custard-filled Pinwheels

1 egg yolk
1 tablespoon flour
1 teaspoon cornstarch
1 tablespoon sugar
½ cup, plus 2 tablespoons, milk
3 drops pure vanilla extract
⅓ recipe Danish Pastry dough, as above

Beat the egg yolk lightly in a bowl and work in the flour and cornstarch and 4 tablespoons of the milk. Pour the remaining milk into a saucepan and heat it to just below boiling point. Gradually stir the hot milk into the yolk mixture. Return everything to the saucepan and stir over low heat until you have a thick, bubbling sauce. Remove the sauce from the heat and beat in the vanilla extract. Cool the mixture completely.

To make the pinwheels, roll out the dough to a thickness of ¼ inch and cut it in 6-inch squares. Cut from each corner to within ½ inch of the center. Place a portion of the filling in the center. Fold alternate sections to the middle so the points slightly overlap, and seal them by gently pressing down in the center.

Baking

Lay the pastries on floured baking sheets and leave them in a warm place for 20 minutes to rise. Preheat the oven to 400°F. Bake the pastries for 20 minutes or until they are golden-brown. Cool them on wire racks.

Finishing

The pastries can be served as they are or drizzled with a simple icing made from ¼ cup confectioners' sugar and a little water. Halved glacé cherries may be used as a decoration.

The basic Danish pastry dough can also be made into the old-fashioned butter cake. This is made in a round cake pan and consists of a circle of dough topped with more dough made into circles, spirals or other elaborate shapes. Sometimes a hole is left in the center and filled with butter, dark brown sugar and raisins.

Old-fashioned Butter Cake

To make one 8-inch-diameter cake:
¼ cup (½ stick) unsalted butter, softened
¼ cup firmly packed brown sugar
2 teaspoons pure almond extract
½ quantity Danish pastry dough, as above
8 ounces confectioners' sugar, 1 tablespoon butter or margarine and 2 tablespoons boiling water, for icing

Beat together the butter, sugar and almond extract.

Divide the dough in half and roll one piece into an 8-inch circle. Press it into a shallow, 8-inch-diameter cake pan. Roll the remaining piece into a 14-inch square and spread half of it with the butter mixture. Fold the other half of the dough over the top and seal the edges. Cut the folded dough in 2-inch-wide strips and roll up each one. Tuck the ends of the strip underneath the roll to prevent them from unwinding in the oven. Place the rolls of dough on top of the round of dough in the pan, evenly spaced and with one in the center.

Leave the cake for 20 minutes in a warm place to rise.

Preheat the oven to 350°F.

Bake the cake for 45 minutes or until it is golden-brown and crisp.

Cool it on a wire rack. Make up the icing and drizzle it all over the top before serving.

● *Semla*

Danish pastries are eaten at coffee time, alongside other enriched breads such as the *pulla* (see page 107) or the *kringle* which, besides cardamom, contains raisins, candied citrus peel and almonds.

A similar mixture of nuts and fruits is used to make the *julekage*, Christmas cake.

Julekage

To make one large round loaf or two braided loaves:

1 ounce fresh yeast or 1 tablespoon dried
1¼ cups warm milk
2 eggs, beaten
grated rind ½ lemon
6 cardamom seeds, freshly crushed
½ teaspoon ground cinnamon
¼ cup sugar
½ teaspoon pure vanilla extract
4 cups (1 pound) all-purpose flour
½ teaspoon salt
½ cup (1 stick) butter, softened
2 ounces candied fruits, chopped
2 ounces slivered almonds
2 ounces golden raisins
1 egg, beaten, for glaze

Place half the milk in a large mixing bowl and sprinkle over the yeast. Leave it five minutes for fresh yeast and 15 for dried. Add the remaining milk, the eggs, lemon rind, cardamom and cinnamon, the sugar and vanilla extract. Add the salt to the flour and then gradually mix them into the milk mixture. Knead the dough in the bowl until it is smooth. With it still in the bowl, knead in the butter, candied fruits, almonds and raisins. Cover the dough and leave it in a warm place for 1½ hours or until it has doubled in size.

Preheat the oven to 350°F. Knead the dough on a floured work surface. Either form it into a ball and put it on a floured baking sheet or divide it in two and form each piece into a braid (see page 18), again laying the finished loaves on a floured baking sheet. Leave the loaves to rise for 20 minutes in a warm place. Brush them with the beaten egg.

Bake the large loaf for 45 minutes and the smaller ones for 35 minutes. They will be well browned and should sound hollow when tapped. Cool them on a wire rack.

SWEDEN

The Swedes have a wide variety of breads, most of which are based on rye flour or meal. They range from rich pumpernickel types to the lighter ones made from the finer grades of rye flour. Crispbreads, called *knackebrod*, are extremely popular, as are the twice-baked rolls called rusks or crisprolls, which are similar to the *kavring* from Norway (see page 120).

Traditionally, Swedish bread has a bitter sweet flavor, the result of a combination of rye flour and molasses, but nowadays, mainly due to a large immigrant population, there is a greater variety of unsweetened bread in the stores. Caraway and fennel seeds are also popular flavorings.

The Swedes have many special-occasion breads. On Shrove Tuesday, the following buns, called *semla* or *semlor*, are served as a dessert. Traditionally, they should be served in a bowl of milk, but if bread and milk is not to your taste, the milk can be omitted. Without it, they make a delicious teatime treat, rather like English cream buns. The buns themselves are soft and golden, with a thin, crisp crust.

Semla

To make sixteen small round buns:

½ ounce fresh yeast or 2 teaspoons dried
½ cup warm water
1 egg, beaten
¾ cup warm milk
¼ cup sugar
4 cardamom seeds, freshly crushed
½ cup (1 stick) butter, softened
4 cups (1 pound) all-purpose flour
½ teaspoon salt
1 egg, beaten

Filling:

½ cup ground almonds
½ cup superfine sugar
2 tablespoons beaten egg
½ teaspoon pure almond extract
½ cup, plus 2 tablespoons, heavy cream, whipped

Finishing:

2 tablespoons confectioners' sugar for dusting (optional)
hot milk

In a large bowl, dissolve the yeast over the water and leave it for 5 minutes. Beat in the egg, milk, sugar, cardamom and butter. Mix the flour and salt together. Gradually beat the flour into the yeast mixture. Knead the mixture in the bowl until it is smooth and shiny (see page 13). Cover it and leave it in a warm place for 1 hour or until it has doubled in size.

Preheat the oven to 400°F. Knead the dough on a floured work surface, divide it in sixteen pieces and shape each piece into a round bun. Place the buns on floured baking sheets without flattening them. Leave them in a warm place for 20 minutes to rise. Brush the buns with the beaten egg and bake them for 15 minutes or until they are golden-brown. Cool them on wire racks.

To make the filling, mix together the almonds, sugar, egg and almond extract. Divide it in sixteen pieces and form each piece into a disc shape.

Slit each bun in half horizontally, leaving one side joined. Place a portion of the almond paste inside and top it with the cream. Sieve confectioners' sugar over the top of the buns if wished.

To serve, spoon hot milk into small dishes and place a filled bun in the center.

Lussekatter

To make eight cats or one wreath:
1 ounce fresh yeast or 1 tablespoon dried
4 tablespoons warm water
¾ cup milk
1 teaspoon saffron threads
½ cup (1 stick) butter, softened
½ cup sugar
2 eggs, beaten
4 cups (1 pound) all-purpose flour
4 ounces golden raisins
1 egg, beaten

Decoration

for cats: 24 raisins
for wreath: 2 tablespoons slivered almonds, 2 tablespoons sugar

Many Swedish specialty breads are made around Christmas time. *Prastens har* (priest's hair) is white wheat bread shaped like a curled wig with raisins in the curls. *Munkar* (monks) are deep-fried yeasted doughnuts, and *kringlor* are twist-shaped buns. *Tunnbrod* (thin bread) is a thin, round, flat bread that is baked on a griddle and folded or rolled. It used to be made only once a year and piled in stacks for keeping, each stack made from 1½ barrels of flour.

The thirteenth of December is St. Lucia's day, when the oldest girl of each family dresses as the Queen of Light, with a crown of candles on her head, and gives saffron buns to the rest of the household. These buns have been made in many different shapes, but the most popular has always been the cat, and so the buns are now called *Lussekatter* (Lucy's Cats). The spiral patterns from which the shape is formed are very old, making the probable origin of the buns pre-Christian. The basic spirals can be placed together to make one large loaf, or the dough can be made into a braided wreath. The buns themselves are soft and sweet and a beautiful yellow color.

● *Lussekatter*

In a small bowl, add the yeast to the water and leave it to stand – five minutes for fresh yeast and 15 for dried. Place the milk and saffron in a saucepan. Set them over low heat and bring them slowly to a boil, stirring, so that the milk turns golden. Strain the milk into a large mixing bowl. Stir in the butter and sugar and cool to lukewarm. Stir in the yeast and eggs.

Mix the flour with the salt and beat it into the yeast mixture. Add the raisins. Knead the dough in the bowl until it is smooth (see page 13). Cover it and leave it in a warm place for 1½ hours, or until it has doubled in size.

Preheat the oven to 375°F. Knead the dough on a floured work surface and divide it in 16 pieces. To make the cats, roll each piece of dough in a sausage shape about 10 inches long. Form eight of the pieces in an "S" shape, curling round the ends to make spirals, the top spiral slightly smaller than the bottom one. Form the other eight pieces in reverse "S" shapes and spiral the ends as before. Cross one forward-facing piece diagonally over one reverse-facing piece, and press lightly down in the center. Place the formed cats on to floured baking sheets and press three raisins into each one to make the eyes and nose. Leave them in a warm place for 20 minutes to rise.

To make the wreath, take off about one-eighth of the dough and reserve it. Divide the rest in three pieces. Roll each one into a rope about 25 inches long and braid them. Form the braid into a ring, joining the ends securely. Roll the reserved piece of dough into a long rope. Loop it over the seam and form it into a bow. Place the wreath on a floured baking sheet and leave it in a warm place to rise for 20 minutes. Brush it with the beaten egg and scatter it with the almonds and sugar.

Bake the cats for 20 minutes and the wreath for 35 minutes, or until they are golden-brown and sound hollow when tapped.

The traditional dish for serving on Christmas Eve is a home-cooked, lightly-salted ham and the stock in which it is cooked is still saved for the family custom of *doppa y grytan*, dipping in the pot. Sometimes, this is simply a dip into the stockpot to bring good luck and food for the coming year; in other households, the stock is specially made into a clear soup that is served in a large tureen, and surrounded by bread that has been torn in small pieces in readiness for dipping. Once, the bread was always made at home, but now you can go out and buy small round loaves especially made for the Christmas "dip in the pot," known simply as *doppbrod*.

Doppbrod

To make four small round loaves:
1½ ounces fresh yeast or 1½ tablespoons dried
¼ cup, plus 2 tablespoons, warm water
4 cups (1 pound) rye meal
2½ cups (10 ounces) all-purpose flour
1 tablespoon salt
1 tablespoon fennel seeds
1 tablespoon aniseeds
1¾ cups, plus 2 tablespoons, warm milk
2 tablespoons sugar
2 tablespoons butter, softened

In a small bowl, dissolve the yeast in the water and leave it to stand – five minutes for fresh yeast and 15 for dried. In a large bowl, mix together the rye meal and all-purpose flour, salt and fennel and aniseeds. Make a well in the center. Pour in the yeast mixture and begin to mix in a little flour from the sides of the well. Add the milk, sugar and butter, and mix everything to a dough. Turn the dough on to a floured work surface and knead it until it is smooth. Return it to the bowl, cover it and leave it in a

● *Flourishing wheat field, Denmark*

warm place for approximately 1 hour, or until it has about doubled in size.

Preheat the oven to 400°F. Knead the dough again and divide it in four equal pieces. Form each piece into a round loaf and place it on a floured baking sheet. Leave the loaves in a warm place to rise for 20 minutes. Bake them for 30 minutes or until they sound hollow when tapped. Cool them on wire racks.

FINLAND

Most of the bread in Finland is made from rye flour. It has been proved to be the most nutritious in the world, and from it the Finnish stamina and strength of character is said to derive.

At one time, all bread was made in the home and there were many regional differences. In the east of the country, for example, bread was made once a week. In the west, baking days were much less frequent and bread could be stored for several months before being eaten.

The following two breads are typical of the Finnish style. The first, *suomalaisleipa*, is a leavened rye bread, mid-brown in color, light in texture and best eaten when fresh.

● *Fertile soil for agriculture*

Turn the dough on to a floured work surface and knead it, using the remaining rye meal. Return the dough to the bowl, cover it and leave it in a warm place for 1 hour, or until it has doubled in size.

Preheat the oven to 375°F. Knead the dough again and form it into a round loaf. Put it on a floured baking sheet and leave it in a warm place for 20 minutes to rise.

Bake the loaf for 40 minutes, or until it has a hard brown crust and sounds hollow when tapped. Cool it for a while on a wire rack.

The second bread – literally "Rye-bread rounds" – is of the type that is made into rings and would once have been strung on poles and stored in the rafters of the roof. It is made by a sourdough method with rye meal only, and is close-textured, dark, strong-flavored, but surprisingly soft, and delicious with butter, cheese and cold smoked meats.

Nowadays it is eaten fresh, but in the old days, during storage, it would have become like a crisp rusk. Large batches of this type of bread were often made during springtime, before the ice melted, and kept in store for the summertime.

Suomalaisleipa

To make one round loaf:

1 ounce fresh yeast or 1 tablespoon dried
1¼ cups warm water
1 tablespoon dark brown sugar
1 tablespoon butter, softened
2 cups (8 ounces) all-purpose flour
1½ cups (6 ounces) rye meal
1½ teaspoons salt

In a large mixing bowl, sprinkle the yeast over half the water and leave it to stand – five minutes for fresh yeast and 15 for dried. Stir in the remaining water, the sugar, butter, all the all-purpose flour, 1 cup of the rye meal and the salt. Knead the mixture in the bowl to make a smooth dough (see page 13). Cover it with a clean, dry cloth and leave it in a warm place for 10 minutes.

Ruisreikaleivat

To make three rings
and three small buns:

First Day:

4½ cups water
1 ounce fresh yeast or 1 tablespoon dried
3 rye crispbreads
4½ cups (18 ounces) rye meal

Second Day:

2 ounces fresh yeast or 2 tablespoons dried
2 tablespoons salt
4 cups (1 pound) rye meal

● *Ruisreikaleivat*

On the first day, dissolve the yeast in the water, crumble in the crispbreads and stir in the 4½ cups rye meal. Cover and leave in a warm place overnight.

On the second day, with the dough still in the bowl, knead in the yeast, salt and further rye meal. Turn the dough on to a floured work surface and knead it. It will be soft and sticky, but keep going. You may have to use quite a bit of extra flour for your hands and the work surface. Return the dough to the bowl, cover it and leave it in a warm place to rise for 1 hour or until it has doubled in size.

Preheat the oven to 450°F. Knead the dough again. It may still be very moist. Divide it in three and make each piece into a round, flat loaf. Using a pastry cutter dipped in flour, stamp out a 2½-inch round from the center of each one. Put the loaves and the middles on floured baking sheets and leave them to rise for 30 minutes.

Bake the loaves for 25 minutes and the middles for 10 minutes. Cool them on wire racks.

Wheat and barley flours are also used in Finland, but in much smaller quantities. The *rieska*, made in the north of the country, is a flat, unleavened barley loaf and the *ohraleipa* is a leavened loaf made from a mixture of wheat and barley flour, and milk. The American whole-wheat graham flour is also used, in conjunction with either white wheat or rye flour. Potato bread became popular after the rather late introduction of the potato in the eighteenth century and there are also many varieties of crispbreads and rusks.

A definite Finnish specialty is the filled loaf, made with a leavened or unleavened dough and filled with either savory or sweet mixtures. The most traditional fillings are fish, a mixture of pork and fish, or pork and rutabagas or turnips, or local berries such as lingonberries and blackberries. The filling is sealed inside the dough which is frequently basted with melted lard during a long baking. When the loaf is served, the crust is separated from the filling, broken in pieces and buttered, and the filling is served alongside it. The *kalakukko*, below, is a typical example. The filling is very rich and so a little will go a long way. As an alternative, replace the fish with 1 pound of rutabaga, cut in small, thin pieces. Some doughs for this type of dish are made simply of rye meal and water.

Kalakukko

To make one large filled loaf:

1 ounce fresh yeast or 1 tablespoon dried
1¼ cups warm water
4 cups (1 pound) rye meal
2 teaspoons salt
8 ounces pork belly slices
1 pound small oily fish such as sprats or sardines
2 tablespoons salt
⅓ cup lard, melted

● *Rich arable land, Finland*

In a large mixing bowl, sprinkle the yeast over half the water and leave it – five minutes for fresh and 15 for dried. Add the rest of the water and then the flour and salt. Turn the dough on to a floured work surface and knead it until it is smooth. Return it to the bowl, cover it and leave it in a warm place for 1 hour or until it has doubled in size.

Remove the rind from the pork slices and cut in 2-inch pieces. Head and gut the fish and remove the backbones.

Preheat the oven to 400°F. Roll out the dough in a large round, reserving about one sixteenth. Layer the fish and pieces of pork in the center of the dough, sprinkling them liberally with the salt. Fold over the edges of the dough and seal them. Turn the dough packet over, place it on a baking sheet and form it into an oval shape. Leave it in a warm place to rise for 30 minutes.

Place the loaf in the oven for 10 minutes. Turn the heat to 300°F and bake the loaf for a further 4 to 5 hours, basting it frequently with the melted lard.

Should the loaf leak, plug up the holes with the reserved dough to keep the juices inside.

Much bread in Finland is now commercially made, but the local specialties still survive. *Verileipa* (blood bread or black bread) was once made all over western Finland at the time of the autumn slaughters, using animal blood to enrich and color; and there is a barley bread in Lapland made by steeping barley in buttermilk, mixing in egg and baking the mixture to make a rich, chewy flat bread.

NORWAY

Flat breads, called *lefse*, are the specialty of Norway, particularly in the rural areas. They are baked on a griddle and served with fish, mutton, cheese and pickles. Sometimes they are baked as crumbles served with sour cream, as a dessert. They are made from flour or flour mixed with mashed potato, and should be soft and pliable. Often they are made in batches to be stored and dipped in hot water to soften them before serving. Many Norwegian housewives have a special *lefse* rolling pin which is ridged to make a crinkled pattern on the thin round of dough.

Lefse

To make sixteen round flat breads:
2 cups milk
¼ cup (½ stick) butter
1 teaspoon salt
2 cups (8 ounces) plain cake flour

Place the milk, butter and salt in a saucepan (make sure that the saucepan is large enough to take the flour later). Set them over low heat and stir until the butter has dissolved. Bring them to a boil and stir in the flour all at once. Stir on the heat until the mixture is very thick. Take it from the heat and cool it completely.

● *Special-shaped loaves, Sweden*

Divide the dough in 16 pieces and, using plenty of flour on your work surface and rolling pin, roll each piece into a flat round. Bake the rounds on an ungreased griddle, pre-heated over medium heat, until they are speckled brown and dry looking. Stack them up as they are done.

If you are making them in advance, stack them and wrap them in wax paper and store them in a cool, dry place. They will become dry and crisp. Just before serving, dip them quickly in hot water and stack them with a layer of plastic wrap or a clean, dry cloth between each one.

The *lefse* can be served with savory dishes or they can be covered with a mixture of melted butter, ground cinnamon and sugar, or raisins, and served rolled up like a pancake.

At country weddings in the Voss area, the local wedding cake, called *brudlaupskling*, is traditionally made from huge flat white breads, layered with a mixture of butter, cheese, heavy cream and syrup, and served cut in squares. The tradition goes back to the days when white bread was a luxury that could only be enjoyed on special occasions.

For sandwiches, the Norwegians prefer bread made with whole-wheat flour or rye meal, often slightly sweetened with molasses, syrup or brown sugar. The following bread has a light, soft texture and slightly sweet flavor.

Hvetekake

To make two 1-pound loaves:

1 ounce fresh yeast or 1 tablespoon dried
2½ cups warm water
¼ cup dark brown sugar
3 cups (12 ounces) all-purpose flour
3 tablespoons butter, softened
2 teaspoons salt
3 cups (12 ounces) whole-wheat flour

In a large bowl, stir the yeast into 2 cups of the water. Leave it five minutes for fresh yeast and 15 for dried. Stir in 1 tablespoon of the sugar and all the all-purpose flour. Cover the mixture and leave it in a warm place for 30 minutes to form a sponge. In a small bowl, dissolve the rest of the sugar in the remaining water. Stir in the butter and salt. Beat the mixture into the sponge and gradually knead in the whole-wheat flour. Turn the dough on to a floured work surface and knead it until it is smooth. Return it to the bowl, cover it and leave it in a warm place for 1 hour or until it has doubled in size.

Preheat the oven to 350°F. Cut the dough in two equal pieces and form them into loaf shapes. They can be made into round or long loaves to be baked on sheets or put into loaf pans. Leave the shaped loaves in a warm place for 20 minutes to rise.

Brush the tops of the loaves with water. Bake them for 40 minutes or until they sound hollow when tapped. Cool them on wire racks.

Like all Scandinavians, the Norwegians are fond of crispbreads and rusks. This recipe, although specifically from Norway, is typical of those from all the countries in the region. You can serve these crisp kavring rolls with butter and cheese, but they also make a wonderful accompaniment to a light snack, such as a salad.

Kavring

To make twenty-four rolls:

1 ounce fresh yeast or 1 tablespoon dried
1¼ cups warm water
2 teaspoons sugar
1 teaspoon salt
2 tablespoons butter, softened
2 cups (8 ounces) whole-wheat flour
2 cups (8 ounces) all-purpose flour

In a large bowl, sprinkle the yeast over half the water and leave it – five minutes for fresh yeast and 15 for dried. Add the rest of the water, the sugar, salt, butter and flours. Mix them to a dough. Turn it on to a floured work surface and knead it. Return it to the bowl, cover it and leave in a warm place for 1 hour or until it has doubled in size.

Preheat the oven to 425°F.

Knead the dough again, divide it in 12 pieces and form each piece into a round bun. Lay the buns on floured baking sheets, without pressing them down. Leave them in a warm place for 20 minutes to rise. Bake the buns for 12 minutes, or until they are golden-brown.

Cool them on wire racks.

Turn the oven down to 250°F. Put the buns back on the floured baking sheets and, using two forks to avoid burning yourself, tear them apart. Leave the halves split-side up and place them in the oven for 1 hour so they dry out and become very crisp. They should only color very lightly. Once again, cool them on wire racks.

These rolls stay crisp if they are stored in an airtight container. Do not freeze them.

A natural bread oven in the volcanic terrain of northeast Iceland

ICELAND

Bread in Iceland is a mixture of the old and the new. The indigenous breads are the various kinds of flat bread that were once baked on hot stones but are now made on a griddle, and the dark, Pumpernickel types that have a sweet-sour flavor. The newer types have been introduced only within the last twenty years, mainly from Germany.

Very little grain has ever been grown in Iceland, so most is imported, a fact which for many centuries determined the diet of the Icelandic peoples. In the thirteenth century, Iceland had an agreement with Norway by which Norway sent in six loaded food ships each year. At the beginning of the fifteenth century, however, this ceased, and for a long time no food was imported. Apparently the poor then ate dried fish instead of bread and this continued until around 1800. Even then, bread was made almost exclusively only by the better-off town dwellers. Consequently, there are only a few Icelandic bread recipes to be found.

The first recipe here is an example of a flat bread, the simplest of which are made with rye meal and water only. When mixed with milk, the breads become soft-textured. They can be served with all kinds of savory dishes, with cheese and with paté. They are also good topped with jam.

Flatbread with Milk

To make thirty-two round flat breads:

1¾ cups (7 ounces) rye meal
1¾ cups (7 ounces) whole-wheat flour
1¾ cups (7 ounces) plain cake flour
4 teaspoons baking powder
1 teaspoon salt
2 cups hot milk

Place all the flours in a bowl with the baking powder and salt. Make a well in the center and pour in the hot milk. Mix everything to a dough and knead it until it is smooth. Divide the dough in 32 pieces and roll each one of these into a thin, 7-inch round.

Cook the rounds on a preheated, ungreased griddle, over medium heat, until they are cooked through and speckled brown but still soft. Serve them hot, spread with butter.

Laufabread

To make eighteen flat cakes:

4 cups (1 pound) plain cake flour
1 teaspoon baking powder
1 tablespoon sugar
2 tablespoons butter
1 cup hot milk

Place the flour, baking powder and sugar in a bowl and rub in the butter. Make a well in the center and pour in the hot milk. Mix everything to a dough and knead it until it is smooth. Divide the dough in eighteen pieces and roll each piece into a flat round. Using a sharp knife, cut a circle of eight pointed, radiating petals in each flat cake. Use the cut-out pieces to make extra cakes.

Deep fry the cakes in hot oil until they are golden-brown, crisp and puffy. Drain them on paper towels and serve them hot.

Laufabread (leaf bread) are deep-fried flat, slightly sweet breads, traditionally served at Christmas to accompany the seasonal dish of salted lamb.

THE UNITED STATES AND CANADA

American and Canadian cookery have their roots in the pioneer days when families, first from Britain, Holland and France, and later from all over Europe, trekked westwards across a brand new country, adapting their own foods and cooking styles to the availability of ingredients and the rigors of cooking over open fires and in makeshift ovens.

Europe's ideal bread-making grain has always been wheat, and this was taken over to the New World by the early settlers. Even as early as 1585, a colony founded by Sir Walter Raleigh, from England, planted wheat on Roanoke Island, off North Carolina; the Pilgrim Fathers, from Plymouth, carried wheat and rye to the New World in 1620; in 1634 the first watermill was built at Boston, and Dutch settlers quickly established a large wheat-growing area around New York.

The success of these new wheat crops, however, was by no means guaranteed. Many times in these early years, when new land was put under the plow, the climate and conditions proved inhospitable and the settlers had to fall back on the skills and knowledge of the local Indians. Through them they were introduced to Indian corn, or maize, which was to save them from starvation in difficult years. Maize grew well in the local climate and conditions. It was easy to carry, and could be made quickly into small cakes for cooking on a "spider" (like a frying pan with legs) over hot ashes. The new Americans acquired a taste for it and, even when wheat *was* readily available to all, corn bread remained an essential part of American cuisine.

Farmers not only grew the corn that they were first given by the Indians, but they also developed and perfected new varieties – until there were literally hundreds. These could be divided into five families of corn – flint, dent, soft, sweet and popcorn. The two most used for bread were flint corn, which grew in the north, and Boone Country White, a dent corn (so-called because dents develop in the kernel as it dries), which grew in the south.

There are a wide variety of corn breads, many of which do not rely on yeast for rising. Yeast could be obtained where beer had been brewed, but trekkers in the prairies would rarely have had access to it. The earliest corn breads, therefore, consisted simply of cornmeal mixed to a dough or paste with water. Later, buttermilk, a little fat and a rising agent such as baking soda (or, after 1856, baking powder) were added.

In 1862, a publication called *The Nebraska Farmer* listed thirty-three ways of preparing fresh or dried corn, and many recipe books from the nineteenth and early twentieth centuries would state alongside a bread recipe which type of corn was the best one to use.

The simplest corn bread made today is corn pone. The name, according to William Strachey, who in 1612 wrote about travelling in Virginia, comes from the Indian *apone*, a variety of cornmeal and water cake that was cooked in hot ashes. These were copied by the settlers and called pone or ash cakes. Because they were often cooked on a hoe, held over the flames, they came to be known as hoe cakes.

 Wheat storage-elevators

in 8 pieces and form each one into a round, flat cake. Place them on a floured baking sheet and bake them for 20 minutes, or until the edges are brown.

They are wonderful hot and buttered, but are also very good cold.

Johnny cake was another pioneer specialty. It was usually baked in a flat pan in the oven, although some recipes call for a spider or a griddle. There are many variations of Johnny cake. Its main ingredient is cornmeal, but some contain molasses, some sour cream, and others a mixture of flours. Indeed, it seems to have been made originally from any suitable ingredients available.

The origin of the name Johnny cake has never been proved. Some say it is a corruption of "journey" cake; others, that it comes from the Indian tribe of Shawnee, from whom the original idea may have come.

Johnny cake has a rich, nutty flavor, it is crisp on the outside and soft in the middle, and it is recommended that it should be eaten hot and buttered. It will accompany anything from jelly or boiled eggs to a stew of meat and beans.

Corn Pone

To make eight small cakes:

2 cups (8 ounces) cornmeal
1 teaspoon salt
1 teaspoon baking soda
2 tablespoons lard or shortening
1/2 cup, plus 2 tablespoons, boiling water
1/2 cup, plus 2 tablespoons, buttermilk

Preheat the oven to 350°F. Place the cornmeal, salt and baking soda in a mixing bowl and rub in the lard or shortening. Make a well in the center. Pour in the boiling water, stirring in the cornmeal from the sides of the well. Add enough of the buttermilk to make a soft, but moldable, dough. Divide the dough

Johnny Cake

To make one 8 × 10-inch loaf:

1 1/2 cups (6 ounces) cornmeal
2 cups (8 ounces) plain cake flour
2 teaspoons baking powder
1 teaspoon salt
1 tablespoon sugar
1/3 cup shortening
2 cups, plus 2 tablespoons, milk, or 1/2 milk and 1/2 water

Preheat the oven to 350°F. Place the cornmeal, flour, baking powder, salt and sugar in a mixing bowl and rub in the shortening. Make a well in the center and pour in the milk gradually, mixing everything to a thick batter as you do so. Pour the batter into a greased 8 × 10-inch baking pan.

Bake the cake for 30 minutes, or until it is golden-brown on top and a skewer inserted into the center comes out clean.

Spoon bread is really a cross between a bread and a pudding. It is unsweetened, baked in a deep dish, and has a crispy top and a delicious custardy middle. The story goes that in the pioneer days a housewife was making both cornmeal mush and corn bread and somehow mixed the two together. In fact it was probably a way of making leftover eggs and milk into a substantial meal. Spoon bread can be used as an accompaniment to a meat dish, in a similar way to the English Yorkshire pudding. The following recipe is based on an old one from Ohio, which suggests: "Serve it with maple syrup or just plain.... It is simply swell served with creamed mushrooms, or creamed chicken or tuna fish, or even dried beef."

Spoon Bread

To make one "pudding":

¾ cup (3 ounces) cornmeal

3 tablespoons butter

1 teaspoon salt

1 cup boiling water

1 cup milk

3 eggs, separated

● *Johnny Cake (see page 123)*

Preheat the oven to 375°F. Place the cornmeal, butter and salt in a bowl and pour in the boiling water. Gradually beat in the milk and then the egg yolks. Stiffly whip the egg whites and fold them into the mixture.

Pour the batter into a buttered 2-pint ovenproof dish and bake it for 40 minutes, or until it is golden-brown, risen and set. Serve the spoon bread hot.

The new wheat fields in Canada, meanwhile, were flourishing. The French around Quebec had produced 738,000 bushels of grain with their first wheat crop. Then, in 1812, the Scottish Earl of Selkirk arrived in Canada with many of his clan, made homeless by the Highland clearances. They settled in the Red River valley and attempted to grow the staple foods of their Scots upbringing – turnips, potatoes, wheat and barley. They survived two disastrous crop failures due to birds, locusts and various fights with Indians and trappers, and eventually their wheat crops far excelled any that they could have achieved in Scotland. The acreages of wheat expanded, new varieties were developed, machinery was gradually introduced for planting and harvesting, and railways opened up communications. This happened not only in Canada but all over what was to become the United States. Wheat was available to all and white bread, so greatly desired in Britain and Europe, became the norm in many households.

Baking soda, baking powder and various sourdough starters were far more common than yeast, and enabled some breads to be made very quickly and easily. The Selkirk settlers brought the bannock from Scotland and it became a favorite food for trappers in the north. The bannock was made either with whole-wheat or white flour and a simple rising agent or none at all. Egg is sometimes added to modern recipes. Even now, at the winter carnivals in northern Manitoba, there are bannock-baking competitions.

Bannock

To make two 7-inch or one 10-inch bannock:

3½ cups (14 ounces) plain cake flour
2 teaspoons baking powder
½ teaspoon salt
3 tablespoons lard
¾ cup water

Place the flour, baking powder and salt in a mixing bowl and rub in the lard. Make a well in the center and pour in the water to make a soft, slightly sticky dough. Knead the dough lightly on a floured work surface. Divide the dough in two equal pieces and roll each piece into a ½-inch-thick, 7-inch-diameter circle.

Heat a greased griddle over low heat and cook each bannock for about 7 minutes on each side, or until it is just browned and cooked through. It will sound hollow when it is tapped.

To cook the bannock in the oven, roll the whole piece of dough to a thickness of ½ inch. Lay it on a floured baking sheet and place it in a preheated 350°F oven for 20 minutes, or until it is golden-brown.

Both the area round the St. Lawrence River in Canada and that around Boston in New England lay claim to having invented steamed brown bread. The Boston version contains cornmeal, rye meal and whole-wheat or graham flour. For the Canadian version – Shediac brown bread – the rye meal is replaced by all-purpose flour. Both contain molasses and in the Boston version there are optional raisins. Steamed brown bread is moist and savory-sweet and goes excellently with baked beans and bacon.

Boston Brown Bread

To make one 12-ounce loaf:

½ cup (2 ounces) cornmeal
½ cup (2 ounces) rye meal
½ cup (2 ounces) whole-wheat or graham flour
½ teaspoon salt
½ teaspoon baking soda
3 tablespoons molasses
1 cup cultured buttermilk or sour milk
2 ounces raisins, optional

Place the cornmeal, rye meal, whole-wheat flour, salt and baking soda in a bowl and mix in the molasses and buttermilk. This will make a thick batter. Mix in the raisins if you are using them.

Pour the batter into a greased 2½-cup pudding mold. Cut a large circle of aluminum foil and a large circle of wax paper. Lay the paper on top of the foil and butter it. Make a 1-inch pleat through both layers (this allows space for expansion of the loaf). Cover the basin with the paper and foil, paper side down. Tie the cover down with string, making a handle for easy lifting. Bring a large pan of water to a boil and place a trivet in the bottom. Lower the mold on to the trivet. Cover the pan and boil the bread for 3 hours, topping up the water as and when necessary.

Lift out the mold and turn out the bread. Serve the bread hot, with baked beans.

For the pioneers, yeast was scarce, forcing them to develop alternative methods of leavening. The breads they subsequently produced, using a variety of starters, were so good that, even when yeast was readily available, non-yeast breads were still demanded and enjoyed alongside the newer, lighter ones.

In her book *The Country Kitchen*, published in the United States in 1938, Della Lutes says, 'My father did not like yeast bread… and did not eat it. He said there was nothing to get your teeth into, and that it wasn't fit for a dog… He wanted Salt Risin' Bread and he wanted it fresh… My mother thoroughly disliked making Salt Risin' Bread. It was temperamental, required longer rising and took more time to bake… He and I would feast our corporeal selves on the nutty richness of Salt Risin' Bread, and stock our souls with memories against another day.'

Her mother was right, Salt Risin' Bread is tricky to make; but her father was right too, it is exceptionally good. It is certainly more dense than white wheat bread, but is very soft inside with a thin crisp crust. The crumb is a pale creamy-yellow color and there is a definite taste of cornmeal even though so little is used in the mixture.

When you start to eat Salt Risin' Bread it is difficult to stop, but despite the pleasure it gives, I wouldn't like to have to make it every day or even every week. For an occasional change, however, it is wonderful. It goes particularly well with a hot, savory soup, stew or chowder, and is a delicious complement to traditional American country cooking.

When the mixture has risen, knead in the remaining flour and the shortening. Form the bread into a loaf shape and put it into a 2-pound loaf pan. Leave it in a warm place for about 30 minutes or until it has risen above the top of the pan.

Preheat the oven to 350°F.

Bake the loaf for 50 minutes, or until it is golden brown. Cool it on a wire rack.

The recipes that I have given in this section are largely pioneer breads, that have been enjoyed in North America for a century or more. Since then, of course, many different races have come into both countries, enriching their culture and their cuisine. They have all had their own ethnic breads, some of which are to be found elsewhere in this book. Here, however, must be included the Bagel. Bagels first came from Austria, where they were called Beugeln, which means rings. You will probably never find them now in an Austrian cookery book, but they are certainly to be found wherever there is a Jewish community. They are popular in both the United States and also in Australia. Like Pretzels (see page 39), Bagels are poached briefly before they are boiled, giving them a firm, light texture and a shiny, golden brown surface. They are usually eaten sliced through the middle to give two ring shapes, buttered and, classically, spread with cream cheese and topped with smoked fish. The halves are also good toasted.

Salt Risin' Bread

To make one 2-pound loaf:

¼ cup plus 2 tablespoons (1¾ ounces) cornmeal
2 teaspoons sugar
2 teaspoons salt
1 cup milk, boiling
3 cups all-purpose flour
½ teaspoon baking soda
2 tablespoons shortening

Place the cornmeal in a bowl with 1 teaspoon each of the sugar and salt. Pour on the boiling milk. Cover the bowl and leave it in a warm place for 12 hours. After this time the mixture should have bubbles in it.

Add 1 cup of the flour, the remaining salt and sugar and the baking soda. Leave the mixture in a warm, draft-free place for it to rise. (Old recipe books once recommended that the bowl should be stood in a larger bowl of hot water, and kept at a constant temperature by changing it and topping up. Nowadays, placing the mixture on the central heating boiler or by a wood-burning stove is adequate.) The mixture could take anything up to 3 hours to rise and may smell rather unpleasant, but don't be put off.

Bagels

To make sixteen Bagels:

1 cup milk, boiling
¼ cup (½ stick) butter
2 tablespoons superfine sugar
½ ounce fresh yeast or 2 teaspoons dried
½ teaspoon salt
1 egg, separated
3½ cups (14 ounces) all-purpose flour
poppy or sesame seeds, or coarse sea salt, optional

Pour the milk into a mixing bowl, stir in the butter and sugar and cool the mixture to lukewarm. Sprinkle in the yeast and leave it to stand – five minutes for fresh yeast and 15 minutes for dried. Stir in the salt and egg white and gradually beat in the flour to make a soft dough. Turn the dough on to a floured work surface and knead it until it is smooth. Return it to the bowl, cover it and leave it in a warm place for 1 hour or until it has doubled in size.

Knead the dough again and divide it into sixteen even-sized pieces. Form each one into a round. With one round on the work surface, flour your forefinger and gently press it through the middle of the

● *Salt Risin' Bread*

● *Bagels (see page 126)*

round. Then gently work it round in a circle to make a hole. Make the hole bigger by twirling the bagel round and round, until it makes up about one third of the diameter. When all the bagels are done, cover them with a clean cloth and leave them for 10 minutes.

For bagels, which are wet, you really need to grease your baking sheets to prevent them from sticking. Preheat the oven to 400°F. Bring a large pan of water to a boil and turn the heat to simmer so that the water is just trembling. Gently drop the bagels in the water, a few at a time so that there is no danger of their touching each other. Leave them in the water for about 15 seconds or until they begin to swell. Lift the bagels out with a wide, perforated spoon and place them on the prepared baking sheets.

Bake the bagels for 20 minutes, or until they are golden-brown. Transfer them to wire racks to cool.

The idea of making a sourdough to leaven bread must have come originally with settlers from northern Europe. It was readily taken up throughout America, but never more so than in Alaska where the prospectors carried their ball of sourdough starter wherever they went. Sourdough bread was their staple food and they eventually became known as "sourdoughs" themselves. A popular way of carrying the starter was to make a hollow for it inside a sack of flour, where it would keep warm. When the time came to make a batch of bread, water was poured into the hollow to mix with the starter and surrounding flour to make a soft dough. Most of the dough was taken out and baked and a little left behind to form a new starter.

The following bread is a modern sourdough bread that is sometimes called San Francisco sourdough. It uses not only sourdough but yeast and baking soda as well! "If two out of three fail then the third may work," seems to be the philosophy, but it makes a loaf that is soft and rich, with a characteristic sour-sweet flavor.

Sourdough

To make one large or two small loaves:

Starter:

1 cup (4 ounces) all-purpose flour
2 teaspoons sugar
1 cup water

Loaf:

1 ounce fresh yeast or 1 tablespoon dried
1½ cups warm water
6 cups (1½ pounds) all-purpose flour
2 teaspoons salt
2 teaspoons sugar
½ teaspoon baking soda

To make the starter, place the flour and sugar in a bowl and stir in the water. Cover the bowl and leave it in a warm place for 1 to 2 days, or until it begins to bubble and rise.

To make the loaf, pour the water into a mixing bowl and sprinkle over the yeast. Leave this to stand – five minutes for fresh yeast and 15 for dried. Stir in the starter, 4 cups of the flour, the salt and the sugar. Stir the mixture for 3 minutes, then cover it and leave it to rise for about 2 hours or until it has doubled in size.

Mix the baking soda with 1 cup of the remaining flour and stir it into the dough. Knead the dough on a floured board, adding the remaining flour as you do so. Shape the dough. Lay it on a floured baking sheet and leave it to rise for 20 minutes. Preheat the oven to 400°F. Bake two small loaves for 35 minutes and a single large loaf for 45 minutes. Cool them on a wire rack.

● *Bagel factory, Quebec, Canada*

The Scandinavians, Germans and eastern Europeans who came to Canada and America, brought with them a preference for rye bread, which is still popular today. The following recipe, made with yeast, is based on one which appeared in *The Original Boston Cooking School Book* by Fannie Farmer, which was first published in 1896.

Fannie Farmer's Rye Bread

To make one 2-pound loaf:

4 tablespoons warm water
½ cup scalded milk
¾ cup boiling water
3 tablespoons butter
2 tablespoons dark brown sugar
2 teaspoons salt
1 ounce fresh yeast or 1 tablespoon dried
1½ cups (6 ounces) all-purpose flour
3 cups (12 ounces) rye meal

In a large mixing bowl, sprinkle the yeast over the 4 tablespoons of water. Leave this to stand – five minutes for fresh yeast and 15 for dried. In another bowl, mix together the scalded milk and boiling water, and stir in the butter, sugar and salt. Cool the mixture to lukewarm and then stir it into the yeast. Stir in the flour and leave the mixture in a warm place for 30 minutes until it begins to bubble up the sides of the bowl. Add the rye meal and knead it in. Then knead the dough on a floured work surface. Return it to the bowl, cover it and leave it in a warm place for 1 hour or until it has doubled in size.

Preheat the oven to 400°F. Knead the dough again and form it into a rectangular loaf. Place it in a 2-pound loaf pan and leave it for 20 minutes in a warm place to rise. Bake the loaf for 45 minutes, or until it is golden-brown and sounds hollow when tapped. Cool it on a wire rack.

In eastern America, there were unlimited supplies of white flour, and yeast was used in preference to sourdough starters. The result of this was the development of more sophisticated bread recipes. The following buns were a favorite in Philadelphia. They are soft, sweet and spicy, with a sweet, dark-brown shiny top.

Philadelphia Sticky Buns

To make about eight buns:

1 ounce fresh yeast or 1 tablespoon dried
4 tablespoons warm water
1 cup warm milk
½ cup (1 stick) butter, softened
½ cup sugar
2 egg yolks
4½ cups (1 pound 2 ounces) all-purpose flour
1 teaspoon ground cinnamon
1 teaspoon salt

Filling and Glaze:

½ cup water
¾ cup dark brown sugar
1 tablespoon butter
3 ounces chopped walnuts or currants

In a large mixing bowl, sprinkle the fresh yeast over the water. Leave it to stand – five minutes for fresh yeast and 15 for dried. Stir in the milk, butter, sugar and egg yolks and then the flour, cinnamon and salt. Knead the mixture in the bowl (see page 13) until it is smooth. Cover it and leave it in a warm place for 1 hour to double in size.

To make the glaze, put the water, sugar and butter in a saucepan and stir them over low heat until the sugar and butter have dissolved.

Preheat the oven to 350°F. Butter a 10-inch-diameter cake pan. Knead the dough on a floured work surface and roll it into a rectangle 12 inches long and ½ inch thick. Gradually pour about half the sugar glaze over the surface. If you are using currants, sprinkle them all over the top; if chopped walnuts, then only sprinkle on two thirds of them. Quickly roll up the dough and cut it in 1-inch-thick slices. Pour the remaining glaze into the buttered pan and scatter in the remaining walnuts. Place the rolled slices of bun on top. Leave them in a warm place for 20 minutes to rise.

Bake the buns for 30 minutes, or until they are well browned on top. Turn the whole lot together on to a wire rack and leave them, sticky side up, to cool. To serve, gently ease the buns apart with a knife.

● *Parker House Rolls (see page 132)*

● *Harvesting in Minnesota, USA*

Small white rolls, in many shapes and sizes, became popular in America's fashionable restaurants. The Parker House Restaurant opened in Boston in 1855 and its Parker House rolls became essential fare at smart dinners all over the country. They are basically a light roll, enriched with milk, eggs and a little butter. Their chief distinction from any other type of roll is their folded shape.

Parker House Rolls

To make about twenty rolls:

1 ounce fresh yeast or 1 tablespoon dried
4 tablespoons warm water
1 cup warm milk
1 egg, beaten
4 cups (1 pound) all-purpose flour
1 teaspoon salt
2 tablespoons butter, melted

In a large mixing bowl, sprinkle the yeast over the warm water. Leave it to stand – five minutes for fresh yeast and 15 for dried. Stir in the milk and egg and then the flour and salt. Mix everything to a dough. Turn it on to a floured board and knead it. Return it to the bowl, cover it and leave it in a warm place for 1 hour or until it has doubled in size.

Preheat the oven to 400°F. Knead the dough again and roll it out to a thickness of about ½ inch. Stamp it into 3-inch rounds with a pastry cutter. Brush each with the butter. Using the back of a knife, make a deep groove across each round, then fold the round in half and press the edges together.

Place the rolls on floured baking sheets and leave them in a warm place for 20 minutes to rise. Bake them for 20 minutes, or until they are golden-brown. Cool them on wire racks.

Both the Canadians and the Americans are fond of sweet breads and it is very often difficult to distinguish what is bread and what is cake. There are many different recipes, both old and modern for what the British would call tea breads – sweetened breads, raised with soda and baking powder and containing dried fruits and nuts. One from Quebec, Canada, is mixed with beer and contains walnuts and dates; another, called Paradise lemon bread, can be found in households in Paradise Valley, Alberta, Moncton, New Brunswick and Montreal.

Muffins and doughnuts also fall in the middle ground between being cakes and being breads. The doughnut recipe below comes from a descendant of one of the Scottish communities who settled in Compton County in eastern Quebec in about 1840. Doughnuts were a favorite breakfast on both sides of the border. Eat these warm, either plain, or sprinkled with sugar or drizzled with warm maple syrup.

Old-fashioned Doughnuts

To make about thirty-six doughnuts:

1 cup sugar
2 tablespoons shortening or lard, melted
2 eggs, beaten
½ teaspoon pure vanilla extract
4½ cups (1 pound 2 ounces) plain cake flour
2 teaspoons baking powder
1 teaspoon baking soda
1 teaspoon salt
1 teaspoon ground nutmeg
1½ cups cultured buttermilk or sour milk
oil for deep frying

Place the sugar in a large mixing bowl and beat in the shortening or lard, eggs and vanilla extract. Mix the flour with the baking powder, baking soda, salt and nutmeg. Beat it into the sugar mixture, a little at a time, alternately with the buttermilk or sour milk. You should have a very moist dough. Place this dough, still in the bowl, in the refrigerator for 1 hour to chill and firm.

Turn the dough on to a floured work surface and coat it well with flour. Roll it out to a thickness of about ½ inch. Stamp it into 2½-inch rounds and stamp a ½-inch hole in the center of each one. You can use a doughnut cutter for this or a large and a small pastry cutter or, if you do not have a small enough pastry cutter, use an apple corer for the center hole. The dough will still be quite sticky, so flour the cutters well by dipping them in the flour bag and handle the cut doughnuts gently, lifting them with a palette knife. Keep your fingers well floured as well.

Heat a pan of oil over high heat. Place the doughnut rounds in the pan about three at a time. Cook them for about a minute, until they are golden-brown on one side. Turn them over and brown the other side. Lift them out with a slotted spoon and drain off the excess oil by placing them on paper towels.

Muffins

To make ten muffins:

1 cup (4 ounces) plain cake flour
1 cup (4 ounces) whole-wheat or graham flour
1 teaspoon salt
2 teaspoons baking powder
2 tablespoons dark brown sugar
1 cup milk
1 egg, beaten
3 tablespoons shortening, melted

Preheat the oven to 400°F. Place the flours in a bowl with the salt, baking powder and sugar. Make a well in the center and beat in the milk, egg and shortening. Mix to make a thick batter. Half fill 10 muffin pans or muffin cases with the mixture. Place on baking sheets. Bake the muffins for 20 minutes or until they are risen and cooked through.

Another sweet specialty is muffins. The muffins in Fannie Farmer's cookbook are very similar to English Muffins, made with a moist dough and cooked on a griddle. However, over the years, traditional American muffins have developed.

In a book called *Breads and More Breads*, compiled in 1941 from recipes submitted by cooks all over America, there are no fewer than thirty variations in flavorings, some of which, for example ketchup, pickle, or pepper relish, sound rather odd. Others, such as banana, sweet corn or spice, sound delicious. Here is the basic muffin recipe, plus a few suggestions.

Variations and Flavorings:
- use all-purpose flour or all whole-wheat or graham flour.
- add 4 ounces raw blueberries.
- add 4 ounces raw cranberries, halved and mixed with ⅓ cup confectioners' sugar.
- gently stew 1 large, chopped cooking apple to a purée with ¼ cup sugar and add this to the mixture.
- add 4 ounces raisins, or chopped dates.
- add 3 ounces chopped nuts.
- add 3 ounces chocolate chips.
- add 4 ounces grated cheese.
- add 4 ounces chopped, fried bacon.

• *Old-fashioned Doughnuts*

CENTRAL AND SOUTH AMERICA

The Spanish conquered Mexico some five hundred years ago, and were amazed at many of the things they found – including the food. There were previously unknown vegetables and fruits, chocolate that was used to flavor not just drinks but rich meat dishes as well, and the most important energy provider in the diet of the native South American Indians – corn.

Corn was so essential to the lives of the Mayans that they even believed that man had been created from corn dough. Later, explorers found corn in Cuba, where it was grown in small fields and called something which sounded like "may-ees" by the local population. To the Europeans, it therefore became "maize."

Maize had been developed by the native Indians of Central and South America from a variety of coarse grass which is now extinct. It bore small, inch-long ears, each wrapped in a separate husk, and had edible kernels similar to very small peas. By the time the Spaniards arrived, the Indians had developed hundreds of different varieties to suit all climates and altitudes – among them white, yellow, red and black corn, sweet corn and popcorn. There are even more varieties known today: some are best for drying and grinding into flour and others for eating.

Corn or maize meal differs from flour made with wheat in that it contains only very small amounts of gluten and other protein. However, the Indians overcame this by adding accompanying foods. Freshly-prepared maize meal was made into flat, unleavened breads, similar to the early European hearth cakes. Once cooked, these cakes were typically wrapped around nutritious foods such as beans, meat or fish, so providing the constituents of a healthy diet. These cakes are called tortillas, and they are the same today as they were five hundred years ago.

Tortillas are Mexico's national bread. The name comes from the Spanish, meaning "little cakes." The Indians originally called them long, complicated names, according to the type of corn used in them. White corn tortillas were *iztactlaolli*, and those made from black corn were *yauhtlaolli*. It was much easier to call them all tortillas and, as the languages and races blended, the name became universal.

The Indians developed the technique for making tortillas centuries ago. The first process involves soaking the corn kernels in a solution of lime. The kernels swell considerably and the husks loosen, to form a mixture known as *nixtamal*. This is then pounded and ground to a paste or moist dough, called *masa*.

Every Mexican woman once knew how to shape and fashion a tortilla. She would take a small ball of masa dough, about the size of a golf ball, and pat it between her hands until it was thin and flat, before transferring it to a hot griddle. It is said that the early morning sound of Mexico was the patting of tortillas for breakfast.

Nowadays, tortillas are still prepared by hand, but there are also tortilla factories and tortilla stores which provide them in various stages of making. The masa is rarely prepared at home, but can be bought, moist and freshly prepared. For those without the time or experience to fashion the dough, a tortilla press can be used, or tortillas can be bought already shaped but uncooked, or completely cooked and ready to eat.

● *Lime-soaked maize for tortillas*

It is impossible to buy fresh masa in most countries outside of Latin America, but masa harina, dried masa, is available in specialty food stores and those selling Mexican goods. The best brand is the white masa harina, produced and packaged by the Quaker Oats company.

In the recipe below, the amount of water you need may vary with the type of masa you are able to get.

Tortillas de Maiz

To make twelve 6-inch corn tortillas:

2 cups masa harina
1¼ cups warm water

Place the masa harina in a bowl and make a well in the center. Add the water a little at a time and check the consistency of the dough. It should hold together and be moist enough to handle and roll without pieces crumbling away. Leave the dough in the bowl, cover it with a clean, dry cloth and let it rest for 15 minutes. This makes it more workable.

Form the dough in twelve pieces about the size of golf balls. Place one piece in the palm of your left hand and begin to pat it with your right (or the other way round if you are left handed). As the tortilla begins to get larger, turn it round a little and pat it from hand to hand, gently pushing the edges round the bottom of your palm. (Apparently Mexican women used to make very thin, large tortillas by stretching them over their knee!) Continue doing this until you have a 6-inch round. After several tortillas you will begin to get the knack but, if it still proves impossible, put the ball of dough between two pieces of plastic wrap and roll it with a rolling pin.

Heat an ungreased griddle over low heat. Place one tortilla at a time on the griddle and cook it for about one minute on each side or until it is cooked through and the sides look dry and speckled brown. Lay a clean, dry cloth over a large plate. Lay the tortilla on it and cover it up while you cook the next. Build up a pile of tortillas on the plate, covering them up each time.

Serve the tortillas warm. If you want to make them in advance you can wrap them in plastic wrap and store them in the refrigerator. To reheat them, sprinkle them lightly with a few drops of water and place them on the griddle again.

There are variations on the plain tortilla. To make black tortillas, for example, you can replace plain water with the liquid left from cooking black beans plus some of the beans mashed up. Blue tortillas are made in Mexico from special blue-black colored corn kernels. You may not fancy this, but a spiced tortilla is another matter and easily made by adding chili powder and paprika to the dough.

Once you have made your tortillas, you have a passport to many different and exciting meals. The first thing to remember is that tortillas are both your food and your eating utensils. Numerous foods from around the world can be folded into a tortilla – in Mexico, even soup.

Tortillas can also be made into tacos, tostadas, tostaditas, enchiladas and quesadillas.

TACOS: These are basically tortillas wrapped around a savory filling. You can leave the tortillas soft, or fold and deep fry them to make a crisp, filled package.

TOSTADAS: Deep fry whole tortillas, stack them on a plate with spiced and savory fillings in between and fresh salad vegetables on the top.

TOSTADITAS: Cut the tortillas in wedges and deep fry them to accompany dips, salads and savory meat and bean dishes.

ENCHILADAS: Day-old tortillas are first softened by being dipped for a few seconds on each side in hot oil. After this they can be dipped in a spiced sauce, but this is not always the case. They are rolled around a savory filling, a sauce is poured over them and they are baked in the oven.

QUESADILLAS: Uncooked tortillas are wrapped around a filling of cheese before being fried in oil or on a griddle.

If you cannot find any masa harina, you can make *Tortillas de Harina* (wheat-flour tortillas). These are popular in the northern area of Sonora and also in the extreme southwest of the United States. They are often served with robustly-flavored dishes of meat or with refried beans. When, along with the beans, they also contain crumbled Mexican cheese, raw onion and a spicy sauce, they are known as burritos. A flour tortilla, rolled around a filling and deep fried is called a chimichanga and this can be either savory or filled with a sweet fruit mixture.

Tortillas de Harina

To make ten 6-inch tortillas:
2 cups (8 ounces) plain cake flour
1 teaspoon salt
1 teaspoon baking powder
¼ cup lard
¾ cup hot water

Place the flour in a bowl with the salt and baking powder and rub in the lard. Make a well in the center and pour in the water. Mix everything to a dough and knead it lightly in the bowl. Cover it and let it rest for 10 minutes.

Form the dough into ten round pieces. Roll each piece in flour and flour your hands well. Using the method above for *Tortillas de Maiz*, pat each piece of dough into a 6-inch round.

Heat an ungreased griddle over medium heat. Lay a tortilla on the griddle and cook it until the surface begins to bubble and the underside is speckled brown. Turn it over and brown the second side. Stack them under a cloth as they are done and eat them warm.

● *Pan Dulce*

When the Spaniards brought wheat flour to Mexico, it was readily taken up by the Indians, who learned to make bread in the European fashion. There are over two thousand breads and biscuits in present day Mexico, divided into *bolillo* (plain bread) and *concha* (sweet breads and biscuits). Plain wheat flour is the main ingredient and most of the flours are what are known as "smooth," or similar to plain cake flour. Stronger flours, however, are beginning to be imported.

These *bolillos* are the everyday rolls served in town restaurants. They are soft and sweet, much sweeter than ordinary bread rolls.

are many of them, each with their own name. They are served in hotels and cafés for breakfast and can be bought at markets and in the *panaderias* or local bakeries.

The following recipe for *pan dulce* produces buns that are soft and very sweet with a golden-brown topping similar to a crumble.

Whole-wheat flour is used on a small scale in Mexico. The *semitas* buns are really good, with a faintly spicy flavor and a dark, shiny top.

Bolillos

To make twelve rolls:

1 ounce fresh yeast or 1 tablespoon dried
1¾ cups warm water
2 teaspoons salt
2 tablespoons sugar
5 cups (1 pound 4 ounces) all-purpose flour
¼ cup lard, softened

In a small bowl, sprinkle the yeast over about one third of the water and leave it – five minutes for fresh yeast and 15 for dried. Stir the salt and sugar into the remaining water. Place the flour in a mixing bowl. Make a well in the center and pour in the yeast mixture and the salted and sugared water. Add the lard, in small pieces. Mix everything to a dough. Turn it on to a floured board and knead it until it is smooth. Return the dough to the bowl, cover it and leave it in a warm place for 1 hour or until it has doubled in size.

Preheat the oven to 375°F. Knead the dough again and divide it in twelve pieces. Form each piece into a rectangle and then point each end. Lay the rolls on floured baking sheets and leave them in a warm place for 20 minutes to rise. Bake them for 20 minutes, or until they are golden-brown. Cool them on wire racks.

The Mexicans have a very sweet tooth. The Indians kept bees for honey and produced corn syrup from some varieties of corn, but sweet breads weren't made until sugar cane, brought by the Spaniards, became widely grown. Columbus planted the first sugar cane in South America and the first large sugar-cane producer in Mexico was Hernán Cortez. It is now grown all over the country on a large scale, with small patches grown by peasant farmers and taken to old-fashioned cane mills in the villages for local use. Sweet breads are called *pan dulce* and there

Pan Dulce

To make twelve small buns:

½ ounce fresh yeast or 2 teaspoons dried
½ cup, plus 2 tablepoons, warm water
3½ cups (14 ounces) all-purpose flour
1 teaspoon salt
½ cup sugar
2 tablespoons lard, softened
2 eggs, beaten

Icing:

¼ cup lard or shortening
⅓ cup confectioners' sugar
1 egg
4 tablespoons light cream
¾ cup (3 ounces) plain cake flour
1 teaspoon ground cinnamon

In a large mixing bowl, mix the yeast with the water and leave it – five minutes for fresh yeast, 15 for dried. Add 2 cups of the flour and the salt. Cover and leave for about 30 minutes to rise. Beat in the remaining flour, the sugar, lard and eggs. Mix everything to a dough. Turn it on to a floured board and knead it until it is smooth. Return it to the bowl, cover it and leave it in a warm place for 1 hour or until it has doubled in size.

To make the icing, beat the lard or shortening with the sugar. Beat the egg with the cream and mix the flour with the cinnamon. Beat these mixtures, alternately and a little at a time, into the sugar and lard.

Preheat the oven to 350°F. Knead the dough again and make it into twelve small, round buns. Spread the icing over the buns and place them on floured baking sheets. Leave them in a warm place for 20 minutes to rise. Bake them for 20 minutes, or until they are golden-brown. Cool them on wire racks.

Semitas

To make sixteen small buns:

1 ounce fresh yeast or 1 tablespoon dried

¾ cup warm water, plus 4 tablespoons

2½ cups (10 ounces) whole-wheat flour

2½ cups (10 ounces) all-purpose flour

1 teaspoon ground cinnamon

¾ cup dark brown sugar

¾ cup warm milk

¼ cup lard, softened

In a small bowl, sprinkle the yeast over ¾ cup of water and leave it five minutes for fresh yeast, 15 for dried. Place the flour in a large mixing bowl and add the cinnamon and half the sugar. Make a well in the center and pour in the yeast mixture and the milk. Add the lard. Mix everything to a dough. Turn it on to a floured work surface and knead it until it is smooth. Return it to the bowl, cover it and leave it in a warm place for 1 hour or until it has doubled in size.

Preheat the oven to 375°F. Knead the dough again and form it into sixteen small round buns. Place them on floured baking sheets and leave them in a warm place for 20 minutes to rise.

To make the glaze, place the remaining sugar and 4 tablespoons water into a small saucepan and set over low heat. Stir it until the

● *Peineta*

sugar has dissolved and then bring to a boil. Take the pan from the heat and keep the glaze warm.

Bake the buns for 20 minutes, or until they are golden-brown, and lift them on to wire racks. Brush them immediately with the dark sugar glaze and leave them to cool.

There are many festivals in Mexico and each has its own special bread. There are breads for religious occasions, such as Holy Week bread, in the form of small rolls. On Palm Sunday each person puts one roll, together with medicinal herbs, the local wine and sometimes money, into a basket and takes it as an offering to church. A bread called *las cueglas* is made for weddings. The most popular special bread of all, however, is *pan de muertos* (bread of the dead) which is baked for the Day of the Dead celebrated on the 1st and 2nd of November. It is a rich, soft, sweet bread, decorated with dough shapes, either of bones, animals or plants.

Pan de Muertos

To make one loaf:

1/2 ounce fresh yeast or 2 teaspoons dried
3/4 cup warm milk
3 cups (12 ounces) all-purpose flour
1 teaspoon salt
grated rind 1/4 orange
1/2 teaspoon ground anise
3 tablespoons sugar
1/4 cup (1/2 stick) butter, softened
1 egg
2 egg yolks
2 eggs, beaten, plus 2 teaspoons sugar

In a small bowl, sprinkle the yeast over half the milk and leave it – five minutes for fresh, 15 for dried. Place the flour in a large mixing bowl with the salt, orange rind, anise and 3 tablespoons sugar. Make a well in the center, pour in the remaining milk and add one egg and the yolks, the butter and the yeast mixture. Mix everything to a dough. Turn it on to a floured board and knead it until it is smooth. Return it to the bowl, cover it and leave it in a warm place for 1 hour, or until it has doubled in size.

Preheat the oven to 350°F. Knead the dough again and divide it in two pieces of one third and two thirds. Form the larger piece

into a ball and put it on to a floured baking sheet. Divide the smaller piece in three. Roll two of these into long sausage shapes that will lie over the top of the ball from side to side. Mold the ends of each one to form them into depressed knob shapes, like the ends of long bones. Lay the "bones" over the bread in a cross. Form the remaining piece into a skull shape and place it in the center of the bone cross. Leave the loaf in a warm place for 20 minutes to rise. Brush it with the beaten egg and sprinkle it with sugar. Bake the loaf for 30 minutes, or until it is golden-brown. Cool it on a wire rack.

Besides the many small buns, there are large breads in many different shapes. There are, for example, round egg breads decorated with a face of flour paste. This comb-shaped bread looks extremely attractive. It is rich and soft with a thin golden crust and is excellent with jelly and preserves.

Peineta

To make one loaf:

1/2 ounce fresh yeast or 2 teaspoons dried
1/2 cup warm water
1/4 cup, plus 2 tablespoons, warm milk
2 tablespoons lard, softened
1 tablespoon sugar
1 egg, beaten
3 cups (12 ounces) all-purpose flour
1 teaspoon salt

In a large mixing bowl, sprinkle the yeast over the water and leave it – five minutes for fresh yeast and 15 for dried. Add the milk, lard, sugar and egg. Mix the flour with the salt and stir it into the bowl. Mix everything to a dough, turn it on to a floured work surface and knead it until it is smooth. Return it to the bowl, cover it and leave it in a warm place for 1 hour or until it has doubled in size.

Preheat the oven to 350°F. Knead the dough again. Form it into a neat ball and then roll it flat into a round about 9 inches in diameter and 3/4 inch thick. With a sharp knife make 3/4-inch-long cuts all round the edge of the dough 1/2 inch apart. Fold the round in half so that one edge overlaps the other by about 3/4 inch. Lift the loaf on to a floured baking sheet and ease the corners round so that it becomes a crescent shape and the segments at the edges spread apart. Leave the loaf in a warm place for 20 minutes to rise. Bake it for 30 minutes, or until it is golden-brown. Cool it on a wire rack.

THE WEST INDIES

The West Indies form a chain that stretches from Cuba, off the Florida peninsula, to Trinidad, off central America – separating the Caribbean sea from the Atlantic. They were first discovered by Christopher Columbus, in 1492, who marveled at their beauty and their abundance of native fruits and spices. The generous islands were home to a generous and gentle people who were very soon exploited by Europeans. The Spanish, Portuguese, French and Dutch all scrambled to claim islands as their own and to take a share in their riches.

The Carib Indians combined hunting and gathering with farming. The islands were rich in fruits, nuts, hot and sweet peppers, avocados and spices, and the cooking of the Islands still utilizes these to the full. The staple of the Indians' diet was cassava bread, which is still made by the Indians who survive on the Windward Island of Dominica. Cassava is a starchy tuber, also called *manioc*. There are two types, sweet and bitter. Raw cassava can be poisonous, but the preparation and cooking process renders it harmless. To make cassava bread, the tubers are first peeled and then grated, either using a homemade grater or, increasingly, a food processor or blender. After grating, the cassava was once put into what was known as a cassava canoe, a wooden container very similar to the dug-out canoes of the Indians. However it is laid out, the grated cassava is left to stand for a while and is then squeezed in a cloth to extract the acidic juices. Sun-drying is the next process, before the cassava is ground to make meal. The meal is then mixed with water to make flat cakes which are cooked on the equivalent of a griddle and once more left to dry in the sun.

● *A bakery in the Dominican Republic*

Cassava bread is also commercially made and it can be bought throughout the West Indies and the United States, in places where there are large ethnic populations. Apparently it has an earthy flavor and it can be eaten plain or, as in Jamaica, fried for breakfast.

Although the foods of the Islands were abundant, they were not sufficient to feed the growing European population. The new inhabitants sent for flour, wine, vinegar, oil and meat. They brought in plants and began growing new crops: breadfruit, oranges, limes, mangoes, rice, coffee and, most importantly, sugar cane. Workers were needed to harvest it and so African slaves were shipped to the Islands, bringing with them their own foods and methods of cooking. Okra, taro, callaloo and akee were added to the crops of the islands. The Africans soon discovered the spices and hot peppers of the Caribs and used them to flavor the poor food on which they were fed, so adding yet another aspect to Caribbean cooking.

After the slaves were freed they no longer wished to work in the plantations, and so their previous owners looked elsewhere for cheap labor. They found it in the East. Chinese, East Indians and Indians from the Indian continent all came to work with the sugar. They brought with them curries, flat breads and a preference for rice.

As in most countries, much everyday bread is now commercially made, but there are still many housewives who enjoy baking specialty breads. A great favorite for home baking are the sweet, quick breads, many of which combine ingredients and methods from all over the world. The main flour is wheat flour, but it may well be mixed with maize, cassava flour, breadfruit flour or banana flour.

Coconut bread uses the native coconuts, European flour, baking powder and butter, plus locally grown sugar. Coconuts on the Islands are very much moister than they are by the time they have been shipped to North America or to Europe, and if you use a fresh one you will get a far better flavor and texture than if you buy a packet of desiccated coconut. This bread is moist and not too sweet, with a rich coconut flavor. Serve it plain as a light snack.

Coconut Bread

To make one 2-pound loaf:
1 small coconut
2 cups (8 ounces) plain cake flour
2 teaspoons baking powder
½ teaspoon each of ground cinnamon and cloves or 1 teaspoon pure vanilla extract
½ teaspoon salt
½ cup sugar
½ cup (1 stick) unsalted butter, melted
¼ cup, plus 2 tablespoons, coconut water
¼ cup, plus 2 tablespoons, evaporated milk
3 ounces raisins, optional

Preheat the oven to 350°F. Skewer two eyes of the coconut and pour out the coconut water into a jug. Break open the coconut with a heavy hammer. Take out the flesh and peel away the outer brown skin with a potato peeler. Grate the white flesh, either by hand or in a food processor.

Place the flour, baking powder, spices (if using them), salt and sugar in a bowl and toss them together. Mix in the grated coconut. Make a well in the center and add the butter and vanilla extract. Gradually beat in the coconut water and evaporated milk. Mix in the raisins, if you are using them.

Place the mixture in a greased, 2-pound loaf pan. Bake the bread for 40 minutes or until it is golden-brown and a skewer inserted in the center comes out clean.

The native banana is used all over the Caribbean Islands in both sweet and savory dishes. Bananas are put in stews, fried, flamed and baked in their skins. In Jamaica, ripe bananas are made into banana bread, a delicious moist, sweet bread, best eaten plain. Banana bread is also, of course, extremely popular in parts of the United States.

Banana Bread

To make one 2-pound loaf:

½ cup (1 stick) unsalted butter
½ cup sugar
1 egg, beaten
2 cups (8 ounces) plain cake flour
1 tablespoon baking powder
½ teaspoon salt
½ teaspoon ground nutmeg
1 pound ripe bananas
1 teaspoon pure vanilla extract
2 ounces raisins
2 ounces pecan nuts, chopped

Preheat the oven to 350°F. In a large bowl, cream together the butter and sugar and gradually beat in the egg. Mix together the flour, baking powder, salt and nutmeg. Peel and mash the bananas. Beat the flour and the bananas alternately into the butter and sugar, beating and blending well. Mix in the vanilla extract, raisins and the chopped pecan nuts. Place the mixture in a greased, 2-pound loaf pan. Bake the loaf for 50 minutes or until a skewer inserted into the center comes out clean.

Sweet corn is indigenous to the area. The native Indians used to cook it with water and leave the mixture to firm, in the same way as polenta is made in Italy. It was then cut into shapes and fried. The Africans now make a similar dish called fungee or funchi.

This corn bread comes from Dominica and, again, it contains ingredients from all sections of the population. There is European flour and baking powder plus local spices and coconut, and limes (that were first planted in the sixteenth century). It is a delicious bread. The basic mixture is not too sweet and it has that wonderful, crumbly, slightly grainy yet chewy texture, similar to a crumble topping on fruit, and it is full of moist, sweet coconut and dried fruits. The method may be rather long-winded, but it really is worth making it.

• *Loaves and joined buns, Haiti*

● *Banana Bread*

● *Market at Port au Prince, Haiti*

Pan Dulce de Harina de Maiz

To make one 2-pound loaf:

1 small coconut
1½ cups (6 ounces) cornmeal
½ cup (2 ounces) plain cake flour
1 tablespoon baking powder
½ teaspoon ground cinnamon
½ teaspoon ground nutmeg
½ teaspoon ground cloves
¼ cup sugar
½ teaspoon salt
grated rind 1 lime or lemon
3 tablespoons butter
3 tablespoons lard
2 eggs, beaten
4 ounces raisins, golden raisins and citrus fruit peel, mixed

Skewer the "eyes" of the coconut and drain out the water. Break the coconut. Peel it, using a potato peeler, extract all the white flesh, and grate it. Reserve 1 cup of the grated coconut. To make what is known as coconut milk, place the rest of the coconut in a blender, pour on an equal volume of hot, but not boiling, water and blend until you have a smooth, white liquid. Strain it through a sieve, pressing down hard. This is far more than you will need for the recipe, but you can keep the remainder in the refrigerator for up to two days and use it for making curries.

Preheat the oven to 350°F. Mix together all the dry ingredients, including the sugar and the lime rind. In a large mixing bowl, cream together the butter and lard and gradually beat in the dry mixture. Beat in ¼ cup, plus 2 tablespoons, of the coconut milk and the two eggs. Mix in the grated coconut and the fruits and peels. Place the mixture into a greased 2-pound loaf pan. It will come half to three-quarters of the way up the sides. Bake the loaf for 35 minutes, or until it is golden-brown and a skewer inserted into the center comes out clean.

When the Europeans first sent for flour, they used it to make the breads to which they were accustomed, risen with yeast and with as much white flour as possible. These dinner rolls sound very English. You can imagine a planter's family sitting down to dinner with a roll beside each plate.

Dinner Rolls

To make twelve rolls:

1 ounce fresh yeast or 1 tablespoon dried
4 tablespoons warm water
1 cup warm milk
2 teaspoons sugar
1 teaspoon salt
2 tablespoons shortening
4 cups (1 pound) all-purpose flour

● *Pan Dulce de Harina de Maiz*

In a large mixing bowl, sprinkle the yeast over the warm water and leave it to stand – five minutes for fresh yeast and 15 for dried. Stir in the milk, sugar, salt and shortening. Add the flour and mix everything to a dough. Turn it on to a floured work surface and knead it until it is smooth. Return it to the bowl, cover it and leave it for about 1 hour or until it has doubled in size.

Preheat the oven to 400°F. Knead the dough again. Divide it in twelve pieces and form each one into a round or oval roll. Lay the rolls on floured baking sheets and leave them in a warm place for 20 minutes to rise.

Bake the rolls for 20 minutes or until they are golden-brown. Cool them on wire racks.

● *Floats*

Another very European bread which arrived in the nineteenth century is the *pan de Majorca*. In 1848, an immigrant from Majorca opened up La Mallorquina restaurant in San Juan, Puerto Rico, and started to make the rolls that in his native country were called *enseimadas* – sweet rolls enriched with lard and dusted with sugar. Every morning, a plate of freshly-baked *enseimadas* were placed on the breakfast table. They came to be known as *pan de Majorca* and can now be bought from bakers' stores in San Juan.

Pan serra, a very close-textured loaf, is the specialty of Curaçao where it is served with the rich fish stew called *sopito*. It is apparently ideal for soaking up the last remnants in the bowl.

Modern breads of the Western world have spread to all countries and the standard brown and white yeasted breads are commercially baked in most of the Islands. Baking bread dough is not, however, the only thing that you can do with it. You can also deep fry it. Floats are deep-fried circles of rich dough that puff up and become crisp and golden. In Trinidad they are the accompaniment to *accra*, cakes made with salt-fish and batter. *Accra* and floats, you could say, is the Trinidadian equivalent of the British fish and chips.

The Indians brought with them their own flat breads. The *chapati* changed over the years to become what are now called *roti* (which simply means bread), 10-inch-diameter flat cakes which are cooked on a griddle. Traditionally, they are served with curries. The Indian population provides the food for the local carnival in Port of Spain. They prepare *roti* literally by the stack, and fill them with spoonfuls of savory mixtures such as beef stewed in tomatoes, potato curry and split-pea purée.

Roti are soft with a buttery outside. In Jamaica, the Indians would use their authentic ghee, a butter that has been clarified. You can clarify butter by melting and skimming it, but you can simply use plain melted butter.

Floats

To make twenty floats:

½ ounce fresh yeast or 2 teaspoons dried
1½ cups warm water
4 cups (1 pound) plain cake flour
1 teaspoon salt
½ cup lard
oil for deep frying

In a small bowl, sprinkle the yeast over about ½ cup of the water. Place the flour and salt in a large mixing bowl and rub in the lard. Make a well in the center and pour in the yeast mixture and the remaining water. Mix everything to a dough. Turn it on to a floured work surface and knead it until it is smooth. Return it to the bowl, cover it and leave it in a warm place for 45 minutes, or until it has doubled in size.

Knead the dough again and divide it in 20 small balls about 1½ inches in diameter. Place them on a floured board or baking sheet, cover them and leave them in a warm place for 45 minutes, or until they have doubled in size. Without any further kneading, roll each ball into a flat round about 3 inches in diameter. Heat a pan of deep oil over high heat. Put in the floats, one at a time, and fry them for about 1 minute on each side until they are golden-brown and puffy. Drain them on paper towels and serve them warm.

Roti

To make about four roti:

2 cups (8 ounces) plain cake flour
1 teaspoon baking powder
1 teaspoon salt
3 tablespoons butter or shortening
½ cup, plus 2 tablespoons, cold water
⅓ cup butter or ghee, melted

Place the flour, baking powder and salt in a bowl and rub in the butter or shortening. Make a well in the center and add the water, a little at a time, to make a stiff dough. Place the dough on a floured work surface and knead it until it is smooth. Return it to the bowl, cover it and let it rest in a warm place for 30 minutes.

Knead the dough again and divide it in four pieces. Form each one into a ball and then roll it into a 10-inch round. Fold the round in half and then in half again. Leave the folded rounds for 15 minutes. This makes the *roti* firm and easy to handle. Using your hands and a rolling pin, roll the folded pieces once more into circles.

Heat a griddle over medium heat. Place one *roti* on the griddle and cook it for 1 minute so that it is dry, but not at all colored on the underside. Turn it over and brush it with the ghee or butter. Cook it for about three minutes longer, brushing on more ghee after the first 2 minutes. The top will bubble and sizzle. Turn the *roti* over and finish cooking the first side for about 2 minutes, or until it just begins to brown. The *roti* should be firm and pliable. Should the outside be too crisp, lay the *roti* on a work surface and bang it with a wooden spoon or wooden mallet to make the outside flaky.

Place the *roti* on a clean, dry cloth and fold the sides of the cloth over it. Cook the other *roti* in the same way, adding them to the first one inside the cloth as they are done.

THE MIDDLE EAST
(INCLUDING GREECE AND TURKEY, EGYPT, TUNISIA AND MOROCCO)

*There are many different peoples and cultures, three different religions and a wide variety of
foods in the area that we now call the Middle East.*

*There has never been an official agreement as to where the Middle East begins and ends, but
when, for the purposes of the Second World War, the British moved their Middle East
Command to Egypt, the term came to include the countries that are at the eastern end of the
Mediterranean, including Greece, Turkey and Cyprus.*

*The northern North African countries, Morocco, Algeria, Tunisia, Libya and Egypt, share
many of the same cooking styles and they too have been included in this section.*

148

The foods common to most of these countries are olives and their oil, beans, lentils and lamb. There is a preference for yogurt rather than for fresh milk, and the main source of carbohydrates is bread made from wheat flour. Rice comes a close second, but bread, or *khobz*, as it is called in so many of the countries, is eaten more than meat, vegetables or fruit, and its consumption is rising even now. In the Middle East, bread has kept its traditional characteristics – and in many of the countries the white sliced loaf, so common throughout the Western world, has never been popular.

Bread is seen in many Middle Eastern countries as a gift from God, and if any piece is found on the floor it is picked up with reverence and put into a place where it will not be trodden on. Indeed, housewives baking bread say a prayer before kneading and again before putting their bread into the oven, to make sure that it will be successful.

Bread is eaten with every meal. Flat breads are folded over ingredients, to become both eating utensil and food. Thicker breads are dipped into the communal pot to soak up the gravy and rich juices, and pockets of bread are filled with a variety of meats, beans and fresh salad vegetables. Leftover breads are diced, crumbled or toasted to make a base for a variety of dishes.

There are hundreds of different breads in the Middle East and North Africa, but the most common, and also the oldest, is *lavash*, a thin, slightly crispy bread which is baked in ovals and rounds of varying sizes, even up to 24 inches wide.

Because *lavash* is crisp, it lasts for a long time; and in many households enough is made to last a family for up to four months, wrapped in linen for storage. *Lavash* is normally baked in a clay oven called a *tonir*, which is similar to the Indian tandoor, but when made out in the open, it is cooked on a *saj*, a cast-iron dome that is heated from underneath with a fire of wood chips and camel dung.

Lavash can be baked with all-purpose flour, whole-wheat flour or a mixture. Serve it plain with curries or other hot dishes, with dips, or buttered with a salad.

● *Flat breads made for a wedding, Turkey*

149

● *Lavash*

Lavash

To make ten Lavash:

1 ounce fresh yeast or 1 tablespoon dried

1¼ cups warm water

4 cups (1 pound) plain cake flour

1½ teaspoons salt

In a small bowl, sprinkle the yeast over half the water. Place the flour and salt in a mixing bowl and make a well in the center. Pour in the yeast mixture and remaining water. Mix everything to a dough, turn it on to a floured work surface and knead it well. Return it to the bowl, cover it with a cloth and leave it in a warm place for 1 to 1½ hours or until it has doubled in size.

Preheat the oven to 400°F. Knead the dough again, divide it into ten equal pieces and form them into balls. Roll each ball into a flat round, 8 to 10 inches in diameter. Prick each one all over with a fork. Line a baking sheet with aluminum foil and put it in the very bottom of the oven to heat. Lay one of the dough rounds on the foil and put it in the oven for 3 minutes or until it is cooked through and bubbly. Wrap the bread in a clean, dry cloth and cook the others in the same way, adding them to the first one as they are done. Serve the lavash warm.

The second most popular bread is *khobz Arabi*, literally Arab bread, and this has become well-known in the West in recent years as pita bread, from the Armenian variation of *khobz Arabi* known as *pideh*. *Khobz Arabi* can be made with white flour, whole-wheat flour or a mixture. This is the recipe that I have been using for many years.

Khobz Arabi

To make eight pita breads:

basic bread dough (see page 12) made with 4 cups all-purpose or whole-wheat flour or half and half

Mix and knead the dough and leave it to rise for 1 hour. Preheat the oven to 450°F. Knead the dough again and divide it in eight pieces. Roll each piece into an oval of 5 × 8 inches. Leave the pieces covered with a cloth and let them rise for 20 minutes.

Flour enough baking sheets to take all the breads and place them in the oven for 5 minutes so they become really hot. Lay the breads on the baking sheets and put them in the oven for 15 minutes, or until they are only just beginning to brown.

If the breads are to be served immediately, wrap them in a clean cloth to keep them warm. You can also cool them on wire racks and warm them under the grill when needed.

● *Sifting grain (left) and baking (center) in Cyprus. Stall in Istanbul, Turkey (right)*

GREECE

Many people regard Greece as being a Western country, but most of its influences, including culinary ones, have come from the East. Pita bread has become almost synonymous with Greek food in recent years. The other Greek everyday bread is a crusty plain loaf, sometimes round and sometimes oval, golden-brown and often sprinkled with sesame seeds.

The main religion in Greece is Orthodox Christianity and the highlight of the Orthodox year is Easter. During the seven weeks of Lent, devout Christians in Greece abstain from meat and fish and sometimes also eggs, butter, milk and cheese. Easter, then, is a time of great feasting as well as religious celebration. To accompany the Easter lamb there are salads, yogurt, feta cheese, hard-cooked eggs dyed red, and the special, rich bread called *tsoureki*. Tsoureki is baked in many different shapes, the most common of which is the spiral with a red egg in the center.

I must admit that I wondered about baking a hard-cooked egg, but I needn't have worried. The egg nestled comfortably in the dough and didn't explode, but made the loaf look rather turban-like when it came from the oven. The bread itself is soft, rich and sweet and, personally, I prefer the lemon flavoring to the caraway. We divided the egg up. It tasted just like a hard-cooked egg, except that the part that stood up from the dough was slightly browned on top and tougher than ordinary boiled white. *Tsoureki* makes an unusual Easter treat in any country.

Tsoureki

To make one 8-inch-diameter loaf:
1 ounce fresh yeast or 1 tablespoon dried
4 tablespoons warm milk
2½ cups (10 ounces) all-purpose flour
2 eggs, beaten
½ teaspoon salt
¼ cup sugar
½ teaspoon caraway seeds, or grated rind ½ lemon
⅓ cup butter, unsalted, softened
1 egg, hard-cooked with red food coloring in the water
1 egg yolk

Sprinkle the yeast into a large mixing bowl. Add the milk and 2 tablespoons of the flour. Cover the mixture and leave it in a warm place for 20 minutes to form a sponge. Mix in the eggs, the remaining flour, salt, sugar and caraway seeds or lemon rind. Knead in the butter. Turn the dough on to a floured work surface and knead it until it is smooth. Return it to the bowl, cover it and leave it in a warm place for 1 hour to double in size.

Preheat the oven to 350°F. Knead the dough again. Roll it into a long sausage shape about 1½ inches in diameter. On a baking sheet, coil it round into a tight spiral about 6 inches in diameter. Press the dyed hard-cooked egg into the center and brush the loaf with the egg yolk.

Bake the loaf for about 45 minutes, or until it is golden-brown.

The Greeks also bake a special bread on New Year's Eve. Called *vassilopitta*, it is sometimes made by the same recipe used for *tsoureki*, but sometimes with different proportions of milk, butter and eggs. It is baked in a round pan called a *tapsi*, brushed with egg white and sprinkled with sesame seeds. All the family assemble to eat this special bread, which is cut by the head of the household. The first piece for Christ, and the second, for the house, are put aside. The third piece, is for the head of the house and the fourth for his wife, and so on according to age, and boys before girls, until every member has a slice.

TURKEY

One of the everyday breads of Turkey is a sourdough bread made with white wheat flour which was once baked in outdoor brick or clay ovens.

The following recipe comes from Arto der Haroutounian's book, *Middle Eastern Cookery*, published in 1982. It is, he says, a specialty of Antakya (the once famous Antioch). It is also popular in Greece where it is eaten during Lent to relieve a monotonous diet. In Cyprus it is called *elioti* and in Armenia, *tsit-hats*, and it can also be found in northern Syria where it is called *khobz-el-zeytoun*.

Essentially, this is a white bread dough, rolled around a filling of olives and onions. It is excellent with salads and soups.

Zeytin Ekmegi

To make two 16-inch-long olive breads:

basic bread dough (see page 12) made with 4 cups (1 pound) all-purpose flour
3 tablespoons olive oil
1 medium onion, finely chopped
20 black olives, halved and pitted

Mix and knead the dough, let it rise and knead it again. Preheat the oven to 375°F.

Divide the dough in two and roll each piece into a rectangle about 8 × 16 inches. In a small frying pan, soften the onion in the oil. Stir in the olives and take the pan from the heat. Divide the olive mixture between the two rectangles of dough, spreading it evenly over the surface, but leaving a gap of about ¾ inch all round the edge. Roll up each piece of dough from one long side and seal the ends to make a long loaf with pointed ends. Cut two crosses on each loaf and leave the loaves in a warm place to rise for 20 minutes.

Bake the loaves for 30 minutes, or until they are golden-brown and sound hollow when tapped.

SYRIA

Syria borders on southern Turkey, so it is no wonder that the countries share similar tastes and recipes. This onion bread from Syria has similar flavorings to the Turkish olive bread, and is actually made on both sides of the border. The differences are that the dough is made with baking powder and baking soda instead of with yeast, and chopped olives and raw onions are actually incorporated into the mixture. It is a good savory loaf for lunches and picnics, and is easily and quickly made.

Khobz Basali

To make one 1-pound onion loaf:

2 cups (8 ounces) plain cake flour
½ teaspoon salt
1 teaspoon baking powder
1 teaspoon baking soda
½ teaspoon ground cumin
¼ teaspoon chili powder
1 teaspoon chopped thyme (or ½ teaspoon dried)
10 black olives, pitted and chopped
1 small onion, finely chopped
½ cup, plus 2 tablespoons, water
5 tablespoons olive oil

Place the flour in a mixing bowl and add the salt, baking powder, baking soda, cumin, chili powder, thyme, olives and onion. Mix them together. Make a well in the center and add the water. Mix everything to a dough. Turn the dough on to a floured work surface and knead it until it is smooth. Knead in the oil, a tablespoon at a time. Place the dough in an oiled mixing bowl, cover it and leave it for 30 minutes.

Preheat the oven to 350°F. Place the dough in a greased 1-pound loaf pan and bake it for 40 minutes, or until it is golden-brown. Turn it on to a wire rack to cool.

● *Zeytin Ekmegi*

LEBANON

From the Lebanon, comes *mannaeesh* – small circles of white bread dough topped with a mixture of thyme and marjoram. These are definitely an acquired taste, as the larger quantities of dried thyme give a rather bitter flavor. For western tastes you could use one quarter the amount.

Mannaeesh

To make ten 5-inch rounds:

basic bread dough (see page 12) made with 4 cups (1 pound) all-purpose flour and ½ ounce fresh yeast or 2 teaspoons dried

Topping:

¼ cup olive oil
1 tablespoon dried thyme
½ tablespoon dried marjoram
3 tablespoons sesame seeds

Knead the dough for the first time and let it rise. Preheat the oven to 450°F.

Knead the dough for a second time. Divide it in ten pieces, make them into balls and roll them flat into 5-inch-diameter circles. Leave them in a warm place for 20 minutes to rise.

Brush the circles with some of the oil. Mix the remaining oil with the thyme, marjoram and sesame seeds and spread the mixture evenly over the dough circles.

Preheat two floured baking sheets in the oven. Place the mannaeesh on the hot sheets and cook them for about 8 minutes or until they are cooked through and only lightly colored.

ISRAEL

Israel is a relatively new country, made up of peoples of eighty or more nations, all of whom have contributed to the country's cuisine. Their religion and religious customs and festivals bind them together. *Cholla* is made to welcome the Jewish Sabbath. It is a light, soft bread with a thin, golden, crisp crust.

Cholla

To make one braided loaf:

1½ ounces fresh yeast or 1½ tablespoons dried
½ cup, plus 2 tablespoons, warm water
5 cups (1 pound 4 ounces) all-purpose flour
1 tablespoon sugar
2 teaspoons salt
3 eggs, beaten
3 tablespoons shortening
1 egg yolk, beaten with 1 tablespoon water
poppy seeds, optional

In a small bowl, sprinkle the yeast over the warm water and leave it to stand – five minutes for fresh yeast and 15 for dried. Place the flour, sugar and salt in a mixing bowl and make a well in the center. Add the yeast mixture, eggs and shortening. Mix everything to a dough. Turn it on to a floured work surface and knead it until it is smooth. Return it to the bowl, cover it and leave it in a warm place for 1 hour or until it has doubled in size.

Preheat the oven to 400°F. Knead the dough again and divide it in four equal pieces. Shape each piece into a rope about 22 inches long. Form these pieces into the arms of a cross, joining the ends in the

● *Cholla*

center. Then make a four-part braid. Lift the ends of two opposite pieces and fold them over so that they change places. Do the same with the other two pieces. Continue doing this, angling the lengths of the vertical strip slightly to the right as you cross them over each other, until all the lengths are used up. Tuck the loose ends underneath and place the loaf on to a floured baking sheet. Leave it in a warm place for 20 minutes to rise.

Brush the loaf with the egg and water mixture and scatter it with the poppy seeds, if you are using them. Bake the loaf for 15 minutes. Then turn the heat to 375°F and bake for a further 30 minutes, or until the cholla is golden-brown and cooked through. Cool it on a wire rack.

YEMEN, MUSCAT AND OMAN

Flat, round breads are popular throughout the Middle East, and the specialty in these countries is to top them with a pounded mixture of fresh coriander and soaked fenugreek seeds. The result of this is a curry-like aroma and flavor, and breads that go well with dishes that have rich, spicy sauces.

Khobz-el-Saluf

To make ten 7-inch rounds:

basic bread dough (see page 12) made with 2 cups whole-wheat flour and 2 cups all-purpose flour, kneaded and risen

Topping:

2 teaspoons fenugreek seeds, soaked in ½ cup water overnight
1 clove garlic
2 ounces chopped fresh coriander leaves
½ teaspoon salt
1 tablespoon lemon juice
2 tablespoons water
¼ cup (½ stick) butter or ghee, melted

While the bread dough is rising, drain the fenugreek and place it in a blender with the garlic, coriander, salt, lemon juice and water. Blend the mixture to a paste, place it in a bowl and refrigerate it until it is needed.

Preheat the oven to 500°F. Heat two floured baking sheets. Knead the dough and divide it in 10 pieces. Form the pieces into balls and then roll each one flat, into a 7-inch circle. Prick the circles four times with a fork and brush them with the melted ghee

or butter. Divide the fenugreek and coriander paste between the circles and spread it evenly. Place the circles on the heated baking sheets and bake them for 5 minutes. Khobz-el-Saluf are at their best when served warm.

IRAN

The Iranian version of the flat *lavash* bread is called *nane lavash*. The proportion of flour in the basic dough is the same as for *lavash* (see page 150), but a large amount of whole-wheat flour is used. *Nane lavash* is only made commercially, as the dough is rolled into rounds that are too large and unwieldy to bake in a domestic oven.

In the commercial bakeries, the worktops are made of a stone compound and have up to thirty large, round rubs built into them. The dough is left to rise in these until it comes above the level of the bench. Pieces are then cut off by apprentice workers who roll them out into round or oval shapes. The rolled dough is then taken to a more experienced baker who throws it from hand to hand, making it even bigger and flatter. He lays it on a table and rolls a spiked wheel, called a *jella*, across it three times before throwing it on to a *manjak* – a slightly domed, oval cushion that measures about 12 × 24 inches. The cushion is used to carry the bread to the oven without it splitting apart or stretching even further. The oven is a large, domed, clay construction called a *tannour* or *tonir*. The baker holds the cushion by a pocket at the back and presses it on to the hot wall of the oven. In just over half a minute, when the bread is bubbling, golden-brown and crisp, another baker with a metal hook on a long rod, called a *mengash*, pulls off the cooked bread and flicks it through an opening into the store – where it is sold, still hot and crisp.

The same bread is made at home in smaller rounds which are called *taftoon*.

Taftoon

To make ten taftoons:

1 ounce fresh yeast or 1 tablespoon dried
1¼ cups warm water
3 cups (12 ounces) whole-wheat flour
1 cup (4 ounces) plain cake flour

In a small bowl, sprinkle the yeast over half the water. Leave this to stand – five minutes for fresh yeast and 15 for dried. Place the flours into a mixing bowl and make a well in the center. Pour in the yeast mixture and remaining water. Mix everything to a dough, turn it on to a floured work surface and knead it well. Return it to the bowl, cover with a cloth and leave in a warm place for 1 to 1½ hours or until it has doubled in size.

Heat the oven to 400°F. Knead the dough again, divide it in ten equal pieces and form them into balls. Roll each ball into

● *Selling Bagels in the streets of Jerusalem, Israel*

a flat round, 8 to 10 inches in diameter. Prick each one all over with a fork. Line a baking sheet with aluminum foil and place it in the very bottom of the oven to heat. Lay one of the dough rounds on the foil and place it in the oven for 3 minutes or until it is cooked through and bubbly. Wrap the bread in a clean, dry cloth and add the others as they are done. Serve the taftoon warm.

Sangyak is another bread made using these ingredients (usually with a large proportion of whole-wheat flour), and it is shaped in the same way. The rolled, flat loaves are brushed with oil and patterned with fingertip indentations before being baked on a bed of hot pebbles so that they become bubbly and crisp.
Barbari are long, flat, plain loaves with four deep slits along their length.

Barbari

To make four 5 × 12-inch loaves:

1 ounce fresh yeast or 1 tablespoon dried
1½ cups warm water
5 cups (1 pound 4 ounces) all-purpose flour
2 teaspoons salt
1 tablespoon olive oil, plus extra for shaping

In a small bowl, sprinkle the yeast over 4 tablespoons of the water. Leave this to stand – five minutes for fresh yeast and 15 for dried. Place the flour and salt in a mixing bowl and make a well in the center. Pour in the yeast mixture and about half the remaining water. Mix in a small portion of flour from the sides of the well. Leave the bowl in a warm place for 20 minutes until the liquid in the center is frothing. Add the remaining water and the oil. Mix everything to a dough. Turn it on to a floured work surface and knead it until it is smooth. Return it to the bowl, cover it and leave it in a warm place for 1 hour or until it has doubled in size.

Preheat the oven to 425°F. Turn the dough on to an oiled work surface and divide it in four equal pieces. With oiled hands and an oiled rolling pin, roll each piece into a rectangle about 5 × 12 inches and ½ inch thick. Lay the loaves on floured baking sheets. Brush the tops with oil and make four parallel cuts down each loaf, stopping ¾ inch from the ends. Make the cuts wider by running a finger down them. Leave the loaves for 5 minutes and then bake them for 15 minutes, or until they are golden-brown. Cool them on wire racks.

EGYPT

The first leavened bread was made in ancient Egypt, where the basic loaf was made of wheat or barley flour with the additions for the wealthier of mashed dates or honey. Egypt's consumption of bread is still large. *Semit*, bread rings coated with sesame seeds, are sold in the streets of Cairo today, by vendors who carry them strung on poles. The following recipe is described in Claudia Roden's *Middle Eastern Food*.

Semit

To make ten 7-inch-diameter rings:

1 ounce fresh yeast or 1 tablespoon dried
½ cup, plus 2 tablespoons, warm water
4 cups (1 pound) all-purpose flour
2 teaspoons salt
1 tablespoon butter
1 tablespoon lard
½ cup, plus 2 tablespoons, warm milk
1 egg, beaten
3 ounces sesame seeds

In a small bowl, sprinkle the yeast over the water and leave it to stand – five minutes for fresh yeast and 15 for dried. Place the flour and salt in a mixing bowl and rub in the butter and lard. Make a well in the center and pour in the yeast mixture and the milk. Mix everything to a dough. Turn it on to a floured work surface and knead it. Return it to the bowl, cover it and leave it in a warm place for 1 hour or until it has doubled in size.

Preheat the oven to 450°F.

Cover baking sheets with oiled aluminum foil. Knead the dough again and divide it into ten pieces. Form each piece into a ring about 7 inches in diameter and ¾ inch thick.

Brush them on both sides with beaten egg and dip them in sesame seeds. Place the rings on the prepared baking sheets and leave them in a warm place for 20 minutes to rise. Bake them for 10 minutes. Turn the heat to 350°F and continue baking for 15 minutes or until the rings are golden-brown.

Cool them on wire racks.

TUNISIA

Khobz Arabi is the most popular everyday bread in Tunisia, but a specialty is a bread made entirely of semolina. It is really golden, with a soft, creamy-colored crumb, gently flavored with sesame and anise.

Semolina Bread

To make one round 2-pound loaf:

1½ ounce fresh yeast or 1½ tablespoons dried

1 cup warm water

4 cups (1 pound) fine semolina

1 teaspoon salt

2 tablespoons olive oil

1 tablespoon lard, softened

1½ tablespoons sesame seeds, toasted in a dry frying pan over medium heat for 2 minutes and cooled

½ teaspoon aniseeds

1 egg, beaten

In a small bowl, sprinkle the yeast over the water and leave it to stand – five minutes for fresh yeast and 15 for dried. Place the semolina in a mixing bowl and add the salt. Rub in the oil and lard. Make a well in the center and pour in the yeast mixture. Mix everything to a dough. Turn it on to a board sprinkled with semolina and knead it. When you first start to knead the loaf it will feel very grainy, almost as though your dough is made from a mixture

of sand and flour. Keep kneading for about ten minutes and it will become as smooth as ordinary bread dough. Return it to the bowl, cover it and leave it in a warm place for 1 hour or until it has doubled in size.

Preheat the oven to 450°F. Knead the dough again and knead in the sesame and aniseeds. Form the dough into a round loaf. Place it on a baking sheet that has been scattered with a little semolina and leave it in a warm place for 20 minutes to rise.

Brush the loaf with the beaten egg. Bake it for 15 minutes. Lower the heat to 350°F and bake it for a further 15 minutes, or until it is golden-brown. Cool on a wire rack.

MOROCCO

Morocco is in the far northwest corner of Africa, and its culinary influences come, in the north, from Spain, and, in the south, from Africa.

The everyday bread of Morocco is called *kisra* or *khboz*. It is round or conical shaped, often spicy and with a slightly heavy texture. For home use, it is made with whole-wheat or barley flour. White flour bread is reserved for visitors and for special occasions.

The great character of Moroccan bread is that it is used to soak up the juices from richly-spiced dishes such as *tangines*. These dishes are often served in a communal pot and meals are eaten with the fingers. Bread is always on the side for scooping and dipping and also for wiping fingers on.

Bread is made at home in most Moroccan households and then taken to the communal bakery for cooking. Every morning, housewives knead their dough in a large, unglazed earthenware pan called

● *Bedouin in the Sinai desert, Egypt*

● *Barbari (see page 157)*

a *qas'a*. The loaves are shaped and stamped with the family's special mark and then arranged on linen-covered trays. These are carried to the bakery on the heads of the children of the house who wear padded caps to help to balance them.

Kisra

To make two small conical loaves:

1 ounce fresh yeast or 1 tablespoon dried
1 cup warm water
4 cups (1 pound) all-purpose flour
1 cup (4 ounces) whole-wheat flour
2 teaspoons salt
1 teaspoon sesame seeds
1 tablespoon aniseeds
½ cup warm milk
oil for greasing
cornmeal for dusting

In a small bowl, sprinkle the yeast in the warm water. Leave this to stand – five minutes for fresh yeast and 15 for dried. Place the two types of flour in a mixing bowl, add the salt, sesame seeds and anise seeds and toss them together. Make a well in the center. Pour in the yeast and milk. Mix everything to a dough. Turn it on to a floured work surface and knead it until it is smooth. Divide the dough in two pieces and leave them on the board for 5 minutes.

Oil a clean mixing bowl. Roll one of the balls of dough around in the bowl so that it becomes covered with oil. Partly by rolling it around the sides of the bowl and partly by manipulation with your hands, form the dough into a cone shape. Place the cone on a baking sheet that has been sprinkled with cornmeal. Shape the other piece of dough in the same way. Cover the loaves with a clean, dry cloth and leave them in a warm place for 1 hour or until they have doubled in size.

Preheat the oven to 400°F. Using a fork, prick each quarter of each loaf, holding the fork so that the holes made by the tines are in vertical lines up the side of the loaf. Bake the loaves for 10 minutes. Reduce the heat to 300°F and continue baking for a further 30 minutes or until they are golden-brown and sound hollow when tapped. Cool the loaves on wire racks.

AFRICA AND SOUTH AFRICA

In many parts of Africa, bread is a luxury, and, even in the relatively well-off African countries such as Nigeria, it takes second place to other carbohydrate foods such as cassava, millet, rice, maize and sorghum.

There are troubles enough in South Africa, but at least most people there have adequate supplies of food. Athough it has a greater African than European population, South Africa is probably the most "Europeanized" of all African countries and its traditional recipes reflect this.

To find out about African bread I looked at Laurens van der Post's *African Cooking*, one of Time-Life Books' "Foods of the World" series. It was published in 1970, when Ethiopia was at peace and food supplies were sufficient to ensure that no one starved. At the time there were many different sorts of bread in Ethiopia because the soil was fertile and the climate kind – making it possible to grow wheat and barley alongside millet. Flours produced from these grains were made into leavened and unleavened breads of many different types, shapes and sizes – all specific to local areas.

The most popular kind of bread throughout Ethiopa was the round, flat *injera*, made from *teff*, a very high grade of refined millet flour. The *injera* was made both in bush homes and city restaurants. To make it, the flour was mixed with water to make a batter, and then left in a warm place to ferment for three or four days. When ready, the batter was poured, in a spiral fashion, into a large heated ceramic griddle. When a thin layer had covered the bottom, a lid was put on and sealed all round with a damp cloth. In just a few minutes the *injera* was ready, pale-yellow colored, soft enough to fold, and with a bubbled surface. Apparently *injera* have a faintly sour flavor and are made to be eaten with a variety of cooked dishes and at the same time used as an eating utensil.

Another bread in Ethiopia was *dabo kolo*. Wheat flour was made into a thick dough by gradually stirring water into it, and the mixture was sometimes flavored with *berbere*, a hot spice paste. Cooking oil was kneaded into it and the dough was rolled and cut into small rounds which were baked until brown.

For a quickly-made snack to eat with the local *talla* beer, barley flour was roasted, mixed with salt and rolled between the fingers into large, round pellets.

SOUTH AFRICA

The original South African inhabitants grew millet. This was pounded into a type of thick porridge which is still eaten today. The European influence came from the Dutch, French Huguenots, Scots, English and Germans, while the Malays, who were brought in as slaves, later added their style to South African cooking.

The first European settlers in South Africa were Dutch. They arrived in 1652, with Jan van Riebeek, to establish a supply port for Dutch ships which regularly called at the Cape. The settlers grew wheat, barley, oats and rye, and also maize, which came to be known locally as mealie. This was as successful with the Africans as it was with the settlers, and mealie meal porridge soon rivalled millet porridge in popularity.

In their first homes around the Cape, Dutch housewives had to bake enough bread each week to cater for large families, employees and servants. Ovens had to be big and were constructed outside the house. They were made of red brick, about eight feet long, with a high-domed roof, and soon became known as "Dutch ovens."

Yeast and rising agents were hard to come by, so breadmakers devised ways of making their own. There were various ways of making sourdough bread and there was also salt rising bread, different from the American version in that no milk was needed for the initial mixing and wheat flour or maize meal was used as a starter. This is a modern recipe for salt rising bread. Whole-wheat and mixed-grain breads are popular in South Africa today and so a choice of flours is given. Salt rising bread is close-textured with a rich, nutty flavor.

● *Washing maize, Zambia*

Salt Rising Bread

To make two 2-pound loaves:

First Day:

2 teaspoons salt

1 tablespoon sugar

1¼ cups boiling water

½ cup, plus 2 tablespoons, cold water

1 cup (4 ounces) whole-wheat flour or mealie meal (cornmeal)

Second Day:

1¼ cups hot water

8 cups (2 pounds) whole-wheat flour or all-purpose flour or a half and half mixture

In a large mixing bowl, mix together the salt, sugar, boiling water and cold water. Sprinkle the whole-wheat flour or cornmeal over the top and cover with plastic wrap. Leave the mixture in a warm place for 24 hours.

The next day, stir in the hot, but not boiling, water and then beat in the flour to make a very moist dough, almost like a thick batter. Leave the dough in the bowl and sprinkle a little more flour over the top. Cover the bowl and leave it in a warm place for 1 hour for the dough to double in size.

Preheat the oven to 400°F. Divide the dough between two 2-pound bread pans and leave it in a warm place for about an hour, or until it rises almost to the top of the pans. Bake the loaves for 40 minutes or until they are browned on top and sound hollow when tapped. Cool them on wire racks.

Rusks, both sweetened and unsweetened have always been popular in South Africa. *Boerbeskuit* (farmers' rusks) are savory, and are made with a salt-rising starter. They keep for a long time and are good with butter and cheese. They are also particularly good when they first come out of the oven, have just been separated from each other and are still quite warm.

Boerbeskuit

To make about 32 rusks:

4 cups (1 pound) all-purpose flour

1 teaspoon salt

½ cup salt-rising starter (see above)

½ cup warm milk

½ cup (1 stick) butter, softened

2 tablespoons butter, melted

Place the flour and salt in the bowl. Make a well in the center and add the starter, the milk and the butter. Mix everything to a dough. Turn it on to a floured board and knead it until it is smooth. Return it to the bowl, cover it and leave it in a warm place for 1 hour or until it has doubled in size.

Preheat the oven to 350°F. Knead the dough again and roll it into a long rope about 1½ inches in diameter. Cut it in pieces about 1½ inches long. Lay half the pieces on a floured baking sheet, packed closely together, with the cut sides top and bottom. Brush them with melted butter and put a second layer on top. Brush the top layer with the butter. Leave the rusks in a warm place for 20 minutes to rise.

● *Tuareg, baking in the Sahara, North Africa*

● *Boerbeskuit*

● *Mosbolletjies*

Bake them for 40 minutes or until they are golden-brown and crisp on the outside. Separate the rusks and cool them on wire racks. Place them on the baking sheets again, this time well apart from each other. Place them in a preheated 200°F oven for 30 minutes or until they are golden-brown and completely dry. Cool them on wire racks again.

The *mosbolletjie* is unique to South Africa and it was first introduced by the Protestant Huguenots from France. *Mos* is the word for grape juice which is in its first stage of fermentation. A *bolletjie* is a small bun. *Mos* contains natural yeasts and makes a good rising agent. Where no fresh grapes were available, settlers used raisins soaked in warm water. The process is a surprisingly easy one, involving only long waiting periods. The buns are soft and sweet with a light texture that is slightly more substantial than that of buns made with yeast. Baking them close together ensures that they stay soft all through.

Mosbolletjies

To make sixteen buns:

Mos Starter:

1 ounce raisins

2 cups warm water

Buns:

4 cups (1 pound) all-purpose flour

½ cup, plus 2 tablespoons, mos

½ cup, plus 2 tablespoons, warm milk

¼ cup (½ stick) butter, softened

½ cup sugar

½ teaspoon aniseeds

1 egg, beaten with 2 tablespoons milk

To make the *mos*, place the raisins in a jar and pour in the water. Cover the jar and leave it in a warm place for 3 to 4 days to ferment. When it is ready, the raisins will have floated to the top.

Place 1½ cups of the flour in a mixing bowl. Make a well in the center and mix in the *mos*. Cover the bowl tightly and leave it for 8 hours so the mixture forms a sponge. Mix in the milk and the remaining flour and the butter, in small pieces. Knead everything together to make a dough. Turn it on to a floured work surface and knead it until it is smooth. Return it to the bowl, cover it and leave it in a warm place to rise for a further 8 hours.

Preheat the oven to 400°F. Knead the dough again and knead in all but 1 tablespoon of the sugar and the aniseed. Divide the dough in sixteen even-sized pieces and form them into long roll shapes. Place the rolls next to each other on a floured baking sheet, setting them on their shortest ends (they will sink to form a tray of joined round buns) to rise. Brush them with the egg and milk and sprinkle them with the remaining sugar.

Bake the rolls for 20 minutes or until they are golden-brown. Slide them on to a wire rack, and leave them, still stuck together, to cool. Separate the buns only as you want to eat them.

As early as 1657, land outside the immediate Cape area was granted to officials, who were known as free burghers, on the understanding that they would grow wheat and other cereal crops. To get to these areas, whole families had to trek many miles through the open country, taking with them only the minimum of survival equipment. On the trek there were no ovens and cooking utensils had to be improvised. They took with them supplies of long-keeping *boerbeskuit*, but when this ran out more bread had to be cooked. The trekkers occasionally found and excavated an anthill which could be used in a similar way to a Dutch oven, but usually they relied on their camp cooking pot, which was three-legged and made of cast iron. All their cooking, including the baking of bread, was done in this pot over an open fire. *Potbrood* (pot bread) is still popular today and is cooked at *braais*, which can only be described as barbecue parties.

Three-legged pots, together with fitting lids, can be bought from hardware stores and agricultural suppliers in South Africa. Before use they must be seasoned by gently melting meat fat in the bottom of the pot and then smearing the fat all round the sides. The pot is wiped clean with paper towels and after this should only be washed lightly, without detergent, and never scoured. If you are unable to get hold of such a pot, a cast-iron casserole dish, with a lid, is a good substitute.

Pot bread is made from basic bread dough (see page 12), often with a mixture of whole-wheat and white flours. After the dough has risen, it is kneaded and placed in the pot, covered, left to rise, and given a brushing of melted butter. The lid is replaced and the pot set in a hole on top of the hot coals. A few coals are heaped on top and the bread left to bake for 45 minutes to 1 hour, depending on the heat of the fire.

If you have no open fire, you can still make *potbrood*.

Potbrood

Use a cast-iron casserole with a good fitting lid. Grease it and put in the dough. After the first rising and brushing with butter, cook the loaf in a preheated 400°F oven for 45 minutes. When you take off the lid, a rich yeasty flavor wafts out. The loaf is well-risen and rounded, with a soft bouncy texture and a thin crisp crust.

Another way of cooking bread dough on a trek was to roll it round a stick which was then held over an open fire. This method is still a great favorite with children at *braais*.

Griddle cookery was also possible over camp fires, and the Scots introduced their bannock (see page 81) which quickly became popular. Another griddle-cooked bread was *roosterkoek*, made by cutting a long rope of bread into slices. The secret of well-cooked *roosterkoek* is not to let the rolls brown too much before they are cooked through. They are delicious split and buttered straight off the griddle.

Roosterkoek

To make about 20 rolls:

basic bread dough (see page 12) made with 4 cups whole-wheat or all-purpose flour, or a mixture

2 tablespoons lamb tail fat, melted; or butter, softened

When the dough is made, knead in the fat or butter. Leave the dough to rise. Knead the dough again and roll it into a long rope about 1½ inches in diameter. Cut it in diagonal slices of the same thickness. Lay the pieces on a floured surface and leave them for 20 minutes to rise.

Heat an ungreased griddle over medium heat. Cook the roosterkoek for about 6 minutes on each side, or until they are cooked through and lightly browned. Serve them hot and buttered.

Rusks, *potbrood* and griddle-cooked breads accompanied the trekkers into the bush, and all are popular even now.

The South Africans are fond of whole-wheat and sifted meal breads. Many different types are made alongside the more standard white loaves, including health breads which contain a mixture of flours plus sesame and sunflower seeds.

The following brown bread has a rich, heavy texture and unusual sweet-sour flavor brought about by the vinegar, which also appears in older South African recipes. It is good buttered as a semi-sweet bread and is also excellent toasted as a base for baked beans. In many ways it is similar to the steamed brown breads of America and Canada.

Brown Batter Bread

To make one 2-pound loaf:

1 ounce fresh yeast or 1 tablespoon dried

¾ cup, plus 2 tablespoons, warm water

3½ cups (14 ounces) whole-wheat flour

1 teaspoon salt

¼ cup dark brown sugar

¾ cup, plus 2 tablespoons, warm milk

¼ cup vinegar

1 tablespoon oil

● *Potbrood (see page 165)*

In a small bowl, sprinkle the yeast over the water and leave it – five minutes for fresh yeast and 15 for dried. Place the flour, salt and sugar in a mixing bowl. Beat in the yeast mixture, milk, vinegar and oil. Pour the batter into a greased 2-pound loaf pan and leave it in a warm place for 1 to 1½ hours to rise to the top of the pan.

Preheat the oven to 400°F. Bake the loaf for 50 minutes or until a skewer inserted in the center comes out clean.

Vetkoek is a popular snack in South Africa and it can be eaten hot or cold. It is deep fried bread, crisp and flaky on the outside and rich and soft in the middle.

Vetkoek

To make twenty-four vetkoek:

basic bread dough (see page 12) made with 4 cups (1 pound) all-purpose or whole-wheat flour, risen

oil for deep frying

Knead the dough and divide it in twenty-four small pieces. Roll the pieces into balls and gently flatten them. Leave them for 10 minutes to rise. Deep fry them in hot oil for about 1 minute on each side or until they are golden-brown, puffy and crisp. Drain them on paper towels and eat them hot.

When you are in a hurry you can make *vetkoek* with baking powder instead. *Vetkoek* made in this way are uneven-shaped golden balls and they can be eaten hot or cold.

The old-fashioned recipe for *vetkoek* was to make them with a plain cake flour and baking powder, a little sugar, eggs and milk, mixed to a thick batter.

The *vetkoek* were eaten either with sweet preserves for breakfast or as a substitute for bread.

Quick Vetkoek

To make about twelve vetkoek:

2¼ cups (9 ounces) whole-wheat or all-purpose flour

½ teaspoon salt

1 tablespoon baking powder

1¼ cups milk for all-purpose flour, 1½ cups, plus 2 tablespoons, whole-wheat flour

oil for deep frying

Mix all the dry ingredients together and add in the milk to make a soft batter. Ladle individual spoonfuls of the mixture into hot oil and deep fry them for about 1 minute on each side, or until they are golden-brown and risen. Drain them on kitchen paper and eat them hot.

● *Quick Vetkoek*

INDIA

India is a land of many peoples, languages, cultures and religions. It is vibrant with color and spice. Its food is the same, varying from region to region and from religion to religion. The staple foods of India are bread and rice and although both can be found all over the country, there is more bread in the wheat-growing north and more rice in the south. There is rarely a meal served without one or both, and, typically, they appear in succession, usually with the rice first.

The traditional bread of India is flat, unleavened and cooked on a form of cast-iron griddle called a *tava*. The Moslems in the north introduced the domed clay ovens called tandoors in which similar or slightly thicker breads could be baked. Later, the Europeans (British, Dutch, Portuguese and French) introduced their own yeasted breads. The Indians called them *dubble roti*, which means double bread, and served them with spiced dishes that had rich sauces in need of mopping up. Sometimes they used the crusted ends of such bread with the crumb removed for use as a filling for other foods.

Wheat is the most used bread flour in India, but there are also breads made from barley, millet, buckwheat and gram (chick-pea) flours. Most of the flour is unrefined and much of it is ground at home. Although whole-wheat, it is more finely ground than Western whole-wheat flours – and its use is essential for the successful cooking of many of the breads. Indian flour can be bought in the West in health and Indian food stores. It is generally sold under the name of chapati flour. If you cannot find any, use a half and half mixture of whole-wheat and plain cake flour.

The chapati was the first Indian bread to be made popular in the West by Indian restaurants. It is a flat, soft bread, unleavened and griddle cooked, thin and between 6 and 8 inches in diameter.

chapati dough is easy to mix, but it improves if it is allowed to stand for a long time, a process which makes the final bread pleasantly soft and pliable.

• *Chapatis*

Chapati dough is also made into *phulkas*, which are almost exactly the same only smaller. There is also a *chapati* made entirely of corn flour (the refined flour, not cornmeal) which is crisp and biscuit-like in texture.

Chapatis

To make 8 chapatis:

2 cups (8 ounces) chapati flour
1 teaspoon salt
¾ cup, plus 2 tablespoons, water

Place the flour in a bowl. Make a well in the center and gradually mix in the water. Check the consistency when you have added about ½ cup and add the remainder, as needed, by the tablespoon. The flour should absorb all the water and it should be possible to knead it to a smooth and elastic dough without the addition of any further flour. Knead the dough on a floured work surface for 5 to 10 minutes. Cover it with wet muslin or with a wet cloth and leave it for at least 30 minutes, or refrigerate it for up to seven hours.

Divide the dough in 8 small balls. Dust each one with flour and roll them out very thinly into rounds about 10 inches in diameter.

Leave them separate and don't stack them whilst you are waiting to cook them, or they will all stick together and you will have to begin again.

Heat an ungreased griddle over medium heat. Warm a dish and a clean, dry cloth. Place one of the chapatis on the griddle and cook it until it begins to bubble in places. Turn it over and leave it until it is cooked through, turning it frequently so that it cooks evenly. Lay the cloth over the heated dish and place the chapati on it. Cover the chapati with the edges of the napkin. Cook the rest, adding them to the first one as you do so.

Chapatis can also be made from gram flour, a chick-pea flour also available from specialty stores. Gram flour chapatis are often flavored with fresh coriander, green pepper or chilies and chopped raw onion. They have a savory flavor with a touch of freshness and are really good with hot, spicy curries.

Gram flour dough is very soft and, because of the pieces of pepper and onion in it, quite difficult to roll out without getting holes in it. You will be more successful if you make gram flour chapatis smaller and thicker than those made with ordinary chapati flour.

Gram Flour Chapatis

To make ten chapatis:

1 cup (4 ounces) gram flour
1½ cups plain cake flour
1 teaspoon salt
1 small onion
1 tablespoon chopped fresh coriander leaves
1 small green chili, or ¼ green pepper
¾ cup, plus 2 tablespoons, ice-cold water
2 tablespoons ghee or shortening, melted

In a bowl, mix together the flours and the salt. Very finely chop the onion, coriander and chili or pepper, and add them to the flours. Make a well in the center and gradually mix in the water to make a soft dough. Divide the dough in 10 round balls and roll them out in circles, 6 to 7 inches in diameter.

Heat a griddle over medium heat and brush it with the melted ghee or shortening. Cook as for the plain chapatis above.

● *Making chapatis*

● *Gram flour Chapatis*

Roti is another plain, flat bread that is served in similar ways to the *chapati*. The dough mixture is the same as for *chapatis* but the cooking method is slightly different. The recipe below is from Madhur Jaffrey's book *Eastern Vegetarian Cooking.*

For tandoori-style *roti*, first make the *roti*, following the recipe below. Instead of using a griddle, heat baking sheets covered with aluminum foil in a preheated 400°F oven. Put the *roti* on the baking sheets, cover them with the hot foil and cook them for 5 minutes. Wrap them in a warmed cloth as soon as they come out of the oven and keep them warm. Dot them with butter and serve hot.

Roti

To make twelve roti:

dough as for plain chapatis, left to rest in the same way

Divide the dough in twelve equal pieces, form the pieces into balls and roll them into 5-inch circles.

Heat a griddle over low to medium heat. Place one *roti* on the griddle and cook it for 1 minute, or until bubbles form inside it. Turn it over and cook the second side for 30 seconds. If you have a gas oven, light a second burner on a medium flame and place the *roti* directly on it. Using cooking tongs, turn the *roti* round so that the whole surface has been exposed to the flame. Do this for about 5 seconds. Turn the *roti* over and repeat for about 3 seconds. The *roti* should puff up.

Wrap the *roti* in a warm cloth and cook the rest in the same way.

If you have an electric oven, place the griddle under the broiler for a few seconds with the *roti* on it.

If your griddle is a large cast-iron one you will probably find that it is either too large or too heavy to be put safely under a grill, so instead you can use a frying pan which fits underneath much better.

● *Rajasthani women sifting*

Chapatis and roti are very thin breads. When something more substantial is wanted there is the *paratha*, which was brought to Delhi and other parts of India by Punjabi refugees. *Parathas* are made with the same flour as *chapatis*, but they are made richer by the addition of milk to the mixture plus a brushing of ghee. Ghee is a special clarified butter from which all milk solids have been removed. It can be bought from the same sort of stores as the *chapati* flour. You can make a substitute by gently melting butter and skimming off all the foam, or you can use a good-quality vegetable oil. *Parathas* can be left plain, or they can be gently spiced with the addition of a few bruised lovage seeds. If these are unavailable, try fennel or cumin seeds.

Parathas

To make six parathas:

2 cups (8 ounces) chapati flour
½ teaspoon salt
12 lovage seeds, bruised, optional
¾ cup, plus 2 tablespoons, water, or milk and water mixed
½ cup ghee or clarified butter, melted, or ½ cup vegetable oil

Place the flour, salt and lovage seeds, if using any, in a mixing bowl and make a well in the center. Mix in the water, or water and milk mixture, a little at a time to make a soft dough. Knead the dough on a floured work surface for 5 minutes. Cover it with wet muslin or a wet cloth and leave it in a cool place for 1 hour or in the refrigerator for up to 7 hours.

Divide the dough in six equal pieces and form each one into a ball. Roll the balls into flat rounds about 6 inches in diameter. Brush them with the ghee or vegetable oil. Bring the sides to the center and twist them together to form a pouch-shape. Turn the dough over, twisted side down and roll it out into a 7-inch round.

Heat a griddle over medium heat and brush it with the ghee or oil. Cook the first *paratha* for about 2 minutes on the first side, or until the top begins to look as though it is drying. Brush it with a little of the ghee and cook for a further minute, or until the underside becomes slightly speckled brown. Turn the *paratha* over and cook it until the second side is speckled and the whole is cooked through. Wrap up the *paratha* in a warmed cloth as soon as it is done and cook the rest in the same way.

Rich Flaky Parathas

Make the dough in the same way. Divide it in six pieces, roll out each piece into a circle and brush it with melted ghee. Fold it in quarters and roll it out again. Repeat the process four times. Cook as for the plain *parathas* above. You may need a little extra ghee for cooking.

Spiced Parathas

The method for these is taken from Madhur Jaffrey's book, *Eastern Vegetarian Cooking*. The addition of spices is my own. Make *paratha* dough in the usual way, omitting the lovage seeds.

When you melt the ghee or clarified butter, add 1 teaspoon each of ground turmeric, ground coriander and cumin seeds. If you are using oil, warm it gently with the spices.

Divide the dough in six pieces and roll them out until they are very thin rounds, about 10 inches in diameter. Brush them with the spiced ghee and then roll each one up tightly into a long rope. Brush the rope with more and then coil it up into a small cone. Flatten the cone slightly to make sure it is going to stay together, put it on a plate and cover it with plastic wrap. Shape the remaining pieces of dough in the same way. Cover and refrigerate them for 1 hour 30 minutes or up to 8 hours.

Roll the cones into rounds about 6 inches in diameter. Heat a griddle over medium heat and brush it with melted ghee or oil. Lay a *paratha* on the griddle and cook it for about 3 minutes, or until the top begins to look dry. Brush the surface with melted ghee and continue cooking, without turning it over, until the underside is speckled brown. Turn the *paratha* over and cook it until the second side is also speckled brown. Wrap the *paratha* in a warmed cloth and cook the rest in the same way.

Stuffed Parathas

To make them even more interesting and substantial, *parathas* are stuffed with a variety of spiced ingredients before being rolled out. In India, grated white radishes, raw and highly spiced, are one of the most popular filling ingredients. Other stuffings are made from cooked ingredients, and include spiced potatoes, spiced minced lamb, lentils or another cooked

● *Spiced Parathas*

vegetable such as cauliflower.

Roll out the *parathas* as in the basic recipe. In the center of each one place about 2 teaspoons of the filling. Bring the sides of the dough together and twist them to form a package. Turn the package over and roll it out as in the basic recipe.

To make radish-stuffed *parathas* you need to buy the long, white radish which is sometimes called mooli. Grate about 3 ounces and mix it with 1 tablespoon chopped fresh coriander, 1 finely chopped fresh green chili, ½ teaspoon each of ground ginger and coriander and ½ teaspoon cumin seeds. Let the mixture stand for 1 hour, so that the flavors can combine, before using.

For potato *parathas*, use 1 cup, cooked potatoes mixed with 1 tablespoon chopped fresh coriander, ½ teaspoon salt, ¼ teaspoon each ground ginger, paprika and chili powder, plus the juice of ½ lime.

Indian bread can also be deep fried to make *puris*. These are puffed and risen, crispy on the outside and soft in the middle, and are eaten with almost all Indian meat dishes. They can be made completely from chapati flour or with a mixture combining chapati and plain cake flours. In India, *puris* are cooked in deep oil in a *karhai*, which is similar to a Chinese wok. Although they are easy to make, it is said that it takes many years of practice to perfect them so that they are delicious and light. A saying in Benares (Varanasi), in the region of Uttar Pradesh, is that if twenty-five *puris* were stacked on a plate and a coin was dropped on them from above, it should still be possible to hear the chink as the coin hits the plate.

A variation on the plain *puri* are banana *puris*, made by mixing mashed banana and plain cake flour. They are slightly sweet and go superbly with curries. They can also be served, sprinkled with confectioners' sugar, as a dessert.

There are also potato *puris*, made by mixing mashed potatoes, curry spices and white flour.

Puris

To make twelve puris:

2 cups (8 ounces) chapati flour

½ teaspoon salt

2 tablespoons melted ghee or vegetable oil

½ cup water, or milk and water mixed, slightly warm

oil for deep frying

Place the flour and salt in a bowl and rub in the ghee or oil. Make a well in the center and pour half the liquid into it and begin to mix in the flour. Gradually add the rest of the liquid to make a stiff dough. Turn the dough on to a floured board and knead it for about 5 minutes, until it becomes smooth and elastic. Return the dough to the bowl, cover it with a damp cloth and leave it in a cool place for 1 hour.

Divide the dough into twelve small balls and roll each one into a 5-inch-diameter round.

Heat a pan of deep oil over medium heat. Carefully drop in one *puri*. It will sink to the bottom and then gradually rise to the surface. Using a perforated spoon, keep pushing it gently under the surface of the oil so it puffs up. Turn it over and, still pushing with the spoon, cook it for about one minute more or until it is evenly puffed and golden-brown all over. Lift it out on to a double layer of paper towels to drain, and cook the rest in the same way.

Kachoris

When a *puri* is stuffed with a spiced mixture it becomes a *kachori*. Use any of the cooked fillings that are given for stuffed *parathas*. Roll the dough into twelve 5-inch rounds and then spread 2 teaspoons of the filling on one side. Fold the rounds in half. Roll them out again in 5-inch rounds, sealing the filling inside. Deep-fry the rounds as for *parathas*.

Kachoris are often served with Hindu vegetarian meals. All the constituents of the meal – different curries, pickles and rice are arranged on large, individual plates called *thalis*. In the center of the arrangement are *kachoris* and *roti*.

Benares (Varanasi) is the city to which Hindu pilgrims from all over India come to celebrate the Festival of Divali, or Festival of Lights, their equivalent of the New Year. Whilst they are there they visit Kachori Gulley, a street where the traders specialize in *puris* and *kachoris*.

One of the few traditional leavened breads you will find in India is *naan*, which is also eaten in Pakistan, Bangladesh and Afghanistan.

There are many different versions of *naan*. Some contain yeast, some baking powder, some baking soda and others a mixture. Some contain eggs and some milk. The similarities are that all use white flour and the main liquid ingredient is yogurt. *Naan* is found only in the north of India where it is baked in the dome-shaped clay tandoors that are found behind every Punjabi home. It is also baked commercially.

The dough for *naan* is mixed and left to rise for a long time, often overnight. Once risen it is kneaded and pulled apart into small pieces. The baker takes a piece of dough and slaps it between the palms of his hands so that it becomes an oval shape, thicker at the edges than in the middle. He scatters it with sesame or poppy seeds and a little chopped onion, and throws it against the sides of the tandoor. Here, because of the dome shape of the oven, it sticks at one point only, becoming tear-drop shaped as it hangs over the fire. After a few minutes cooking, the *naan* will become slightly risen and light brown. The outer parts will be soft and the center parts crisp. The *naan* is taken from the tandoor and eaten while hot and fresh.

● *Naan Bread*

Naan Bread

To make eight flat breads:

4 cups (1 pound) all-purpose flour

½ teaspoon salt

½ teaspoon baking soda

1 cup plain yogurt

½ ounce fresh yeast or ½ tablespoon dried

2 tablespoons ghee or clarified butter; plus extra, melted

2 eggs, beaten

sesame seeds and finely chopped onion, optional

Place the flour, salt and baking soda in a bowl. Gently warm the yogurt and stir in the yeast. Leave this to stand – five minutes for fresh yeast and 15 for dried. Make a well in the flour and stir in the yogurt mixture, the ghee and the eggs. Mix everything to a dough. Turn it on to a floured board and knead it until it is soft and springy (about 10 minutes). Return it to the bowl, cover it and leave it in a warm place for about 2 hours to double in size.

Preheat the oven to 400°F. Knead the dough again and divide it in eight equal pieces. Roll each piece into an oval shape about 10 inches long. Leave them in a warm place for 10 minutes to rise. Spread aluminum foil over baking sheets and lightly oil it. Heat the baking sheets and foil in the oven. Lay the *naan* on the foil and brush them quickly with melted ghee or butter. Scatter them with sesame seeds and/or chopped onion, if you are using them. Bake the *naan* for 7 minutes, or until they are only just browned.

Serve them warm.

In Gujarat, in the northwest of India, millet is the staple grain. It is very often ground at home to make a flour that is said to be more nutritious than wheat flour and one which is much prized by the vegetarian population. To celebrate the new harvest, fresh millet kernels are eaten with sugar balls. Later, when the grains are ground, the flour is made into *batloo*, a flat, dull-brown colored griddle bread which is patterned with indentations made by the ball of the cook's finger. *Dhebras* are flat millet breads, made with a dough that is mixed with chopped spinach and green chilies. Again they are griddle-baked and they are served with plain yogurt and a sweet green mango chutney.

Kashmir, in the far north, is renowned for its wonderful variety of different breads which are very much influenced by the cooking of Afghanistan and Central Asia. Most of the breads are small, like large buns. They are plain, or slightly sweet or salty, and some are scattered with poppy or sesame seeds. *Girda* are chewy and can be served with a type of clotted cream or with a Moslem porridge of meat and grains called *harissa. Kulcha* are made in flat, square shapes and decorated with pricked patterns, and *bakirkhani* are soft with a hole in the center.

The *shirmal* is a tandoor-cooked bread which is a specialty of Lucknow, the Moslem capital of the region of Uttar Pradesh. It is baked in the street bazaars and makes a lunchtime snack or an accompaniment to a main meal. Yesterday's *shirmal* may well turn up for breakfast to be eaten with butter and preserves. Its characteristic is that, when traditionally made, a *shirmal* is gently colored yellow, through the use of saffron. However, according to Madhur Jaffrey in her book *A Taste of India*, saffron is now so expensive that artificial colors are used, producing an orange-red bread the color of tandoori chicken. Much further south, in Andhra Pradesh, *shirmal* are eaten at breakfast with a spiced lamb stew called *nahari*. Here you will also find *feni*, saucer-sized bread which is soaked in milk and eaten with sugar as a dessert.

Shirmal

To make eight shirmal:

4 cups (1 pound) plain cake flour

1 teaspoon salt

2 teaspoons sugar

⅔ cup ghee or clarified butter

1¼ cups milk

a few saffron strands soaked in ½ cup milk for 2 hours

Place the flour, salt and sugar in a mixing bowl and rub in ½ cup of the ghee. Gradually mix in the milk to make a soft dough. Turn the dough on to a floured work surface and knead it until it is soft and smooth. Return it to the bowl, cover it and leave it in a cool place for 2 hours. Knead it again and leave it for 1 hour more.

Preheat the oven to 500°F. In the oven, heat a large, cast-iron frying pan.

Divide the dough into eight small balls and roll them flat, into 6-inch-diameter rounds. Prick them all over with a fork. Place one round on a heated frying pan and bake it for 2 minutes. Sprinkle it with a little saffron milk and cook it for a further 3 minutes. Place it under the broiler for 10 seconds. Sprinkle a little more saffron milk over it and brush it with a little of the remaining ghee.

Wrap the *shirmal* in aluminum foil to keep it warm and cook the others in the same way.

CHINA AND SOUTHEAST ASIA

In China and the other Southeast Asian countries, rice has been the staple food for many centuries and wheat products, especially bread, have always taken second place. However, the Chinese do regularly eat steamed breads – the recipe for which is only slightly different from that for a basic Western bread dough.
Large loaves are a rarity in China. It is more typical for dough to be formed into small buns. Plainer ones are served as accompaniments to other dishes, and sweet ones are eaten as snacks.

● *Springtime bun festival, Cheung Chau Island, China*

CHINA

For culinary purposes, China can be divided into four distinct regions: the north, which includes the provinces of Shantung, Honan, Hopei and the city of Beijing; the coastal area centered on Fukien but including Shanghai; the inland areas of Szechuan and Yunnan; and the southern region of Canton.

Rice is grown in the coastal, inland and southern areas, but in the north, where the climate is colder, conditions are better for wheat-growing than for paddy fields. Although the northern Chinese depend mainly upon wheat for their energy supply, the bulk of it is not made into bread, but into noodles. However, in the far north, where there has been a Mongol influence, you may find bread being served with strips of barbecued lamb.

In most Chinese recipe books you will find no salt used in steamed breads, but a little extra sugar instead; and in some the warm water is replaced with warm milk. The dough is usually formed into small buns which are served as an accompaniment to other dishes. These buns come in many different shapes, two of which are given below.

Chinese steamed breads are usually cooked in a bamboo steamer or over simmering water in a wok. An ordinary steamer can be used. The bread itself is bland. It should be eaten hot, with rich meats and sauces.

Man To

To make thirty-two single or sixteen double steamed rolls:

1 ounce fresh yeast or 1 tablespoon dried
1 tablespoon sugar
1½ cups warm water
4 cups (1 pound) all-purpose flour

In a small bowl, sprinkle the yeast and sugar over 4 tablespoons of the water and leave – five minutes for fresh yeast and 15 for dried. Place the flour in a bowl and make a well in the center. Pour in the yeast mixture and the remaining water. Mix everything to a dough. Turn it on to a floured work surface and knead it until it is smooth. Return it to the bowl, cover it and leave it in a warm place for 1 hour or until it has doubled in size.

Punch down the dough with the back of your fist, cover it again and leave it for a further 20 minutes.

Knead the dough again and shape it into rolls (see below). Bring the water in the bottom of a steamer to the boil. Place the rolls in the steamer, leaving a 1-inch gap between them. Cook them for 10 minutes, or until they are firm and cooked through. Serve them hot.

If the rolls have to be cooked in two batches, cook the first batch and lift them out. When the second batch have been in the steamer for 8 minutes, put the first ones back on top to heat through. Serve them all hot.

Single Flower Rolls:

Divide the dough in half. Roll out and cut each piece into a rectangle about 8 × 12 inches and brush it with sesame oil (sunflower oil can also be used). Roll the pieces up along one long side to make a rolled cylinder about 1½ inches in diameter. With a very sharp knife (the Chinese would use a sharp cleaver), cut the cylinder in pieces about ¾ inch long. Using a chopstick or rounded skewer parallel with the cut, press down in the center of each separate piece. The layers will push out to the sides, making a pattern of two oval spirals joined in the center.

177

● *Man To (see page 177)*

Double Flower Rolls:

Divide the dough in half and roll and cut pieces as above. Place one piece of dough on top of another (because these are on end to end, not cut-surface to cut-surface, they will need to be held in position). Press the chopstick down as before, almost to the bottom of the rolls. The shape will be like two joined spirals with two more spirals underneath. These rolls may need an extra couple of minutes cooking time because of their size.

In some restaurants in China, you might find a richer steamed bread, called *shwieh bai man to*, or snow-white steamed bread, served with "red cooked" dishes. These are joints of meat that are cooked in a casserole with soy sauce, rice wine, sugar, anise and onions. They are rich and highly flavored and go well with the plain taste of steamed bread.

Shwieh Bai Man To

To make thirty-two single or sixteen double rolls:

1 ounce fresh yeast or 1 tablespoon dried
¼ cup sugar
½ cup, plus 2 tablespoons, warm water
½ cup, plus, 2 tablespoons, warm milk
4 tablespoons peanut oil
½ teaspoon salt
4 cups (1 pound) all-purpose flour

Place the yeast in a large bowl. Add 1 teaspoon of the sugar and pour in the water. Leave this five minutes for fresh yeast and 15 for dried. Stir in the milk, oil and salt and gradually mix in the flour to make a dough. Turn the dough on to a floured work surface and knead it until it is smooth. Return it to the bowl, cover it and leave it in a warm place for 1 hour to double in size. Punch the dough down with the back of your fist, cover it again and leave it for a further 20 minutes.

Knead the dough for a second time. Shape and steam, as above.

The basic steamed bread dough is used in China to make steamed filled buns which are part of a selection of dishes called dim sum, a specialty of Canton. Dim sum means "dot on heart" or "to please the heart." The special dishes are made and served only in tea houses as they are thought too complicated to be prepared at home. They include steamed buns; deep-fried filled dumplings called wontons, made with an unleavened flour and egg dough; and spring rolls, deep-fried pancakes. Dim sum dishes are eaten to accompany Chinese tea, usually in the morning but occasionally in the early afternoon.

Steamed buns can have either a sweet or a savory filling.

Steamed Buns with Date and Nut Filling

To make twelve buns:

half quantity of Man To dough (see page 177), risen and kneaded for a second time
2 ounces pitted Chinese red dates (or ordinary dates if these are not available)
1 ounce walnuts
1 ounce almonds
1 tablespoon sesame seeds
2 teaspoons sesame oil

Mince together the dates, walnuts and almonds and mix in the sesame seeds and oil.

Divide the dough into twelve even-sized pieces and roll each piece flat, into a 4-inch round. Place about 2 tablespoons of the filling in the center of each one. Loosely gather up the sides of the dough so that they meet at the top and twist them round to secure the edges and form a pouch shape. Place the buns on a sheet of wax paper, cover them with a clean cloth and leave them for 20 minutes to rise.

In a steamer, bring the water to a boil. Place the buns in the steamer, leaving a 1-inch space between each one. Cover them and steam them for 10 minutes. If you have to cook the buns in two batches, return the first batch to the top of the steamer for the last two minutes, as for the Man To, above.

• *Dining in Yunnan Province, China*

Pork and Water Chestnut Buns

To make twelve buns:

half quantity of Man To dough (see page 177) risen and kneaded for the second time
5 ounces lean pork
3 tablespoons peanut oil
2 tablespoons soy sauce
2 spring onions, finely chopped
4 canned water chestnuts, finely chopped

Very finely chop the pork. Heat the oil in a wok or frying pan over high heat. Add the pork and stir-fry it until it is cooked through. Add the soy sauce and bring it to a boil. Take the pan from the heat and cool the contents. Mix in the spring onions and water chestnuts.

Shape, fill and cook the buns as above.

The traditional accompaniment to Peking duck is Mandarin pancakes. The duck and the crispy skin are served separately, along with bowls of cucumber pieces and scallions. Alongside is a bowl of rich, sweet sauce. The diner takes a pancake and uses a piece of scallion to brush a little of the sauce over it. A piece of duck, skin, cucumber and chopped scallion are placed on the pancake, which is then rolled and eaten with the fingers.

Mandarin Pancakes

To make twenty-four pancakes:

4 cups (1 pound) plain cake flour
1¼ cups boiling water
4 tablespoons sesame oil

Place the flour in a mixing bowl and make a well in the center. Add the water and 1 tablespoon of the oil and stir the mixture gradually into the flour to make a dough. Turn the dough on to a floured work surface and knead it until it is smooth. Leave it for 10 minutes.

Divide the dough in three equal pieces and roll each piece into a sausage shape about 2 inches in diameter. Cut each one in eight slices. Roll each slice into a thin, flat pancake about 7 inches in diameter. Brush one side of half the pancakes with the remaining oil. Sandwich them together with the remaining pancakes with the oil in the middle.

Heat a griddle or heavy frying pan over high heat and then reduce the heat to medium. Cook one pancake sandwich at a time, turning it over when it starts to rise and bubble and when small spots appear on the underside.

When both sides are done, gently peel the pancakes apart and fold each one in half, oiled side inwards. Place the pancake on a heatproof plate in a low oven, to keep warm, and cook the rest in the same way.

The duck and other parts of the meal are served inside the folded pancakes.

● *Family breakfasting on dry bread, Urumchi, China*

SOUTHEAST ASIA

The cooking of Southeast Asia is mainly rice and noodle-based, but in the more Westernized cities, such as Bangkok, there are bakers making Western-type bread. *Pan de sal* are small, round white rolls, speckled with crushed crackers. They look extremely attractive and are good served warm with soup. *Enseimada* is a rich bread, very much like a brioche in texture. The strange mixture of cheese and sugar actually blends very well if they are sprinkled on while the loaf is still very warm.

Pan de Sal

To make sixteen rolls:

1 tablespoon shortening
1 tablespoon salt
1 tablespoon sugar
1 cup boiling water
1 cup warm water
1 ounce fresh yeast or 1 tablespoon dried
4 cups (1 pound) all-purpose flour
4 ounces plain crackers, crumbled

In a large mixing bowl, combine the shortening, salt, sugar and boiling water. Stir, and leave the mixture to cool. Add the warm water and sprinkle in the yeast. Leave it five minutes for fresh yeast and 15 for dried. Gradually mix in the flour to make a dough. Turn it on to a floured work surface and knead it until it is smooth. Return it to the bowl, cover it and leave in a warm place until it has doubled in size. Knead it again.

Preheat the oven to 425°F. Divide into sixteen round buns. Roll the pieces in the cracker crumbs and lay them on floured baking sheets, spread well apart. Leave them in a warm place for 20 minutes to rise.

Bake the buns for 15 minutes and cool them on wire racks.

● *Pan de sal*

Enseimada

To make two 8-inch-diameter loaves:

1 ounce fresh yeast or 1 tablespoon dried
¾ cup warm water
¼ cup, plus 2 tablespoons, sugar
1 teaspoon salt
½ cup (1 stick) butter, softened
6 eggs
6 cups (1 pound 8 ounces) all-purpose flour

Topping:

4 ounces Edam or Gouda cheese, grated
⅓ cup sugar
¼ cup (½ stick) butter, softened

In a large mixing bowl, sprinkle the yeast over the water and leave it – five minutes for fresh yeast and 15 for dried. Stir in the sugar, salt, half the butter, the eggs and 3 cups of the flour. Beat the mixture with a wooden spoon until it is smooth. Gradually add the remaining flour to make a stiff dough. Turn it out on to a floured work surface and knead it until it is smooth. Return it to the bowl, cover it and leave it in a warm place for 1 hour or until it has doubled in size.

Well grease two 8-inch-diameter baking pans. Knead the dough again and divide it in half. Roll each piece into a long rectangle about 6 × 24 inches. Spread them with the remaining butter and roll them up along one long side. Spiral these long rolls into the prepared pans.

Cover the loaves with a clean cloth and leave them in a warm draft-free place for about 1 hour, or until they have approximately doubled in size. Preheat the oven to 375°F. Bake the loaves for 30 minutes, or until they are golden and sound hollow when tapped. Cool them for 15 minutes on wire racks.

To serve, spread the tops of the warm loaves with butter and sprinkle them with the grated cheese and sugar. Cut them into slices.

AUSTRALIA AND NEW ZEALAND

Australia and New Zealand were only discovered by Westerners in the second half of the eighteenth century and consequently were some of the last countries in the world to grow wheat. Their climates were highly suitable and both countries became major producers of the bread-making cereals which had always been the staple food of the European diet.

AUSTRALIA

The first bread cooked by early European settlers in Australia was called Damper. The dough was made with a homemade leaven, was formed into a round, flat loaf, and a cross was cut into the top. This was baked in the coals of an open fire, sometimes literally sitting in the ashes but most often in a round, domed, cast-iron camp-oven which stood on legs over the fire.

Even when permanent towns and settlements sprang up, the Australian way of life continued to be essentially an outdoor one and camping utensils, such as the world-famous billycan, were adapted to the making of bread.

Some of the recipes I have chosen for Australia have been adapted from those I found in a book entitled, simply, *Cookery Book*, produced by the Country Women's Association of Victoria. There are very few recipes for making yeast breads, due, I am told by the Bread Research Institute of Australia, to the fact that bread making at home is not a popular pastime in

Australia. They blame the hot summers and the fact that most people want to be outside as much as possible. Many of the breads are risen with baking powder or baking soda, and the recipes are quick and easy.

The following bran loaf is risen with baking soda and steamed in a billycan. If you don't have a suitable can, use a 6- or 7-inch-diameter cake pan.

Bran Loaf

To make one 1-pound loaf:

1 cup (4 ounces) bran
1 cup (4 ounces) plain cake flour
¼ cup molasses
1 tablespoon black molasses
1 teaspoon baking soda dissolved in 1 tablespoon milk
1 cup milk
6 ounces mixed dark and golden raisins
2 ounces walnuts, chopped

Place the bran and flour in a mixing bowl. Stir in the syrup, molasses, baking soda and milk, and beat to make a smooth mixture. Fold in the dried fruits and walnuts.

Place the mixture in a buttered billycan or 6- to 7-inch-diameter cake pan. Put on the lid of the billycan, or cover the cake pan tightly with buttered wax paper and aluminum foil.

Bring a saucepan of water to the boil. Lower in the billy or cake pan. Cover the saucepan and steam the bread for 3 hours, topping up the water as and when necessary.

Turn out the bread and cool it on a wire rack. Eat it cut in slices and buttered. When cooked in a billy the bread will be a tall cylinder shape, so you can cut circular slices. When it is cooked in a cake pan you will have to cut it in wedges.

Although Australians may be little interested in baking bread, they very much enjoy eating it and the variety that can be bought is tremendous. Australia has many different communities, particularly in the cities, and besides the ordinary sliced white loaf, which is still the most popular, there are pita breads from Greece and the Middle East, focaccia from Italy, steamed Chinese buns, French bread and croissants, and bagels for the Jewish community. All these and many more are available from supermarkets and specialty bread stores. The Bread Research Institute is even looking into the best wheats for making Chinese steamed breads and noodles, so they can not only supply their own population but also export them.

Many of these different communities have their own festivals and accompanying festive breads, which can be found in their own stores and delicatessens. Easter breads, for example, are made by the Italians and Greeks, while people of British extraction buy hot cross buns. At harvest-festival time, large wheatsheaf loaves are made, to be displayed in store windows alongside breads shaped like animals and people.

Over the past twenty years or so, the Australians have become exceptionally health conscious, and this is reflected in their choice of diet — in particular their bread. More people are now enjoying the textures and flavors of whole-wheat and multi-grain breads. These make up 14 percent of the total bread market; white flour with added grains makes up 18 percent, but 68 percent favor plain white. Rye meal, kibbled or cracked (very coarsely milled) grains and extra bran are also added to some loaves.

In my Australian cookery book, I found a recipe for the Grant loaf. Doris Grant has been extolling the virtues of healthy diets with reduced sugar and plenty of fiber since the early 1960s. It seems dated now, but Doris Grant was the original campaigner. When she was first writing, bread in many countries was predominantly of the white-sliced variety and no one ever thought of making their own. This startlingly easy recipe for whole-wheat bread deserves a place here. There is no better section, for Australians have taken to heart her message. Rather than copy someone else's version, I looked in Doris Grant's later book, *Your Daily Food*, published in 1973, for her own recipe. This is it.

The Grant Loaf

To make three 2-pound loaves:

2 ounces fresh yeast or 2 tablespoons dried
5 cups warm water
3 teaspoons brown sugar
12 cups (3 pound) stoneground whole-wheat flour
2 teaspoons salt

In a small bowl, sprinkle the yeast over ¾ cup of the water and leave it for 5 minutes. Stir in the sugar and leave for a further 10 minutes.

Place the flour and salt in a bowl. Make a well in the center and pour in the yeast mixture and the remaining water. Knead the mixture in the bowl (see page 13) until it is smooth, elastic and leaves the sides of the bowl clean.

Divide the dough between three greased 2-pound loaf pans. Cover and leave in a warm place for about 30 minutes or until the dough has risen to the top of the pans.

Preheat the oven to 400°F. Bake the loaves for 40 minutes or until a skewer inserted into the center comes out clean. Turn them on to wire racks to cool.

● *Whole-wheat Apricot and Raisin Loaf*

The following two recipes are real home-baking ones. They contain sugar and fruits and self-rising flour to make them almost like cake, but they are baked in loaf pans and served in buttered slices, so we call them breads. They are both from *Cookery Book*. The first is made from healthy whole-wheat flour and the second, using a can of pineapple, shows the Australians' originality when it comes to cooking.

The Whole-wheat Apricot and Raisin Loaf has a light texture and spicy, semi-sweet flavor. The Pineapple and Date Loaf is slightly heavier and much sweeter, and probably best eaten without butter.

Whole-wheat Apricot and Raisin Loaf

To make one 1-pound loaf:

2 ounces whole dried apricots
¾ cup milk
2 cups (8 ounces) whole-wheat self-rising flour, or plain whole-wheat plus 2 teaspoons baking powder and 1 of baking soda
¼ teaspoon salt
½ teaspoon ground nutmeg
¼ cup (½ stick) butter
¼ cup superfine sugar
2 ounces raisins
1 egg, beaten

Chop the apricots and soak them in the milk for 4 hours. Preheat the oven to 350°F. Place the flour, salt and nutmeg in a bowl and rub in the butter. Toss in the sugar and raisins. Make a well in the center and pour in the beaten egg and the milk and apricots. Mix well to make a soft dough.

Place the mixture in a 1-pound loaf pan and bake it for 30 minutes, or until a skewer stuck in the center comes out clean. Turn the loaf on to a wire rack to cool. Serve it sliced and buttered.

Pineapple and Date Loaf

To make one 2-pound loaf:

1 egg, beaten
¼ cup, plus 2 tablespoons, milk
3 tablespoons butter, melted
one 8-ounce can pineapple and juice, crushed
6 ounces walnuts, chopped
4 ounces dates, pitted and chopped
3 cups (12 ounces) self-rising all-purpose flour
½ cup sugar
½ teaspoon salt

Preheat the oven to 350°F. In a large mixing bowl, stir together the egg, milk, butter, pineapple, nuts and dates. Mix together the flour, sugar and salt, and stir them into the pineapple mixture.

Place the mixture in a buttered 2-pound loaf pan and bake it for 50 minutes, or until a skewer inserted into the center comes out clean.

NEW ZEALAND

Wheat came to New Zealand via Australia. There had never been a variety of grass in the Islands suitable as a good source of grain, and so the Maori people had to wait until the early 1800s before they could grow wheat for themselves. The first wheat in New Zealand was not grown by Europeans, but by Ruatara, chief of the Ngapuhi people. Wheat was, however, grown around mission settlements, and by the 1840s both Europeans and Maoris had well-established wheat fields. Since then, wheat has been one of New Zealand's major arable crops.

The early ovens were the same as in Australia, round and domed and standing on short legs over an open fire. Damper was eaten in New Zealand, too. Sourdough bread was popular and also a bread called *rewena paraoa*, which was raised with a potato starter and was a favorite with the Maoris. *rewena* is the Maori word for leaven and *paraoa* means flour. The bread was first made in the nineteenth century, by Maori farmers who both grew and milled their own wheat. It was baked in the cast-iron camp ovens. *rewena paraoa* is a moist, bouncy, slightly sweet white bread. I cooked mine in an oval casserole and it rose well, developing an attractive cracked top. The bread is very easy to make once the leaven has fermented, as it requires no rising time.

Rewena Paraoa

To make one 2-pound loaf:

Rewena Starter:
4 ounces raw potato, peeled and sliced
2 cups water
1 teaspoon sugar
2 cups (8 ounces) all-purpose flour
Loaf:
2½ cups (10 ounces) all-purpose flour
1 teaspoon baking soda
1 teaspoon salt
1 tablespoon sugar
1 quantity Rewena starter

To make the starter, first boil the potato in the water until it is soft. Keeping it in the water, break it up with a fork or a potato masher. Cool the potato and water to lukewarm and stir in the sugar and flour. Beat the mixture to make a smooth paste. Place it in a bowl, cover it with plastic wrap and leave it in a warm place until it is fermenting. This could take up to four days, depending on the temperature. It may not appear very bubbly, but if you put your ear to it you will hear it working quite loudly.

To make the bread, first preheat the oven to 425°F. Place the flour, baking soda, salt and sugar in a mixing bowl and toss them together. Add the rewena and gradually knead it in to make a soft dough. At first it will seem as though the flour cannot possibly all mix into the starter, but use the kneading in the bowl technique (see page 13) and you will find it goes in easily. The dough will be very sticky, so wash your hands and then coat the dough with flour, after which it should be easy to handle and feel quite springy. Turn it on to a floured work surface and knead it until it is smooth.

Grease a 5-pint cast-iron casserole or ovenproof bowl, and put in the dough. Cover it with greased aluminum foil. Bake the loaf for 40 minutes or until it is risen. Turn it on to a wire rack and return it to the oven for 5 minutes so it becomes golden-brown.

When the European settlements became more established, larger camp ovens were used. These took the form of iron boxes set in brick ovens with a fire top and bottom. Dough mixers came in during the 1890s and the high-speed Chorleywood process, from England, in the 1930s. New Zealand, like every other Western country, went through a stage of favoring white sliced bread from the 1950s to the 1970s and then everyone began to demand bread that was more nutritious.

The New Zealanders, like the Australians, are very health conscious. Even their white flour has a higher extraction from the full grain than that in most of Europe and the United States (78 percent as opposed to 70 percent).

There are now many different types of bread available in New Zealand, many of them made with whole-wheat flour or mixed grains. One of the most popular is what they call a Swiss-style mixed grain bread. The recipes in this section are adapted from *The Cook's Bread Book* by Mary Browne, Helen Leach and Nancy Tichborne. Their mixed-grain bread contains added gluten and is made with quick-rise yeast. I have missed out the gluten and have used fresh or normal dried yeast. If you have difficulty obtaining cracked rye, use all cracked wheat. The bread is moist, with whole pieces of the grain included in the mixture, and with a delicious nutty flavor.

Mixed Grain Bread

To make one 2-pound loaf:

¼ cup (2 ounces) cracked wheat

¼ cup (2 ounces) cracked rye

cold water

1 ounce fresh yeast or 1 tablespoon dried

2 cups warm water

4 tablespoons dry skimmed milk

1 teaspoon salt

4½ cups (1 pound 2 ounces) whole-wheat flour

● *Rewena Paraoa (see page 185)*

Place the cracked grains in a saucepan and cover them with cold water. Bring them to a boil, simmer them for 1 minute, drain them and cool them to lukewarm.

In a large mixing bowl, sprinkle the yeast over about one third of the warm water and leave it – five minutes for fresh yeast and 15 for dried. Stir in the remaining water, the dry milk, the salt and the cracked grains. Gradually mix in the flour to make a very moist dough. Knead it in the bowl until it begins to change texture (see page 13). Transfer the dough to a greased 2-pound bread pan, cover it with a clean cloth and leave it in a warm place for 30 minutes or until it rises to about ½ inch above the top of the pan. Preheat the oven to 400°F.

Bake the loaf for 45 minutes or until it sounds hollow when tapped. Turn it on to a wire rack to cool.

However much bread was baked in commercial bakeries, New Zealanders still enjoyed making bread at home, and there were always bread sections in the local country shows. The more recent interest in ecology and natural living has revived the skill.

The following billycan-baked loaf is slightly similar to the Australian bran loaf, and can be found in old New Zealand cookery books. It is soft and moist, and typical of the loaves made on New Zealand farms in the early part of the twentieth century. It is very slightly sweet and is best cut in slices or wedges (depending on whether you have used a billy or a baking pan) and buttered. It goes equally well with cheese or sweet preserves.

Brown Billy Loaf

To make one 1-pound loaf:

1 cup (4 ounces) plain cake flour
1 cup (4 ounces) whole-wheat flour
1 teaspoon baking soda
2 teaspoons cream of tartar
½ teaspoon salt
½ cup (2 ounces) bran
1½ tablespoons sugar
2 tablespoons butter, in small pieces
1 tablespoon corn syrup
4 tablespoons boiling water
½ cup, plus 2 tablespoons, milk

Preheat the oven to 350°F. Place the flours, baking soda, cream of tartar, salt, bran and sugar in a large mixing bowl and toss together. Place the butter and corn syrup in a jug and stir in the boiling water. Stir until the butter has melted. Stir the mixture into the dry ingredients in the bowl. Stir in the milk to make a thick batter.

Spoon the batter into a greased billy, or into a greased 7-inch-diameter cake pan. Cover it with a greased lid or aluminum foil.

Bake the loaf for 1 to 1¼ hours, or until a skewer inserted in the center comes out clean. Turn the loaf on to a wire rack to cool.

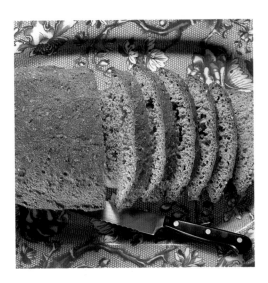

● *Mixed Grain Bread*

INDEX

ACKNOWLEDGMENTS

The publishers wish to thank all individuals, photographers' institutions, and photographic agencies who have kindly supplied photographs for publication in this book.

© **Andes Press Agency**, page 134. © **Bildhuset**, page 119/© Ole Christiansen, page 107. © **Cephas**, page 160, 180/© Stuart Boreham, page 28 (center)/© Nigel Blythe, page 27/© Mick Rock, page 28 (right), 90 (top and bottom)/© Peter Stowell, page 70. © **Robert Estall Photographs**, page 123. © **Chris Fairclough Colour Library**, page 43. © **Robert Harding Picture Library**, pages 37, 45, 62, 65, 67, 69, 111, 115/© Nigel Blythe, page 38/© Nick Servian, page 64. © **The Hutchison Library**, pages 129, 135, 141, 158, 162, 170, 176, 177, 179/© Dave Brinicombe, pages 103, 148/© Sarah Errington, pages 98, 142/© Robert Francis, page 151 (far right)/© Bernard Gerard, page 116/© Jeremy Horner, page 149/© Chris Johnson, page 161/© Bernard Régent, pages 118, 156/© Liba Taylor, pages 95, 100/© John Wright, page 144/© **Images of India Picture Agency**, page 168. **Photobank** © Adrian Baker, page 36/© Peter Baker, page 140. © **Pictures Colour Library Ltd**, pages 15, 25, 88, 151 (far left and center)/© G. Haubois, page 28 (far left). © **John Sims**, pages 49, 55. © **Tony Stone Worldwide**, pages 48, 86, 94, 106, 172/© M. Brylewski, page 26/© Julian Calder, page 22/© Mike Caldwell, page 80/© Joe Cornish, page 59/© Lorentz Gullachsen, page 82/© Gary Irving, page 122/© Zigy Kaluzny, page 9/© Mike McCabe, page 182/© Andy Sacks, pages 6, 8, 13, 132 /© Philip Temple, page 81. © **David Williams Picture Library**, page 121. © **Zefa**, pages 72, 73. © **Zul**, page 50.

We would also like to thank the proprietors of **Ye Olde Tuck Shoppe**, Rye, East Sussex, England, for kindly allowing us to take photographs in their bakery. Thanks also to **Didier Degaille**, from Clarke's Bread, for his invaluable assistance.

The author wishes to thank the many national embassies, agricultural federations and baking institutions who answered questions and provided information. Special thanks too, to **Piers** and **Amanda Garnham** of Bartley Mill, Frant, East Sussex, England, for their help and inspiration.